You, the People

NUMBER TEN
Presidential Rhetoric Series
Martin J. Medhurst, General Editor

You, the People

*American National Identity
in Presidential Rhetoric*

Vanessa B. Beasley

TEXAS A&M UNIVERSITY PRESS   COLLEGE STATION

The paper used in this book
meets the minimum requirements
of the American National Standard for Permanence
of Paper for Printed Library Materials, z39.48-1984.
Binding materials have been chosen for durability.

Library of Congress Cataloging-in-Publication Data

Beasley, Vanessa B., 1966–
You, the people : American national identity in presidential rhetoric /
Vanessa B. Beasley.—1st ed.
p. cm. — (Presidential rhetoric series ; no. 10)
Includes bibliographical references and index.
ISBN 1-58544-277-1 (alk. paper)
1. Nationalism—United States—History.   2. Rhetoric—Political
aspects—United States—History.   3. Group identity—Political aspects—
United States—History.   4. Presidents—United States—Language.
5. United States—Politics and government.   I. Title.   II. Series.
E183.B4   2004
320.54'0973—dc21
2003009577

To Roderick P. Hart,
An uncommon teacher

Contents

Acknowledgments

In the process of writing this book I have been humbled many times. Like any writer, I have been humbled by how much I have not known about the subject matter herein. Henry Steele Commager once wrote that it would take "a thousand essays to penetrate to the truth about America." Although there were times when I took his words literally as I revised this work, most of the time I took them to mean that all any author writing about the nature of democracy in the United States can hope for is to provide a glimpse into part of this truth. If I have met this goal in the pages that follow, it is surely because I have been helped by so many people.

Foremost among these helpers is Roderick P. Hart, to whom the book is dedicated. This work began as a doctoral dissertation under his direction at the University of Texas at Austin. Although the study has been revised and expanded since I finished my doctorate, I will be forever indebted to him for first encouraging me to think imaginatively, broadly, and fearlessly.

While I was on the faculty of the Department of Speech Communication at Texas A&M University, I was also humbled by the intellectual generosity of the many colleagues and students who supported this project. I am especially grateful to Martin J. Medhurst, Kurt Ritter, Leroy Dorsey, and James A. Aune, all members of the Program in Presidential Rhetoric at Texas A&M University. Other members of the department, especially Charles Conrad, Susan Gilbertz, Katherine Miller, Barbara Sharf, Scott Poole, Linda Putnam, Richard Street, and Antonio La Pastina, also provided multiple types of support.

Graduate students enrolled in my course on communication and American political culture at Texas A&M during the fall of 2001 helped me refine some of these arguments, as did the multiple sections of undergraduates enrolled in the course "American Voices." Of this latter group, the incomparably talented Kristin H. Hill later became my research assistant. Within the College of Liberal Arts, James Rosenheim, Mary Ann O'Farrell, Edward Portis, and James Burk were also kind enough to take an interest in this project. Outside of Texas A&M, this work has benefited from the interest and counsel of Davis Houck, Melvin

Laracey, Tarla Peterson, David Ryfe, Mary Stuckey, and Jeffrey Tulis, among others. As I prepared this book for publication after I joined the faculty at Southern Methodist University, Catharine Flagg was an excellent research assistant.

The research presented in this book received institutional support from several sources. First, the LBJ Foundation of the Lyndon Baines Johnson Museum and Library provided a Moody Grant that defrayed some of the expenses of archival work. In addition, I have also received grant support from the Center for Presidential Studies at the George Bush School of Government and Public Service, Texas A&M University.

Some of my research presented here has been previously published. Portions of the introduction appeared in "Making Diversity Safe for Democracy: American Pluralism and the Presidential Local Address, 1885–1992," *Quarterly Journal of Speech* 87 (2001): 25–40. Likewise, chapters one and two feature some material published in "The Rhetoric of Ideological Consensus in the United States: American Principles and the American Prose in Presidential Inaugurals," *Communication Monographs* 68 (2001): 169–83. Finally, earlier drafts of parts of chapter five appeared in "Engendering Democratic Change: How Three U.S. Presidents Discussed Female Suffrage," *Rhetoric & Public Affairs* 5, no. 1 (2002): 70–103.

On a more personal level, I have been sustained by the support of family and friends. Some friends, especially Suzanne Daughton, Joanne Gilbert, Jennifer Long, and Rena Minar, have shared the delights and challenges of balancing academic work and motherhood. Other friends, especially Adam's godparents, Steve Trahan and Ashlea Willet, have kept me sane by listening to me and taking Adam on outings when I needed extra time to work. In this same vein, all of Adam's grandparents have been incredible sources of support for both my husband Trey and me. Apparently it does take a village to raise a child, especially when you are writing a book at the same time.

In coparenting this book, the staff of Texas A&M University Press deserves special mention. They went out of their way to help me on many occasions and were very understanding of my work and my situation. I am especially grateful to Maureen Creamer Bemko for her masterful copyediting.

It has been said before, but I would like to thank Adam, my first son, for making sure it took a long time to write this book. His birth and life have saved me from myself, and he will never know how grateful I have been for that. I would also like to thank my second son, Charlie, who was born while this book was being prepared for publication. From the very beginning, he has forced me to live my priorities on a daily basis. Through it all, my husband Trey has been a consistent and reliable partner, asking at every stage of this manuscript's production what he could do to help. His love humbles me still.

You, the People

Presidential Rhetoric
and the Challenge
of a Diverse Democracy

O n September 11, 2001, as I listened in disbelief to news of the attacks on the World Trade Center and the Pentagon, I could not stop
asking myself two questions: What was happening to us, and what
might we do in response to the attacks?

Like most people, I asked these questions in part because of the attacks'
obvious geopolitical implications. Surely these were calculated acts of aggression, meaning that the United States was likely to go to war, even if it was not
immediately clear against whom. Yet as an observer of language, I was also
struck by something else as I heard myself and others ask these two questions
all day. Although I had been studying the rhetoric of citizenship and national
identity in the United States for almost ten years, I had never before felt the
weight of the pronouns "us" and "we" in quite the same way as I did that
Tuesday. The "we" I uttered and, more to the point, felt so profoundly on September 11 was a different "we" than I might have used on September 10. It was
not a "we" that referred to my most immediate and pragmatic everyday alliances—my family, my friends, my colleagues, and so on—but instead to
something larger, something almost ridiculously ephemeral that was somehow,
on that day especially, overwhelmingly meaningful nonetheless. My September 11 "we" was, in effect, the same "we" of the U.S. Constitution, the mono-
syllabic signifier of a national political community.

But how is this "we," this sense of civic camaraderie, created? In this book
I ask how such a sense has been constructed rhetorically in the United States.
More specifically, this book asks how U.S. presidents have used language to
try to develop and maintain feelings of shared national identity within a wildly

diverse democracy. In other words, this book asks who presidents have told the American people they are. Although I completed the research presented in this book before September 11, 2001, such questions about the relationship between presidential rhetoric and national identity perhaps have taken on a renewed sense of importance after that date. Many of us might recall, for instance, waiting anxiously that evening to hear President George W. Bush speak to the nation in a televised address. On September 11, perhaps more than on any other date in recent memory, the American people needed to hear from their president. They needed to hear a message of reassurance, resolve, and unity that only a president of the United States could provide.

Before September 11, however, it might have been more difficult to speak so plainly about the American people's needs. I certainly would not have presumed to make such sweeping statements about an "us" or a "we" that might constitute "the American people." In fact, I would have used the quotation marks around those phrases primarily to reveal my intellectual awareness that these phrases are themselves reifications, words that generate the feelings that make nationalism possible in the first place.[1] Within rhetorical studies especially, many scholars have been persuaded by Benedict Anderson's claim that nations are only "imagined communities." Even in the smallest of them, Anderson has explained, compatriots "will never know most of their fellow-members, meet them, or even hear of them, yet in the minds of each lives the image of their communion."[2] Similarly, Michael Walzer has suggested that the concept of "the people" is necessarily only a symbolic one that has "no palpable shape or substance."[3]

Nevertheless, as imagined as this fellowship may be, it represents nothing less than the "starting point for politics," according to Walzer.[4] The events of September 11 and their aftermath have demonstrated Walzer's point in obvious ways by showing how powerful the felt communion of a national "we" can be; it is compelling enough for people to willingly sacrifice both their livelihoods and their lives in its name. Although feelings of nationalism are most obvious during times of war and turmoil, they can also be invoked to great effect during more peaceful times, when citizens may take pride in their nation's Olympic athletes, for example, or light fireworks on the Fourth of July or Bastille Day. As these examples reveal, feelings of nationalism can sow powerful seeds of connectedness where there might otherwise be none.

Yet nationalism has an undeniably evil side as well. The ghosts of its twentieth-century manifestations, most notably Nazism and fascism, loom large over contemporary international politics, causing many people to denounce the ancient hatreds fueling violence in the Balkans, the Middle East, Africa,

Northern Ireland, and elsewhere. In spite of such concerns, some countries seem more anxious than ever to protect their allegedly unique national identities. The French government has banned some forms of American popular culture lest their influence erode French cultural identity, just as many Canadians have sought to legislate English as the primary national language. While these latter matters may seem less dangerous than the former, they all suggest that nationalism is ultimately a double-edged sword, an efficient tool for promoting shared identity, perhaps, but one that may also encourage exclusion, intolerance, and even inhumanity.

The challenges of maintaining a balance between these two potential functions of nationalism are strikingly obvious in a country as large and demographically diverse as the United States. Because the American people have never been characterized by the level of ethnic or religious homogeneity that has historically marked the inhabitants of most other nations, Americans have always had to imagine their national political community in alternative yet compelling ways. Throughout U.S. history, however, especially when there existed stark contradictions between the nation's imagined ideals and its citizens' less noble practices, Americans have repeatedly had to confront the limits of their own imaginations. If the United States was idealized as a haven for immigrants, for example, how could members of this type of imagined community justify an interest in restricting certain types of newcomers? Likewise, if the United States was born out of a quest for freedom, how could its people systematically deny the same to an entire race of people? And if equality is the cornerstone of American democracy, why has so much of the nation's history been marked by recurring inequities?

In the weeks after September 11, there were similarly discouraging signs of disjunction between some Americans' self-perceived nature and their actual behavior. For example, even as "United We Stand" billboards and bumper stickers proliferated, the national press started to report incidents of alleged hate crimes against U.S. citizens of Arabic descent. If the terrorist attacks had prompted an unmistakable resurgence of patriotism, they had apparently also led some citizens to a newly heightened fear of immigrants.

When President Bush spoke to a joint session of Congress and to the American people on September 20, 2001, he addressed this contradiction by speaking about both of its impulses directly. The president offered as evidence of the country's strength and united purpose "the courage of the passengers" who sacrificed their lives to prevent a fourth attack and the "endurance of rescuers, working past exhaustion" at ground zero in New York and at the Pentagon in Washington, D.C.: "We have seen the unfurling of flags, the lighting of candles, the giving of blood, the saying of prayers—in English, Hebrew, and Arabic. We have seen the decency of a loving and giving people who have made the grief of strangers their own." Later in the speech, however, the president acknowledged that the American people were fearful too, not just of foreign aggressors but also of each other. "I know many citizens have fears tonight, and I ask you to be calm and resolute, even in the face of a continuing threat. I ask you to uphold the values of America, and remember why so many have come here," Bush implored, with an explicit reference to anti-immigrant sentiment. "We are in a fight for our principles," he continued, "and our first responsibility is to live by them. No one should be singled out for unfair treatment or unkind words because of their ethnic background or religious faith."[5]

With such plain entreaties President Bush urged a shocked and grieving nation to embrace the compassionate fellow-feeling of nationalism without giving in to more destructive reactions such as suspicion and intolerance. Put in terms of my previous discussion of pronouns, Bush offered his listeners an affirming, post–September 11 sense of "us" while urging the American people to resist the temptation to name and blame an internal "them." Although presidential rhetoric alone could not have met this latter goal, Bush's speech demonstrated that the United States' diversity presents certain rhetorical challenges to its leaders, who must persuade their constituents that they are part of a historic, expansive, and enduring national community.

George W. Bush was not the first president to use the bully pulpit to respond to this challenge. Other presidents have done similar rhetorical work in response to crises that threatened the unity of the American people; Abraham Lincoln's Gettysburg Address and Lyndon Johnson's speech on the Voting Rights Act immediately come to mind as two other good examples. Like Bush's address, these speeches are memorable in part because presidents used them to appeal to, in Lincoln's memorable phrase, "the better angels of our nature."[6] In such historic moments, presidents use rhetoric to try to "remake America," in Garry Wills's terms, and to ensure that the nation's democratic unity is strong enough to sustain its diversity.[7]

Yet how is the American "we" made and remade rhetorically by presidents during quieter, less remarkable times? Certainly chief executives cannot afford to engage in constitutive rhetorics of American identity only in times of turmoil. Indeed, whatever the country's fears after September 11, the conditions and frustrations of multiculturalism are not new in the United States, nor are they evident only during times of national or international crises. During times of both war and peace, the American people's cultural differences have always been salient in a democracy whose ethnic diversity is unmatched throughout the world.[8] Similarly, economic disparities and class distinctions have always mattered greatly in the United States, as has gender. We might say, then, that the American "we" has always been a dramatically stratified one, as much of a sociological riddle as a political necessity.

Whatever the citizenry's demographic differences, there are some perennial occasions during which the U.S. president must speak to the citizens—and, more importantly, speak *of* them—as one people. For this book I have chosen to study two such occasions, the inaugural address and the state of the union messages, to trace how presidents rhetorically constructed the "American people" in these discourses from 1885 through 2000. As a result, the analysis I present here is based on close reading of a longitudinal collection of two genres of presidential rhetoric. By focusing on just these two genres, this book invites readers to pay closer attention to some of the platitudinous and perhaps even predictable ways in which multiple presidents have asked the American people to think of their common bonds.

Ultimately, then, instead of asking what individual presidents have said about their constituents' national identity in speeches specifically designed to respond to issues or events that have threatened it, this book looks to two of the most ritualistic genres of presidential speech to ask a slightly different set of questions. What have presidents said about civil rights, for example, when they were not giving civil rights speeches? Likewise, what have they said about the relevance of ethnicity and gender to American citizenship when they were not speaking directly about immigration crises or women's voting rights, but were instead merely expected to report on the nation's values, current state, and future?

In this introductory chapter I make a case for the importance of such questions and explain some of the book's argumentative premises. First, I explain my methodological choices as well as the scope and limits of the analysis. Then I turn to a larger justification of this reading by proposing an alternative approach to a phenomenon known as the "rhetorical presidency." Here I argue that the rhetorical presidency can be understood as an institutional response to the United States' diversity. Rather than "going public" solely to promote specific legislative or policy measures, chief executives may have also used the bully pulpit to "form a mass" out of an increasingly diversifying American people.

RATIONALE, SCOPE, AND FINDINGS

Questions about the creation and maintenance of American national identity are not new, to be sure. Although there can be no complete accounting of any generation's understandings of its nationalistic bonds, some observers have tried to find clues within the nation's canonical texts. Within social science, among the most influential of these studies is Garry Wills's *Inventing America: Jefferson's Declaration of Independence;* among the most recent is Rogers Smith's analysis of citizenship laws in *Civic Ideals: Conflicting Visions of Citizenship in U.S. History.* Within the humanities, Priscilla Wald examined in *Constituting Americans: Cultural Anxiety and Narrative Form* some of the most celebrated writing in U.S. history, including the works of Frederick Douglass, Herman Melville, and W. E. B. Du Bois, for these authors' definitions of American identity. Similarly, Dana Nelson explored a wide range of texts, ranging from the Federalist Papers to medical lectures, for *National Manhood: Capitalist Citizenship and the Imagined Fraternity of White Men,* her study of the ideals of citizenship in the United States during the late eighteenth and early nineteenth centuries. Less explored, however, is an additional set of texts: presidential rhetoric. This omission seems odd, for if the diverse American people have somehow imagined themselves as being united, then surely their visions have been captured in the words that come from the office that presides over all of the American people.

While there might be other elected individuals who would also have an interest in promoting a shared social idiom among the American people, few could deny chief executives' interest in this cause. As Rogers Smith has written, within a democracy, political elites "require a population to lead that imagines itself as being a 'people,' and . . . they need a people that imagines itself in ways that make leadership by [them] appropriate." As sole chief executives presiding over a radically heterogeneous *demos,* U.S. presidents face both of these needs, which ultimately, Smith argues, "drive political leaders to offer civic ideologies, or myths of civic identity, that foster the requisite sense of peoplehood."[9] Such myths, Ernest Gellner has suggested, can result in a view of the nation as not only an "anonymous, internally fluid and fairly undifferentiated, large-scale and culturally homogeneous communit[y]" but also as the "only legitimate respositor[y] of political authority."[10] In other words, for there to be an American nation, an American "we," or even an American presidency at all, U.S. presidents must find ways of breathing life into the otherwise abstract notion of American political community.

Producing myths of civic identity is not unique to the United States, of course. After studying the independence movement in Quebec, for example, Maurice Charland found that "claims for Quebec sovereignty [were based] upon the asserted existence of a particular type of subject."[11] In addition to studying one particular myth of civic identity, Charland has argued persuasively that the investigation of these myths invites a decidedly rhetorical perspective. Heeding Michael McGee's directive to attend to the rhetorical construction of "the people," Charland noted that such rhetoric's constitutive nature requires a Burkean view of rhetoric as something larger than just overtly suasory discourse ("rhetoric as persuasion").[12] This perspective enables critics to grapple with the ways in which discourse, à la Althusser, interpellates its subjects as political beings "through a process of identification in rhetorical narratives that 'always already' presume the constitution of subjects."[13] To find evidence of how presidents have promoted certain forms of American national identity within their discourse, we need not look for overt appeals in which chief executives have told their listeners what to think or which policy to support. Instead, critics can look at ways that presidential discourse subtly reinforces the audience's presumed collective identity as national subjects.

Such constitutive rhetorics are ubiquitous, according to Charland, who calls them "nothing less than the discursive background of social life."[14] So which types of presidential rhetoric might be especially good places to find them? For this analysis I chose to investigate only two genres: inaugural addresses and state of the union messages. As Mikhail Bakhtin has noted, genres provide an extremely useful vantage point through which to view social history; genres, he wrote, are the "drive belts from the history of society to the history of language."[15] Similarly, viewed from a more traditional anthropological perspective, these two highly ritualized instances of presidential speech can be expected to affirm idealized cultural norms. In *The Interpretation of Cultures*, Clifford Geertz recalled Ward Goodenough's influential argument, stating that "a society's culture consists of whatever it is one has to know or believe in order to operate in a manner acceptable to its members."[16] In this sense, I have done this reading under the rubric of what Raymond Williams refers to as the "idealist" approach to culture, in which my purpose has been to view presidential rhetoric in general and these two genres in particular as an "informing spirit" that "manifest[s], in relation with other institutions and activities, the central interests and values of a 'people.'"[17]

In *Deeds Done in Words: Presidential Rhetoric and the Genres of Governance*, Karlyn Kohrs Campbell and Kathleen Hall Jamieson provide a more specific rationale for looking at institutional genres of presidential discourse to find constitutive rhetorics of nationalism and peoplehood. Noting that a focus on genre enables them to "examine the roles that presidents have invited the American people to assume, the people that they have asked us to be," the authors also explain that "when we say that presidents constitute the people, we mean that all presidents have the opportunity to persuade us to conceive of ourselves in ways compatible with their views of government and the world. At the same time, presidents invite us to see them, the presidency, the country, and the country's role in specific ways."[18] As instances of discursive ritual, these two genres of presidential discourse can be expected to teach American culture to its listeners, giving chief executives the chance to remind the American people what they *ought* to know or believe and thus fulfilling the didactic function of rhetoric described by Roderick Hart.[19]

This didactic function is perhaps most evident in inaugural addresses. This genre of presidential discourse is both ritualistic and epideictic, a combination that invites chief executives to promote certain basic understandings of American political community that transcend their own personal agendas and partisan views. As Theodore Sorensen once noted, inaugural addresses should "address the American people of our time but [also] have meaning for all people for all time. . . . they embody the best of our heritage from the past and the best of our hopes for the future."[20] As a result, inaugural addresses as a genre are likely places to find rhetorical linkages between the present moment and the nation's past as well as its future, thereby providing glimpses into both a nostalgic and an idealized vision of American political community.

Yet these speeches are more than merely a forum for the pronunciation of allegedly transcendent national values. They also provide an opportunity for the ritual reenactment of peoplehood. On Inauguration Day, as partisan bickering or other forms of political disharmony are (usually) put aside, Americans are invited to perform their role as a unified people by participating in this ritual, even if their participation is limited to watching the events on television, listening to them on radio, or reading about them in newspapers days later. As Campbell and Jamieson have suggested, inaugural addresses therefore provide "an essential element in the ritual of transition in which the covenant between the citizenry and their leaders [is] renewed."[21] Indeed, Campbell and Jamieson suggest that the constitutive function of these addresses is foremost among their other generic requirements. "The presidential inaugural . . . unifies the audience by reconstituting its members as 'the people' who can witness and ratify the ceremony," they note.[22] In other words, we might suppose that inaugural addresses are important ritualistic moments in which U.S. presidents reassure the American people that they are a people after all.

State of the union messages are also ritualistic, and although these texts may be considered by some to be less epideictic and less didactic than inaugural addresses, Campbell and Jamieson have argued that they can also be characterized as "public meditations on values."[23] "Facts do not speak for themselves," they write, adding that "assessments must be grounded in values. As a consequence, State of the Union addresses not only assess and recomment; they also articulate the values underlying assessments."[24] Thus, state of the union messages are an important set of texts for this analysis exactly because they typically feature presidential recommendations framed within value-oriented terms presumably associated with protecting or advancing a common nationalistic good. Furthermore, if, at any given point in U.S. history, there are contradictions between American policy and American philosophy, these messages might be good places to look to see how presidents dissipate such tensions.

State of the union messages also serve other purposes that are both symbolic and institutional. For example, Campbell and Jamieson write that these messages "ritualistically reaffir[m] the existence of three branches of government" in the United States, thereby reminding "the country that presidents have a unique function in our system of government. They are to view questions in the aggregate and as they pertain to the whole, to the Union."[25] If the inaugural provides an opportunity for the American people to listen as one people, then the state of the union message gives a chief executive the opportunity to speak as the sole and supreme leader, the symbolic guardian of the common good.

The Constitution requires that these executive pronouncements be offered regularly, but it does not require that they be delivered orally. Indeed, in the texts studied in this analysis, the first president to give the address orally was Woodrow Wilson. This difference among texts does not necessarily present a problem for my analysis, however. Even in those years when the messages were only printed and/or read to Congress by clerks, they had symbolic import that went beyond their constitutional or legislative purposes. Campbell and Jamieson recall Charles Beard's insistence that the state of the union or "annual message" is "the one great public document of the United States which is widely read and discussed."[26] Indeed, if Benedict Anderson is correct about the symbiotic relationship between nation-keeping and the rise of print capitalism, then state of the union messages, like inaugural addresses, may be vitally important to the symbolic maintenance of American political community, regardless of whether they were heard by constituents when they were first offered.[27] Both types of speeches are commonly reprinted in newspapers and, more recently, broadcast on television, radio, and Internet sources. Thus, even the production and subsequent dissemination of these messages themselves may be understood as ritualistic processes vital to the reification of imagined political community within the United States.

To summarize the rationale behind my textual choices, I have assumed that both inaugural addresses and state of the union messages are particularly ripe with constitutive rhetorics of American nationalism. If it seems to some readers that there was a bias in my selection of these texts, it was a purposeful bias for two reasons. First, for this analysis I was most interested in the idealized versions of American national identity and the visions of democratic political community that stemmed from them. Any presidential address delivered to the nation is a well-crafted piece of rhetoric, carefully designed to advance specific themes as well as the speaker. Rather than seeing the contrived nature of these speeches as a detriment to what they can reveal about the culture, one might view them instead as *especially* meaningful precisely because they provide information about the ideal. Family photographs, for example, may not tell us much about tired marriages or unhappy childhoods, but they do speak volumes about the high hopes of a clan who purposefully puts aside its everyday problems to dress up for a photographer. Like family photographs, formal addresses record values, providing a rare, unobscured glimpse of a vision of ideal community.

Secondly, although there are other genres of presidential discourse that might also feature such themes, for this analysis I chose to limit the texts to those that occurred with predictable frequency throughout the presidency. Put differently, although Franklin Roosevelt's War Message undoubtedly explained the country's entry into World War II in terms of the United States' characteristics and philosophy (e.g., "the national interest"), I did not include that text in this analysis because other presidents did not have comparable opportunities to craft such messages. Likewise, even though certain presidents have used their veto messages to speak directly to the people when they knew a congressional override was likely, I did not include these messages either. Although I am aware of the potential disadvantages in choosing to limit the data in this manner, I wanted this book to tell a story whose main character was the U.S. presidency in general rather than certain presidents in particular.

Throughout this analysis, I have viewed inaugural addresses and state of the union messages as mythic discourses that bear the implicit imprint of their audiences' perceived characteristics as national subjects, even as they simultaneously attempt to constrain their actions in order to promote a sense of national unity. This critical framework borrows heavily from Edwin Black's notion of a "second persona," the "you" implicitly addressed within this discourse, and it has also been informed by Philip Wander's concept of a more ideologically conscious "third persona."[28] As I read through each inaugural address and state of the union message, then, I looked for rhetoric, both implicit and explicit, that seemed to answer the following types of questions: Who are the American people? How are they explained, defined, and portrayed in these texts? What central and/or defining characteristics are they assumed to share?

Having explained my textual choices and critical framework, I should also explain why I limited the study's temporal scope. Rather than begin with George Washington's first inaugural address in 1789, I chose to focus instead on the years that currently constitute the second half of the U.S. presidency, beginning with Grover Cleveland's first term (in 1885) and ending with Bill Clinton's last year in office (2000). In part this choice was a pragmatic one, because coming to terms with the entire corpus of presidential inaugural and state of the union messages simply seemed too large of a task for one book. It may be, then, that I am guilty of writing volume 2 of this project before writing volume 1.

More importantly, however, focusing on the second half of U.S. presidential history also enabled me to best address specific questions about the role of presidential rhetoric within the United States' diverse democracy. Even if it is true that the American people have always struggled with their own diversity, they did so more obviously during the nation's second century than in its first. By beginning with the late-1880s, for example, I was able to start the analysis with texts produced during the peak years of nineteenth-century immigration and thus see if the growing nativism of the American people was either captured or rebutted in some of its leaders' most ceremonial speech. Likewise, by continuing the analysis through the end of the twentieth century, I was able to follow the ways in which presidents spoke about American national identity in some of their most public messages, even as the "face" of the American people was changing due to demographic shifts, the expansion of civil rights for women and minorities, and another immigration boom.

From 1885 to 2000, there have been many times, of course, when presidents have had to comment specifically about the nation's diversity and its discontents—times when they could neither wait to do so until their next state of the union address nor hope that they would be afforded the opportunity to give another inaugural address. In these moments, presidents may have chosen to respond in various ways, through speech, legislation, or a combination of both. Other scholars have thoroughly studied such responses, to be sure.[29] Yet as I have already noted, here I am using a different set of texts to ask a slightly different set of questions. What have presidents said about American national identity in moments that were "under the radar," that is, ceremonial moments that have required presidents to speak more obliquely about such things? Given the ritualistic and epideictic nature of inaugural addresses and state of the union messages, presidents presumably faced certain constraints in talking about national unity in these speeches. In such moments, for example, they have presumably been eager to steer clear of more direct and/or overly programmatic discussions of such matters, but they also could not ignore them altogether. Instead, they would presumably have had to offer, either explicitly or implicitly, some very basic definitional and even normative answers to some difficult questions: How are Americans supposed to get along with each other within their diverse democracy? What is it, exactly, that holds Americans together?

At first glance, one might presume that presidents giving these high-profile addresses would prefer to answer such questions via platitudes and blatant appeals to patriotism. And sometimes presidents have gotten away with merely that—a fact that I will argue later is not as unimportant as one might initially suspect. But chief executives could not get away with such easy answers all of the time, even within their inaugural and state of the union messages. Consider the constraints they might have faced by virtue of their constituents' diverse heritages, for example, especially when formulating their answers during crises of immigration or race relations. If chief executives appealed too blatantly to their existing constituents' prejudices and fears, they would risk encouraging a dangerous brand of nationalism that lionized intolerance and thus repudiated the allegedly American ideals of equality and individualism. Yet if they ignored popular concerns altogether, they might appear unresponsive to voters' desires and thus risk political suicide. In such moments, the only politically viable solution might be to balance both impulses. In order to preside over a diverse yet peaceful democracy, presidents would have to craft a sense of political community that could both promote an enduring vision of national unity and also respond to the changing needs of a changing constituency. To acknowledge the American people's diversity without allowing it to rhetorically overshadow their democratic bonds, presidents would presumably have to navigate between the Scylla of a pure ideology and the Charybdis of naked pragmatism.

This book is based on my reading of these navigations. Using an interpretive approach, I identified in each text the words and phrases presidents used when describing or otherwise characterizing the "American people." Having made note of these passages, I compared and contrasted them across time in order to search for common themes and/or anomalies within the inaugural addresses and state of the union messages given from 1885 to 2000. In general, I found this discourse to be fairly uniform. Overall, presidents have used these highly ritualized moments to define American nationalism in exactly the ways we might have expected them to: They have promoted an ideational standard for American identity that could easily accommodate diverse constituents. The notion that American identity comes from holding certain principles is not a new one, nor is it uniquely presidential, as I discuss in chapter 1. Just as Crevecoeur, Tocqueville, Hartz, Lipset, and countless other commentators have, U.S. presidents have also repeatedly stated in their speeches that American national identity is based on certain shared beliefs. And they have just as regularly promised that anyone who holds these beliefs is fit to be an American. The appeal of such a definition is obvious. In a country whose citizens may share few of the types of hereditary or biological ties that bind other nations, it makes sense to define national identity ideationally, thus making it available to all comers—at least in theory.

Yet U.S. presidents have not associated American identity with just any type of ideals in these texts. In chapter 2, I argue that they have typically associated it with the nation's traditional civil religious beliefs, an association that I suggest has both advantages and disadvantages. Indeed, after explaining and documenting this type of rhetoric, I spend the remainder of the book focusing on specific examples that underscore some of the more unfortunate implications of this tendency. In chapters 3 through 5, I argue that the conflation of American identity with civil religious themes has sometimes made it far too easy for some presidents to suggest that not all people are worthy of inclusion in the *demos.* Thus, even within the idealized and presumably inclusive discourses chosen for this study, there are times when certain presidents have also suggested that not all types of people are fully equipped to take on the mantle of U.S. citizenship, that there are some who simply cannot be expected to cherish American ideals in the proper way. In chapter 3 I explain how this suggestion has been made during immigration crises, while chapter 4 focuses on times in which presidential rhetoric has implied as much during racial crises. Likewise, in chapter 5 I analyze presidential discussions of the "woman question." Overall, then, although the great majority of the presidential rhetoric featured in this analysis reveals exactly the ideational definitions of national identity that we might expect from presidents, there are also notable moments throughout the second half of U.S. presidential history to date when particular chief executives have offered an altogether different message. Within texts that we might expect to be only inclusive and inviting, I argue, lurks another discourse of exclusivity and dismissal.

Thus, for more than one hundred years and perhaps even longer, in the two genres of presidential rhetoric studied here, chief executives may have simultaneously encouraged tolerance and sanctioned intolerance among the American people. If we can find such a contradictory yet hardy blending of themes within even this type of rhetoric—when presidents are assumed to be talking about the American people in the most positive terms—then what does that mean? In chapter 6 I argue that it might mean that some of the enduring contradictions of American democracy are written plainly into the some of the nation's most ideal-driven texts. If this is so, then, Gunnar Myrdal's "American Dilemma," in which Americans' deeds do not live up to their creed, is such a quintessential part of the U.S. democracy that even presidents cannot overcome it in some of their most well-crafted and rosy messages.

As troublesome as this implication may be, in the pages that follow I will not blame individual presidents for their collective mixed messages. The purpose of this book is less to allege conspiracy or xenophobia among particular presidents than to try to use presidential rhetoric to uncover a dominant cultural logic that may explain some of the more curious contradictions of American nationalism. I will ultimately suggest that this logic may have "used" presidents as much as they have used it, for even their most worrisome messages may be read as being extremely functional. In fact, one of my conclusions is that this curiously contradictory message within presidential rhetoric may in fact be an important kind of glue that holds the American people together, for better and for worse.

Two main concepts central to this book—American national identity and presidential rhetoric—have both been studied before. Legions of scholars have speculated on the roots of American nationalism, for example, and as I have mentioned, I will review some of the most influential arguments in chapter 1. For the moment, though, it is worth noting the main difference between this work and one of the most recent additions to the corpus described above: Rogers Smith's 1997 *Civic Ideals*. There Smith analyzed citizenship laws for their definitions of American character and found that "multiple traditions" of both egalitarian and ascriptive themes were the conflicting yet constitutive basis of the nation's civic ideals. Although Smith uncovers some of the same types of contradictory messages that I explore here, this study is different from Smith's because it is a rhetorical analysis. Whereas Smith used legal, institutionally codified texts for his analysis, this book is based on political speeches, which respond to more public types of exigencies and felt needs and are thus crafted to be both meaningful and motivating to a live audience of citizens.

Likewise, other scholars have studied historical cases of presidential discourse to see how it has enabled chief executives to meet particular challenges. Yet within rhetorical studies especially, most of these types of accounts have focused mainly on one president, administration, and/or distinct historical period.[30] Notable examples of this line of inquiry include David Zarefsky's *President Johnson's War on Poverty: Rhetoric and History* and Martin J. Medhurst's *Dwight D. Eisenhower: Strategic Communicator.* In covering the time period of 1885 to 2000, however, this book differs by offering both an interpretive and a longitudinal reading of the presidency. In other words, by providing critical analysis of the rhetoric of multiple presidents, this book offers an alternative perspective that, while enabling me to offer only relatively minor insights into individual office holders, can hopefully provide a broader lens through which to view the institution of the presidency and, more specifically, its symbolic functions within a diverse democracy.

In describing and defending this reading, I have written mostly as a rhetorical critic in these pages. At times I have asked multidisciplinary questions, to be sure, most often related to history, sociology, and politics. I have asked whether or not the tensions behind the changing norms for U.S. citizenship have been reflected in presidential speech, for example, and I have also used historical evidence to reference specific challenges during the citizenry's growth. As changes in economic, legislative, and other structural conditions affected who was eligible for citizenship from 1885 to 2000, we might expect that presidential descriptions of the voting constituency had to change as well. Or, alternatively, we might suppose that presidents' use of constitutive rhetoric in the speeches studied here did not change at all, as chief executives merely worked harder to assert a particular kind of transcendent national subject in the face of all evidence to the contrary. Here we shall see that although some changes have occurred in this discourse, the second hypothesis seems to be truer than the first.

As a rhetorical critic, however, I have obviously also interpreted this discourse, and my primary purpose throughout this book has been to make a persuasive case for that interpretation. To that end, I have used in the pages that follow numerous textual examples to support my claims. I have not, however, taken care to include one example from every president, nor has that been my goal. Instead, I have tried to select representative examples of presidential discourse that together present a compelling account of how American national identity has been constructed in presidential rhetoric over time, especially during contentious points in the nation's history. Having thus described the book's focus, I should also briefly clarify what this work is not.

First, because this book is not based on a content analytic or otherwise quantitative analysis of presidential speeches, it does not provide a detailed charting of when, where, or how often U.S. presidents have talked about diversity. It does not reveal which president spoke about such matters the most, for example, and it does not attempt to correlate such discussions with campaign strategies, audiences' voting habits, or any other variables. Those are very good questions, but they are not answered here. Instead of documenting such trends quantitatively, this book investigates presidential rhetoric qualitatively by using a historical-critical lens to trace its major constitutive themes regarding American nationalism.

Second, this book does not offer a definitive historical account of the American people's diversity, nor does it attempt to offer a comprehensive account of every federal or otherwise governmental response to that diversity. Other scholars have answered those questions well, and we can assume, happily, that such literature will only continue to grow.[31] Instead, this book recounts the ways in which U.S. presidents have tried to provide such an accounting to the American people at certain points in their history. If this book can be read as a history, then, it is a self-consciously strategic and thus impartial history, told by way of the stories that presidents have themselves told, sometimes at the expense of the actual facts. Although I routinely draw attention to discrepancies between presidential rhetoric and socio-political reality in the pages that follow, my primary critical focus is geared more toward the former than the latter.

Third, this book does not dwell on individual presidents' motives nor does it attempt to provide a detailed recounting of the rhetorical situation that each one faced. In this latter sense especially, this work is not one that easily fits under the umbrella of traditional public address scholarship. Instead, it tries to provide a broader view of the discursive landscape painted by multiple presidents. In other words, this book seeks to provide insights into the nature and implications of a particular strain of presidential rhetoric that has emerged within a particular set of political, institutional, and cultural circumstances. Scholarship on individual presidents is important, to be sure, and I have relied on it heavily in writing this book. Yet here I have been less interested in determining Grover Cleveland's personal feelings about immigration than in seeing what Cleveland's words and, say, Ronald Reagan's—offered one hundred years later on the same subject—had in common. What might we make of their symbolic brotherhood?

Throughout this book I have tried to demonstrate the benefits of listening to past presidents' words as a means toward understanding the past as well as the emergent challenges of the United States' diverse democracy. Some may say that listening to the voices of a group of white men, most of whom are dead, is an odd way to study diversity. In defense of this larger methodological choice, it is worth remembering that, in some respects, the United States is itself an odd place for both nationalism and democracy to flourish. As we will see, both the history and heterogeneity of the United States make it a special case among nations, meaning that its democratic leaders face unique challenges and that we might want to look at their discourse in some new ways. More specifically, as I argue in the following section, we might want to reconsider the reasons why modern presidents in particular would need to speak more often to—and about—the American people.

NATIONALISM AND THE PROBLEM OF THE UNITED STATES: AN ALTERNATIVE ACCOUNT OF THE RISE OF THE RHETORICAL PRESIDENCY

Benedict Anderson has argued that the modern idea of nationalism gained prominence in the eighteenth century with the waning supremacy of both religion and monarchs. After the demise of sacred and feudal communities, he suggests, a new type of union emerged to give individuals sociological solidarity.[32] The "nation" was not merely a substitute collectivity, however. Like its predecessors, it both demanded and promoted a certain way of thinking about individual identity, one inextricably linked to a relatively new technology, the printing press, as well as to an emerging economic system, capitalism.

Print capitalism helped nations disseminate ideas. Whereas churches with illiterate congregations had spread their messages through iconology, and whereas monarchies had employed artisans to portray their magnificence, statist institutions fostered a "national imagination" through books and other works.[33] "Print-capitalism . . . made it possible for rapidly growing numbers of people to think about themselves, and to relate themselves to others, in profoundly new ways," Anderson notes.[34] These new modes of thought were in turn abetted by the rise of state vernaculars. From the fourteenth to the seventeenth century, for example, the Latin language mutated gradually as printed materials written in more specialized, local dialects spread through western Europe. This distribution fostered the development of what are now known as the Germanic languages, and this linguistic diversity in turn hastened the formation of national communities, according to Anderson.[35] By the eighteenth century, then, many believed that individuals who shared language necessarily shared other characteristics and allegiances as well.

But the United States was a different case altogether. The "new American states of the late eighteenth and early nineteenth centuries are of unusual interest," Anderson writes, "because it seems almost impossible to explain them in terms of the two factors . . . which dominated . . . European thinking" about nationalism.[36] First, the American colonists shared a common language with the British, but they rejected the British form of government. Second, the colonists were not peasants, the usual instigators of revolt, but were largely middle class, literate, and relatively well educated. These distinctions are key to the original conceptions of American nationalism, Anderson suggests, which held that even away from their home soil, northern Europeans were better suited for citizenship (and, of course, leadership) than anyone else. Thus the "idea" of America was first perceived as both the product and the exclusive realm of the Protestant, English-speaking colonists.[37]

This belief would cast a shadow over domestic affairs long after the young nation had established its new government. As the country expanded geographically and as more newcomers landed on its shores, its still largely Protestant and all English-speaking leaders would greatly need both the ideological support and willing labor of non-northern Europeans, much in the way feudal barons needed serfs.[38] Yet how could these leaders explain the idea of America to such newcomers? Some immigrants did not speak English, and even those who did were assumed to be incapable of understanding the Enlightenment philosophy of John Locke, for example, or the colonial manifestos of Thomas Paine. Government officials would have to explain citizenship in a way that they thought these newcomers could understand, even if that meant adapting some of these original, allegedly untranslatable principles.

As daunting as this translation process seemed, it would become even more important to the nation's continued stability by the end of the nineteenth century, the time period when this analysis begins. By the late 1880s the United States was swelling with record numbers of immigrants, newcomers whose eagerness and foreignness were equally repellent to more established citizens.[39] In addition, thousands of displaced Native Americans and former slaves struggled to build new lives during this period, even amidst great resentment on the part of many Americans. The women's suffrage movement was also growing, and although women would not win the right to vote nationally until 1920, debates about women's entry into the public sphere were becoming more common and more combative. In short, as the population's differences grew at the nineteenth century's end, so did its discontents. At times, the only thing that the American people seemed to share was a federal government.

Not coincidentally, perhaps, at around this same time U.S. presidents began speaking directly to the American public more and more often. Jeffrey K. Tulis and others have named this historical phenomenon the "rise of the rhetorical presidency" and have attributed the increase in chief executives' speech-making to a few select presidents' shifting views of statesmanship and their constitutional responsibilities at the century's end. Noting that the rhetorical presidency "puts a premium on active and continuous presidential leadership of public opinion," Tulis has suggested that rhetorical presidents have used speech-making to increase their legislative and political power with Congress by garnering popular support for specific policy or agenda items.[40] While Tulis's analysis is persuasive and this function is undeniably important, the rhetorical presidency may serve an additional purpose as well.

Consider the fact that the presidents credited with establishing the rhetorical presidency, namely Theodore Roosevelt, William Taft, and Woodrow Wilson, were all charged with leading a nation that was experiencing rapid growth and, in some areas, fragmentation. Between 1890 and 1909, for example, the decennial immigration to the United States more than doubled, from 3,694,294 to 8,202,388.[41] At roughly the same time, thousands of former slaves struggled with their new freedom—one far newer to some than others, as it took years for news of the Emancipation Proclamation to spread and decades longer for local governments to enforce the Fourteenth and Fifteenth Amendments. Similarly, the American economy felt the Civil War's effects long after its end. Although some parts of the country enjoyed a postwar boom, many southerners were more impoverished than ever, with philosophical resentments compounding their financial woes.

It is perhaps not surprising, then, that both Theodore Roosevelt and Wilson in particular saw an urgent need to "refound" the nation and that both viewed public speech as central to this effort, according to Tulis.[42] Roosevelt, alarmed by the incendiary tactics of demagogues and fearful of the possibility of a national class war, responded by using rhetoric to "act as a brake on public opinion." Wilson went even further, Tulis argues, by "reinterpreting" the Constitution and the presidency so that a chief executive might have "more intimate contact with Congress and the people."[43]

According to Tulis, Wilson advocated this access because he saw interpretation of public opinion as the "core of leadership." For him presidential speech was more than mere translation; a chief executive could also use rhetoric to instruct the American people about collective wishes.[44] Wilson saw this type of leadership as crucial to democratic governance, where "policy—where there is no absolute and arbitrary ruler to do the choosing for the whole people—

means massed opinion, and the forming of the mass is the whole art and mastery of politics."[45] Before he could govern, then, a president first had to "form the mass," an increasingly difficult task in a nation whose population was expanding, and in some cases on the verge of splintering, at unprecedented rates.

Instead of viewing the rhetorical presidency solely in terms of its more obviously political functions, then, we might also view it as involving more subtle ministrations. In this sense, the concept of "going public" might mean something slightly different than it has in the work of Tulis or Samuel Kernell. Kernell, for example, conceptualizes "going public" as "a class of activities in which presidents engage as they promote themselves and their policies before the American public." The point of going public, Kernell continues, is "to place the president and his message before the American people in a way that enhances his success in Washington."[46] Yet if we take a more expansive and symbolic view of the presidency, such as the one offered by Walter Fisher in which it can be viewed as a "symbolic, suasory force, a source of inducement to belief, attitude, value, and action . . . [and] a focal point of national reason and rationality," then chief executives might also be viewed as symbolic guardians of national unity in the United States.[47] If so, then Kernell's influential definition might need to be amended; going public might also function to promote the *idea* of an American people *to* the American people. Especially at times when the American people seem concerned about their own diversity, presidents may be in a unique position to reassure citizens that there is in fact a "national reason and rationality" and that they, too, are a part of it. Such persuading in fact can increase presidents' chances of success in Washington, at least to the extent that they and the Congress continue to preside over a united (and at least partially engaged) democratic public.

Indeed, throughout most of the twentieth century, U.S. presidents appear to have been increasingly charged with managing their constituents' wildly diverse demographic, cultural, economic, and political differences. In spite of Theodore Roosevelt's infamous rejoinder decrying "hyphenated Americans," his executive successors have appeared to become more and more responsive to their constituents' problems of diversity. To wit, even candidates for the presidency in the year 2000 had to carefully craft their responses to the case of six-year-old refugee Elián González, lest they risk the voting-booth fury of a community of Cuban immigrants. It may be, then, that one of the most important but least investigated challenges of the rhetorical presidency has been, in Jean Bethke Elshtain's words, the creation and maintenance of "a political body that brought people together and created a 'we' but still enabled people to . . . respect one another's individualities."[48]

Readers will undoubtedly have their own opinions about how admirable or successful presidents have been in their attempts at using rhetoric to create and maintain such a political body. For my own part, I was ultimately both encouraged and disheartened by the implications of my findings, an ambivalence that may itself be central to American national identity. As banal as presidential constructions of American national identity might seem at times, they may serve an important social function by promoting a sense of enduring democratic unity in the United States. In other words, it may be that presidential platitudes themselves are an important type of "glue" that holds the American people together. If so, there is considerable rhetorical and political genius in that. Nevertheless, to some readers, the rhetorical moves discussed in this book may not seem smart at all; some may be discouraged by the extent to which centuries-old sensibilities regarding ethnic, racial, and gender differences can still haunt more recent pronouncements from the bully pulpit.

Lest this latter conclusion seem too pessimistic, readers might also remember at the outset that the United States' diverse democracy is still very much a work in progress and that its relative stability is as unprecedented as it is unexpected. After all, as Robert Dahl has reminded us, for the ancient Greeks, "the only thinkable site of democracy was, of course, the city-state," with its limited size, shared ethnicity, and exclusively male, property-owning voters.[49] They would never have predicted that democracy could be possible in a place where the *demos* comprises more than 270 million people who may live thousands of miles apart without necessarily sharing any common ethnicity, class interests, gender, sexual orientation, or religious beliefs.[50] That such a political community is possible, even if only in our imaginations, is remarkable. This book explores some of the words that may have made it so.

CHAPTER 1

The Riddle
of the "American People"

merica is truly a shock to the stranger," Gunnar Myrdal wrote know-
ingly in 1944. "The bewildering impression it gives of dissimilarity
throughout and of chaotic unrest is indicated by the fact that few
outside observers—and indeed, few native Americans—have been able to
avoid the intellectual escape of speaking about America as 'paradoxical.'"[1] Even
in the early 1940s, long before the social movements of the 1960s or the culture wars of the 1990s, the United States already seemed wildly diverse and
perplexing to this Swedish observer.

And why not? Nowhere in the European world did so many different types
of people consider themselves part of the same *demos,* and yet there was perhaps nowhere else where the contradictions implicit in a people's union were
so apparent. In a nation founded on principles of equality, for example, everyday practices of institutionalized inequality were all too obvious to Myrdal.
In 1938, while touring the South to research race relations in the United States,
he admitted to a benefactor that he was not prepared for what he saw. "I didn't
realize," Myrdal reportedly confided, "what a terrible problem you have put
me into. I mean we are horrified."[2]

As Myrdal would soon discover, such horrible truths were not limited to
the southern states alone. In 1944, the year his work *An American Dilemma:
The Negro Problem and American Democracy* was published, hundreds of race
riots broke out in more than fifty different U.S. cities. That same year,
Lawrence Fuchs has reported, the University of Denver's National Opinion
Research Center "found that a majority of whites thought that white people
should have the first chance at any kind of job over Negroes."[3] The nation's
internal tensions were not limited to black-white relations. The American
people were especially fearful of their own religious and ethnic diversity

throughout the 1930s and 1940s, when, for example, Protestant clergy were publicly warning their congregations that American Catholics would eventually overturn the U.S. Constitution.[4] Likewise, public opinion polls during the early 1940s regularly reported widespread agreement with the notion that "Jews were more of a threat to the nation than Blacks, Catholics, Germans, and Japanese," with 1942 being the only year that the latter two groups were considered more dangerous than Jews.[5] Indeed, the United States' involvement in World War II only exacerbated an already-budding nativism among its residents, as more than 100,000 Japanese Americans were legally interned in the early 1940s and Mexican Americans were targeted in race riots throughout the United States.

Amidst all of this discord, however, Myrdal also heard a surprising yet unmistakable harmony. "Still there is evidently a strong unity in this nation and a basic homogeneity and stability in its valuations," he reported, his economist's terse style perhaps belying his actual astonishment. "Americans of all national origins, classes, regions, creeds, and colors have something in common: a social ethos, a political creed. It is difficult to avoid the judgment that this 'American Creed' is the cement in the structure of this great and disparate nation."[6]

Myrdal's assessment is now famous, of course, not necessarily because he said anything new—observers had been commenting on Americans' unique yet conflicting beliefs since the eighteenth century—and certainly not because his words solved the problems they were meant to diagnose. In fact, in recent years, as the American people have once again become troubled by their own diversity, some observers have wondered if the problems that so disconcerted Myrdal have only gotten worse. Nevertheless, the Swedish observer's initial appraisal remains attractive because it puts in simple terms two of the most baffling conditions of American nationalism.

First, most thinkers have agreed with Myrdal's observation that the United States is simultaneously divided and unified, a country somehow filled with both "chaotic unrest" and "a basic homogeneity and stability." This fundamental paradox has vexed observers for more than two centuries.[7] Many have asked how the American people can possibly attend to both *pluribus* and *unum*.[8] How can the United States remain sufficiently multicultural and monocultural? Long before anyone was worried about ethnic and racial diversity per se, the founders wrestled with remarkably similar questions of factionalism and federalism as they devised the new nation's government. Even hundreds of years after these debates, Myrdal's description reminds us that to discuss American political community, one has to account for its inherent and enduring tensions, thus begging a question that is perhaps as old as the nation itself: What holds Americans together?

The traditional answer to that question is, in fact, Myrdal's answer—shared beliefs—and this explanation is itself the second reason why his comments still resonate. In the decades since *An American Dilemma* was published, Myrdal's thesis has captured the imagination of a wide variety of scholars, many of whom have passionately debated the exact nature and even the very existence of an "American Creed."[9] Still, within much contemporary scholarship there remains general agreement that shared beliefs, values, and/or attitudes of some sort continue to serve as the "cement" of the American political community, even if these beliefs are themselves transitory, contradictory, and/or hegemonic.[10] Even in an age of heightened awareness of difference and postmodernist skepticism about the possibility of shared meanings, then, it *has* proven very difficult for observers to "avoid the judgment" that some common ways of thinking have in fact held the American people together.[11]

If the American people are ultimately united by a certain set of beliefs, it would obviously be important to know more about what these beliefs are. As I have already suggested and will discuss shortly, there has been a significant amount of scholarly inquiry about their exact nature. And yet as much as we think we know about what these ideals are, we know far less about why they have never truly triumphed in the United States. From the era of Alexis de Tocqueville in the early nineteenth century to the turn of the twenty-first century it has been common for observers to state confidently that Americans believe in equality, for example, but it has been far more difficult for them to explain why so much social inequality has persisted in the United States. (This contradiction was a problem even for Tocqueville, of course, who was troubled by seeing things that were "American but not democratic" in the treatment of Native Americans and slaves.)

For his part, Myrdal believed that the American creed would ultimately prevail.[12] "Americans [will] solve the problem of racial injustice," he predicted in 1944, "or they will cease to be Americans."[13] Obviously, neither of these outcomes has happened, so perhaps something else has occurred. Maybe, as I will argue throughout this book, the American people have learned how to live comfortably with their contradictions. Perhaps they have come to understand American beliefs—and, by implication, American identity—in a way that has helped ease the cognitive dissonance that has presumably accompanied the glaring discrepancies between their creed and their conduct. By learning more about how Americans' allegedly shared beliefs have been transmitted and taught, we might also learn something about the American people's collective compromise (the tacit bargain they may have made to reconcile their national contradiction between "deeds and creed") as well as its potential costs.

In most of this book, I explore this possible reconciliation via a close reading of presidential rhetoric, in which I examine how these elite political actors have explained Americans' shared beliefs, and thus American national identity, to their constituents. Before describing this discourse, however, it might be instructive to first revisit the shared beliefs hypothesis as other voices have articulated it. As Myrdal, Tocqueville, and other commentators' work would suggest, the question of what holds Americans together is neither new nor answered only by presidents. In this chapter I provide a brief intellectual history of this line of inquiry. As we will see, most observers have traditionally taken an ontological approach to the study of American ideals. While popular and beneficial, this approach is also necessarily limited and perhaps even ill-suited to the context, given the social and material conditions of the United States. I conclude by suggesting that a more epistemological and thus more rhetorical focus might address some of these shortcomings. Overall, then, this chapter recounts some of the most influential explanations of American nationalism and then argues that the rhetorical criticism of presidential discourse can add something important to these discussions.

THE SHARED BELIEFS HYPOTHESIS:
ITS ROOTS AND THEMES

Although there has been considerable debate about what kinds of beliefs Americans might share, there has been a surprising amount of agreement that sharing particular ways of thinking has itself been uniquely American. In the words of Sacvan Bercovitch, the American people are commonly assumed to be a "pluralistic, pragmatic people openly living in a dream, bound together by an ideological consensus unmatched by any other modern society."[14] The presumption of some level of ideological consensus has loomed large in most descriptive accounts of American identity and American community, and here I use the phrase "shared beliefs hypothesis" to draw attention to this tendency.[15] Yet most of the accounts that support this hypothesis have been ontological rather than epistemological. That is, most commentators have spent most of their time trying to reveal what these beliefs are: exactly which ideas Americans might share, for example, or which ideals have dominated U.S. political culture. To illustrate this tendency and provide readers with a sense of some of the most popular answers to such questions, in this section I review some of the major themes within this literature.

At the outset, however, it is important to remember that the shared beliefs hypothesis was not invented by scholars. The description of American identity in ideational terms predates not only scholarly descriptions of American nationalism but also the creation of the nation itself. In 1759, for example, Hector St. John de Crevecoeur posed the question, "What then is the American, this new man?" so that he could offer a reply that would emphasize the unique habits of mind that were nurtured and, indeed, necessitated by this new world: "He is an American, who leaving behind him all his ancient prejudices and manners, receives new ones from the new mode of life he has embraced, the new government he obeys, the new rank he holds. The American is a new man, who acts upon new principles."[16] There is no shortage of novelty in Crevecoeur's description, just as there was presumably no shortage of novelty in his everyday existence as an immigrant to the United States in the eighteenth century. Yet notice what he calls "new" and why. Americans have new "prejudices and manners" and even new "principles," born of the new life, new government, and new rank they share. Although presumably everything about their daily practices, tasks, and settings would have been in markedly novel contrast to the environments found in their European homelands, Crevecoeur and others would choose to emphasize their new psyche, their uniquely American minds.

In Crevecoeur's description, such a mindset was as much the product of what was missing in America ("ancient prejudices and manners") as it was a reflection of what was actually there. Subsequent foreign observers would concur. In Tocqueville's influential *Democracy in America,* for example, he noted that Americans were "born equal instead of becoming so" and thus were automatically freed from the multiple and rigid hierarchies of European social life. As James Morone has explained, "In the new world there was no *ancien regime;* no revolutionary tradition to attack it; no reactionary conservatism to counterattack. The result would be a profound faith in individualism. In short, they became unshakable liberals."[17] From the beginning, then, Americans were American because of a shared "profound faith" in certain ideas. This faith itself might have been born out of material necessity and/or novel social conditions, but regardless of its origins or causes, the rhetoric of American identity established in these early accounts defined it as being determined by a shared way of thinking.

The appeal of this definition is clear. In a nation whose citizens may have little else in common, focusing on shared beliefs is an efficient way of accommodating other types of differences. Thus the "ideological character of American nationality," as Philip Gleason has explained, has "meant that it was open to anyone who willed to become an American."[18] In the days of Crevecoeur and Tocqueville, of course, such an invitation would have been nothing short of revolutionary; in European as well as most other nations, identity was based on biology and heredity, bloodline and borders. As the United States fought for and won independence from England as well as European topoi, the unprecedented ideological nature of the rhetoric of American identity became even more exaggerated.[19] Accordingly, Seymour Martin Lipset has pointed to the nation's founding as ground zero for his conception of American exceptionalism. "The United States is exceptional in starting from a revolutionary event, in being 'the first new nation,' the first colony, to be independent, other than Iceland," Lipset writes. "It has defined its raison d'etre *ideologically.* As historian Richard Hofstadter has noted, 'It has been our fate as a country not to have ideologies but to be one.'"[20]

But which ideology, exactly, has the United States been? Which ideas have come to define the American mind? Such questions were the subject of an incredible amount of popular and scholarly attention throughout the twentieth century, although it has recently become fashionable to doubt the benefits of asking them, as I will discuss later in this chapter. Whatever the current fashion, the practice of seeking insights into Americans' shared beliefs has echoed Tocqueville's sense of a certain "patriotism of reflection" among U.S. citizens, whose awareness of national identity has been called assertive and self-conscious and even, by the British statesman James Lord Bryce, "obtrusive."[21] Arthur Mann has suggested that this self-consciousness itself guarantees that questions of national identity remain at the forefront of American public discourse, as it has "locked the American people into a two-centuries-long dialogue with themselves about the meaning and the implementation of their distinguishing idea."[22]

Within the scholarly community such reflection has at times been difficult and even unsatisfactory. "The effort to write about an American mind," Rush Welter has opined, "has proceeded by interpretive devices that seem inadequate to the purpose."[23] Perhaps this is why no less of an authority than Henry Steele Commager once lamented that it would take a "thousand essays to penetrate to the truth about America."[24] Despite such difficulties, at least four interrelated characterizations of American identity have frequently recurred within this literature: an American mission, an American yearning, an American idea, and an American psyche. These themes are so well known as set pieces of Americana that I have discussed them only briefly here via references to some of their most influential proponents' work. Whatever these various authors' particular emphases, however, all four themes share one striking commonality: All presume that American identity is a distinctly cerebral proposition, emanating from the individual or, in some cases, from the ancestral mind into an ephemeral yet somehow enduring national consciousness.

An American Mission

In 1802 John Quincy Adams gave a speech in which he saluted the nation's founders. He did not talk about George Washington, Thomas Jefferson, James Madison, or Alexander Hamilton but instead praised Walter Raleigh, William Penn, William Bradford, and John Winthrop.[25] At least one current observer, Michael Lind, has argued that Adams made the right choices, for this latter group of men comprises the "culture-founders" who "deserve the greatest priority" for their influence over American consciousness. In the case of Winthrop at least, legions of scholars would presumably agree, because his sermonic vision of America as a "city on a hill" articulated a mythic yet supremely influential mission for the young nation.[26]

Robert Bellah has explained that within this myth, America can be viewed as "both a paradise and a wilderness, with all of the rich associations of those terms in the Christian and biblical traditions."[27] For New England Puritans such as Winthrop and Jonathan Edwards, this interpretation of the natural environment clarified the settlers' role as well as their responsibilities. Bellah writes that "they saw themselves on a divinely appointed 'errand into the wilderness' with profound personal, ecclesiastical, and world-historical meaning."[28] These early Americans viewed themselves, in other words, as being on a mission from God, with, as Winthrop warned, "the eyes of all people upon us," in which they were to "build up in the midst of the wilderness" a "foretaste of paradise" and thus create a New Canaan.[29]

As Sacvan Bercovitch and others have noted, such a mission had ideological as well as theological implications. For the Puritans, Bercovitch has explained, it "created a mode of consensus designed to fill the needs of a certain social order."[30] According to Bercovitch, Bellah, and numerous other scholars, however, this ideological function was not limited to Puritan society alone. Instead, it has been used, and continues to be used, to make legitimate a view of Americans as "God's chosen people" with attendant responsibilities within both domestic and foreign affairs.[31] Bercovitch has summarized the lasting influence of the Puritans' vision thus: "This was their legacy: a system of sacred-secular symbols (New Israel, American Jerusalem) for a people intent on progress; a set of rituals of anxiety and control that could at once encourage and confine the energies of free enterprise; a rhetoric of mission so broad in its implications, and so specifically American in its application, that it could facilitate the transitions from Puritan to Yankee, and from errand to manifest destiny and the dream."[32] As a potential source of shared beliefs for Americans, then, the Puritans' mission has imprinted itself on the lives of subsequent generations of Americans as a codified "civil religion," which is manifested in political institutions, and by some accounts, is a normalized Protestantism.[33] According to this explanation, Americans are bound together by certain beliefs born of God's calling and their subsequent covenant with him and with each other.

An American Yearning

Implicit in the Puritan mission was the sense of a deep relationship between the American people and their land. A "love of place was the earliest loyalty brought to the American shores," Max Lerner commented. "For the settlers who had come from the tidy landscapes of Europe," he continues, "[the American landscape] was not a wholly comfortable sight. But it was the right kind of stage-set for the theme and the proportions of the mighty drama to be enacted on it, perhaps contrived for that purpose by a Providential scenic designer with an eye for symbolism."[34] Providential interference presumably being in their favor, the first Americans from Europe quickly tamed the landscape and began to reap its many fruits. It also did not take long for the settlers to seek out new landscapes within the New World. "The expansionist cry of 'Manifest Destiny!'" Lerner notes, "was not only a shibboleth of jingoism but almost a tropism of the American Earth."[35]

It would take slightly longer, however, for scholars to make sense of this peculiarly American yearning. According to Richard Slotkin, "No historian who lived in the heyday of the real Frontier saw as much significance in it as the theorists of a post-Frontier historiography."[36] Foremost among these latter theorists, of course, was Frederick Jackson Turner, who, at the 1893 meeting of the American Historical Society, argued that the material conditions of settling the United States and its ever-expanding borders created "a new product that is American."[37] Such a statement was quite radical for its time; most historians still subscribed to a popular "germ theory" of European influence on American life. Yet Turner supposed that something distinctly un-European had happened to settlers as they tamed the land; there, somehow, American character had sprung up from the ground along with their crops.[38] As George Santayana once asked, "This [American] soil is propitious to every seed, and tares must needs grow in it; but why should it not also breed clear thinking, honest judgment, and rational happiness?"[39]

So compelling was Turner's frontier thesis that it would subsequently be used throughout the twentieth century to explain and criticize all manner of uniquely American phenomena, including topics ranging from U.S. history to international relations to literature.[40] Many of these discussions have underscored the impact of both the reality and the myth of the American frontier on some sort of shared cultural consciousness in the United States, for better and for worse. Some thinkers, for example, have written about the ways in which an American frontier mentality legitimated poor treatment of Native Americans.[41] Others have associated it with a more generalized restlessness among the American people, corresponding with John Steinbeck's characterization of Americans as a perpetually "dissatisfied searching people."[42] Still other authors have made a neo-Turnerian argument by using American geography to explain the nation's relative democratic stability.[43] However it has been filtered through intellectual history, Turner's work has thus contributed to the shared beliefs hypothesis of American identity by locating the genesis of American consciousness within the American landscape. Simply put, in Turner's vision a new land created a new type of men.

An American Idea

Exactly how different this "new man" was from his Old World counterparts suddenly became a very pressing question during the first half of the twentieth century.[44] Although World War I and its isolationist aftermath prompted an increase in exclusionary immigration policies as well as nativist scholarship, World War II left scholars with new sorts of questions.[45] Social scientists as well as humanists of this era worked on projects with an "enlarged sense of purpose and a desire to understand America's character and culture in relation to both her allies and her enemies," according to Luther Luedtke.[46]

According to John Higham, from the 1940s through the early 1960s the "crucial task" of such scholars was to "define the matrix of beliefs and attitudes that shaped American history" and had thus "created a distinctive American people." Not surprisingly, then, this period saw the publication of some of the most ambitious and comprehensive studies of American character to date, including Myrdal's massive project.[47] The books written by his contemporaries reveal the authors' mutual interest in defining Americans' distinctiveness as well as their general agreement about the source of this uniqueness.[48] Following, perhaps, the same impulse that led Henry Steele Commager to write his 1950 classic, *The American Mind*, most observers of this period were interested in understanding American consciousness, especially with regard to its suitability as the basis of democratic political community.

In addition to Myrdal, Louis Hartz was undoubtedly one of the most influential thinkers within this group.[49] His book *The Liberal Tradition in America*, published in 1955, provided what Jennifer Hochschild described as an "analysis of the values and visions that distinguish residents of the United States and pull them together into a single nationality" that still looms large over many subsequent studies of American politics.[50] Simply put, Hartz argued that what made Americans American was allegiance to a Lockean "liberal idea"—in other words, a very specific kind of shared belief—that was thus the "secret root" of U.S. ideology and history.[51] Legions of scholars have agreed. In his 1996 analysis of "American exceptionalism," for example, Lipset lists five quintessentially American ideas (liberty, egalitarianism, individualism, populism, and laissez-faire) whose common roots in liberal philosophy reveal how Hartz's diagnosis continues to be at the center of debate about American nationalism.[52]

One of the reasons Hartz's model of liberalism has been so compelling is its compatibility with American civil religion. As Morone has observed, Lockean liberalism, when combined with the aforementioned Puritan mission, lends itself easily to "a model of economic opportunity and a distinctive political creed: equality, liberty, rights, and consent of the governed." "From this perspective," he adds, "American political history reads like the inexorable (although bumpy) march of liberal democracy" in which individuals have continued to secure individual rights as citizenship has been extended to more and more types of people.[53]

However attractive this explanation might seem, some scholars have rejected liberalism as the quintessential American ideal in order to put other concepts on this pedestal. As Rogers Smith has noted, Bernard Bailyn, Gordon Wood, and John Pocock argued for dominant "traditions of republicanism" in U.S. history "that were not reducible to, and in some respects opposed, Lockean liberalism."[54] Within the colonial period, for example, republicanism, not liberalism, was the rallying cry for the revolutionaries, and neither the vagaries of this political philosophy nor its British roots, Wood has argued, kept some of the earliest American citizens from aligning themselves with its principles.[55]

In terms of shared beliefs, foremost among these principles were "love of our country, resignation and obedience to the laws, public spirit, love of liberty, [and] sacrifice of life and all to the public," according to a 1772 tract attributed to "Preceptor."[56] Although this model clearly detracted from liberalism's emphasis on the individual, notice how even this abridged account of republican philosophy emphasizes the need for citizens to share a commitment to certain ideas. A "successful republic required citizens to be profoundly socialized into certain beliefs, aspirations, and character traits," Smith notes. Within American political culture, such beliefs have been linked to democratic republicanism, and, more recently, communitarianism, with an argument for "a consolidated nation" designed to advance the needs of "the people" rather than the individual.[57]

For his part, Smith has rejected the wholesale versions of both liberalism and republicanism as the defining idea of the American people. Instead, he has argued that another set of beliefs, which he classifies as corresponding to "multiple traditions," has evolved within the United States as "political parties and actors [have] offer[ed] varying civic conceptions blending liberal, republican, and ascriptive elements in different combinations." Smith finds evidence of such ideological hybridization in U.S. citizenship laws, crafted by political actors in response to political exigencies and public fears. This perpetual mixture of ideas inevitably results in civil conflicts, according to Smith, meaning that no one idea reigns supreme within the United States. Rather, there is constant fluctuation between competing ideals, "with the long-term trends being products of contingent politics more than inexorable cultural necessities."[58]

Smith's analysis might at first seem to challenge the shared beliefs hypothesis a bit. How can one speak of a people united by shared beliefs if these beliefs are themselves contradictory and transitory? Ultimately, however, Smith's multiple traditions hypothesis can be viewed as reinforcing the shared beliefs hypothesis as much as it threatens it. Not only does the negotiation Smith documents take place between clearly ideological poles, thus revealing the influence of certain types of ideas within the American consciousness, but it also results in an apparently unique (and presumably uniquely American) way of thinking. In Smith's analysis, then, the negotiation of beliefs may be the "cement" so vital to American political community, making the sharing of such dynamic civic ideals all the more remarkable.

An American Psyche

Whatever the exact nature of their political impulses, the American people are collectively also thought of as being excessively pragmatic; Santayana once described the American as an "idealist working with matter."[59] The previously discussed battles over American ideals may sound overly philosophical, but another group of observers has provided an alternative way of identifying shared beliefs in the United States.

During the second half of the twentieth century, scholars from social psychology, political science, sociology, and speech communication contributed to a line of research often referred to as "value analysis." The results of these research efforts were multiple, comprehensive lists of purportedly American values. During the 1960s, for example, Ethel Albert and Robin Williams conducted now-classic studies of "America's traditional core values" by utilizing research methods from the social and behavioral sciences. Noting that self-reported values "should not be mistaken for the actualities of conduct," the authors nevertheless concluded that prominent values in the United States included an activist approach to life, emphasis on achievement and material success, a moral character ("oriented to such Puritan values as duty, industry, and sobriety"), religious faith, scientific and secular rationality, idealism and perfectionism, equality, self-reliance, tolerance for diversity, and external conformity.[60]

A more recent example of this line of inquiry is sociologist Alan Wolfe's 1998 work *One Nation, After All: What Middle-Class Americans Really Think about God, Country, Family, Racism, Welfare, Immigration, Homosexuality, Work, the Right, the Left and Each Other.* Drawing upon interviews with members of the middle class living in select suburbs, Wolfe paints a picture of a prototypical American mind driven primarily by moderation and tolerance, characteristics also featured in previous studies.[61] Perhaps more telling than his conclusions, however, is his study's primary assumption. Finding out what Americans "really think," according to Wolfe, will also tell us "whether we remain one nation, after all."[62] In this view the strength of a nation can be measured, à la the Likert scale perhaps, by the strength of shared beliefs.

Such attempts to create more or less typological accounts of American values deserve mention within this discussion for at least two reasons. First, the results of these studies typically underscore the sometimes contradictory nature of Americans' shared beliefs, much like Smith's analysis did. Somehow, these studies suggest, Americans can value both individuality and conformity at the same time. Some scholars have even suggested that this perpetual state of negotiating competing concepts may itself be a quintessentially American trait.[63] Erik Erikson once argued, for example, that the "functioning American, as the heir to a history of extreme contrasts and abrupt changes, bases his final ego identity on some tentative combination of dynamic polarities."[64]

Second, at a broader level, this research underscores the depths to which the shared beliefs hypothesis has been both trusted and tested by social scientists. While some critics of American studies have claimed that the research is bedeviled by a lack of rigorous methodology, studies such as these reveal that traditional research methods have been used to identify a list of specific characteristics considered germane to or even constitutive of American identity.[65]

Especially within this fourth category of an "American Psyche," then, much of traditional scholarship on Americans' shared beliefs has provided us with a list or, put differently, an ontological accounting of the "distinctively American way of thought, character, and conduct" that Commager tried to capture in 1950. The simplified list of themes offered here might even be thought of as a rudimentary table of contents for the American mind, with one section devoted to a civil religious mission, one dominated by agrarian yearning, one preoccupied with political philosophy, and one that identifies its own needs and impulses.

As much as such accounts might reveal about what is on the American mind, however, they do not tell us much about how such ideas got there, or perhaps even more importantly, how they remain. As George Herbert Mead suggested, minds do not simply just come into being; they are not found but are instead made by external and largely social conditions.[66] Yet when one considers the social and material conditions of the United States, the preeminence of the shared beliefs hypothesis becomes all the more remarkable. In a nation as diverse, capitalistic, and modernist as the United States, the primary question might not be which beliefs citizens share, but instead how American citizens could be expected to share anything at all.

CHALLENGES TO SHARED BELIEFS IN THE UNITED STATES

In some respects, the United States might be the last place one might expect to find shared beliefs among the citizenry. First, and most obviously, there is no avoiding the historic and demographic facts of Americans' many differences and their attendant discontents. How could such a culturally diverse people be expected to share the same ideals? Second, for all their alleged allegiance to political ideals, whether liberal or republican, Americans are also eager capitalists, trained to vie against other for resources and status. How could such a competitive and economically stratified people be expected to share anything? Lastly, they are hopelessly modern, filled with all of the discontented anomie and restlessness that modernity is assumed to imply. How could such a jaded, disconnected people be expected to believe anything?

On the face of it, then, and despite its undeniable popularity, the shared beliefs hypothesis would seem a wildly inappropriate and misleading way to explain American nationalism. Yet this discomfort itself is an initial reason why we might need to know more not about what these beliefs are but instead about how they could possibly be shared by people who might be otherwise fragmented by problems of diversity, philosophy, and modernity.

The Problem of Diversity

The lure of the shared beliefs hypothesis notwithstanding, some commentators are loath to make "generalizations about the 'American tradition,'" Max Lerner notes, "because there are as many subtraditions as there are national and ethnic groups that came to America, and each has left a heritage."[67] Over time, this diversity has debilitated the American people as much as it has defined them.

Journalist John Elston has noted that "the most salient fact about American history is [that] the ancestors of everyone who lives in the United States originally came from somewhere else."[68] Although Elston's comment ignores the Native Americans, his comments underscore the idea that the conditions of the United States' diverse democracy are as old as the nation itself. Built on the backs of immigrant and slave labor, the United States would also become an endurance test of sorts for its diverse constituents, who have been forced together under conditions of adversity, suspicion, and prejudice from colonial days until contemporary times. Nativism ran just as rampant through the Puritans' "wilderness" as it would throughout the nineteenth and twentieth centuries, for example.[69] The problem of the color line, too, grew out of colonial practices, when the "importation" of slave labor from Africa engendered what Howard Zinn has called "that special racial feeling—whether hatred, or contempt, or pity, or patronization—that accompanied the inferior position of blacks in America for the next 350 years."[70]

The fears and problems that have arisen because of Americans' ethnic and racial differences are well known today, in large part because recent generations of scholars have insisted on telling the stories of the "overlooked voices" of American history.[71] Indeed, some of these stories will be retold in this book. Yet even the telling of these tales, true though they may be, contributes to a certain sense of loss of national unity within the United States, according to some commentators.[72] Noted historian John Higham, for example, who in the 1950s and 1960s had criticized "the cult of American consensus" that tended to homogenize U.S. history so "that all separate particles were blended together in one indistinguishable mass," changed his stance considerably a few decades later. In 1983, Higham lamented that "somewhere in the late 1960s the ruling paradigms of homogeneity and consensus were replaced by the paradigms of fragmentation and heterogeneity," thereby supplanting any sense of "our national unity and our national identity."[73]

Despite this alleged loss, the American people have increasingly sought even more recognition of their manifold heterogeneity.[74] As many Americans continue to call for greater awareness of multiple layers of identity, personal elements such as gender, sexual orientation, age, physical appearance, and physical ability acquire the status of traditionally acknowledged characteristics such as ethnicity and race. As political philosopher Iris Marion Young has noted, "In our complex, plural society, every social group has group differences cutting across it, which are potential sources of wisdom, excitement, conflict, and oppression. Gay men, for example, may be Black, rich, homeless, or old, and those differences produce different identifications and potential conflicts among gay men, as well as affinities with straight men."[75] By cutting across traditional identifications, these more specific features can make the assumption of ideological consensus even more difficult. Individuals may identify with one group's position on one issue and then disassociate themselves from its views on another, making shared beliefs more difficult to identify, even among presumably homogeneous groups.[76] Such shifting bonds can challenge the American people's perception of themselves as a nation "united under God" or anything else, leaving the critic to wonder if the shared beliefs hypothesis is an accurate description of American nationalism.

The Problem of Economics

Perhaps because of the overwhelming nature of the United States' many demographic differences, some observers have explained the enduring union of the nation by invoking a shared philosophical ideal of Lockean individualism, as I have already discussed. Paradoxically, however, by its very nature this presumably shared belief can severely challenge the possibility of a united, interdependent citizenry.

As the product of the marriage between individualism and capitalism, the notion of an "American Dream" is perhaps one of the most revered mythologies in the United States. Achieving this dream is a sign of strength, self-reliance, and the ability to overcome the past, and it is undeniably related to the American yearning for conquest and expansion.[77] Yet the means by which individuals might achieve these goals can be controversial in the United States, where citizens often argue about how equality of opportunity might be promoted within a capitalistic system that is guaranteed to produce inequality of results.

Such a schizoid demand is undoubtedly the product of the same Lockean liberalism long thought to unite the American people, in which the individual is "prior to society, which comes into existence only through the voluntary contract of individuals trying to maximize their own self-interest."[78] Put slightly differently, and in Tocqueville's words, "In ages of equality, every man finds his beliefs within himself." Yet the French observer also warned about this tendency, especially in a democracy, where "isolation of each man from the rest and egoism resulting therefrom stand out clearest."[79] If American individualism threatened the potential for American political community, such problems could only be exacerbated by an attendant economic philosophy.

Much like John Locke had, Adam Smith broke with the traditional theories of his day by focusing on the individual rather than society and by arguing that the basic source of wealth was human labor, not the state.[80] Smith argued that even self-interest, if properly channeled, ultimately benefited the greater community as well through the invisible hand theory, which held that "the individual, intending only his own gain, is led to 'promote an end which was no part of his own intention,' the well-being of society," according to James Bronowski and Bruce Mazlish.[81] This belief has been repeatedly reincarnated in American popular and political culture; nearly two hundred years after Smith's death, for example, it was central to the "trickle-down theory" of Reaganomics in the 1980s. This philosophical tradition allowed Americans to perceive a convenient link between the free-wheeling existential self and a (necessarily) conservative social order. In short, what was good for General Motors—or, more to the point, for Bill Gates or Sam Walton—was also good for the country.[82]

In theory, then, individualism and capitalism would indeed seem to be great social levelers within a diverse democracy. Instead of being locked into a social caste, each person has an equal chance to get ahead in a social hierarchy based on wealth rather than color, gender, or pedigree. Yet an increased awareness of difference seems to frighten Americans who perceive the gains of others as impediments to their own achievement. This interpretation may explain recent popular rejections of laws protecting minorities from discrimination, for example, especially those based on the premise that such policies may grant some groups "special rights." Similarly, policies such as affirmative action seem wrong to some citizens because they distribute rewards based on criteria unrelated to individual merit. Instead of using shared beliefs to catapult themselves and each other toward the American dream, then, Americans seem more likely to depend on mutual suspicions within the zero-sum mindset mandated by their preferred form of capitalism.

The Problem of Modernity

The third reason that the American people might not be expected to share beliefs is because, to some scholars at least, they are ill-equipped to believe in much of anything. Some observers assume that, as modernity's children, Americans lack the psychological and emotional elements necessary for communal bonds.

A number of scholars have suggested that Americans are so individualistic that the only thing they could possibly have in common is narcissism.[83] In Christopher Lasch's famous estimation, for example, Americans "liv[e] in a state of restless, perpetually unsatisfied desire."[84] Observations like these are common. American sociologists in particular have produced some gloomy conclusions about how their compatriots' inner feelings can impede national community.

Some have argued, for example, that Americans face so many choices and constraints in their everyday interactions that there is little possibility for them to sustain meaningful fellowship. American citizens are ultimately little more than alienated, anxious individuals, suggest these accounts. Many scholars attribute this anxiety to the "techno-economic" conditions of the modern, industrialist world.[85] According to this argument, if communities were born out of necessity in earlier times, modern technology has made obsolete many of the practical reasons for erstwhile solidarity.

Peter Berger and coauthors Brigitte Berger and Hansfried Kellner write that the American perceives personal experience as "incomplete, somehow defective [under] constant threat of meaninglessness, disidentification and experiences of anomie" due to the effects of "technological production" on her or his consciousness.[86] Similarly, Daniel Bell has argued that in the United States, as in other modern societies, technological advances have resulted in the objectification of individuals and their labor. Thus, according to Philip Slater, the same economic competition that seemed so healthy and productive in Adam Smith's philosophy has ultimately contributed to the disintegration of individuals' feelings of belonging. Slater suggests that "our society lies near the competitive edge, and although it contains cooperative institutions, we suffer from their weakness and peripherality. Studies of business executives reveal a deep hunger for an atmosphere of trust and fraternity with their colleagues. The competitive life is a lonely one, and its satisfactions short-lived, for each race only leads to another one."[87]

Such dreary characterizations of American life seem to confirm Robert Nisbet's subsequent observation of an increasingly weakening sense of national community in the United States over the course of the twentieth century.[88] Other scholars, E. Digby Baltzell, for example, have simply accepted the premise that "the gradual erosion . . . of the traditional community ties . . . is both the cause and the result of extensive social mobility, individuation, anonymity, and the consequent prevalence of purely monetary social relationships."[89] Most recently, political scientist Robert Putnam has lamented the decline in membership in voluntary associations and suggested that there is an overall decline in social capital, an assessment that supports this diagnosis of anomie.[90]

Summarizing many of the conditions that might make shared beliefs unlikely if not impossible in the United States, Rosabeth Moss Kanter has suggested that

> the fact that modern American culture is at the same time pluralistic and eclectic, surrounding the person with a much greater number of options than in the last century—with respect to careers, consumption, relationships—makes it harder for the individual both to make definitive choices (as of one group or one culture and lifestyle within that group) and to find one set of people with whom he can share every aspect of his life, since everyone else has the same large number of options from which to extract a lifestyle. The individual constructs his own social world out of the myriad choices confronting him, and the chance that many others will construct theirs in exactly the same way is much more limited than in the less diverse environment of the last century.[91]

If Kanter's and these other assessments are correct, the shared beliefs hypothesis might seem like little more than fiction, a rhetoric that, in this case at least, seems to have little to do with reality. The syndromes described in this section—unbridled diversity, capitalist economics, and an alienated psyche—explain why it might simply be impossible for the American people to share any beliefs at all.

In fact, at the twentieth century's end, some contemporary observers seemed willing to agree with this prognosis. For them, the clamoring chaos once heard by Myrdal has finally drowned out any hint of unified harmony in the United States. Throughout the 1990s, for instance, politicians and philosophers alike saw Americans' diversity as causing a loss of community and a breakdown of meaning in public life. "Are we a nation?" was the question Michael Lind asked in his popular 1995 book *The Next American Nation: The New Nationalism and the Fourth American Revolution.* Both Lind's query and his book's title underscored the growing sense of fragmentation among Americans as the twentieth century closed.

Obviously, such feelings were not strong support for the shared beliefs hypothesis. What, then, had happened in the late twentieth century? Had

Americans' shared beliefs somehow evaporated? Was there no longer any sense
of American mission or yearning, for example? Did the principles of liberalism, republicanism, or even the carefully blended pseudo-populist ideals articulated by Adam Smith no longer resonate with the American people? If so,
had they been replaced by something else? Indeed, if any of these possibili-
ties were true, then what did they portend for the ongoing stability of the
United States? What could hold the American people together in the future?

If these questions seem nervous, the 1990s was an anxious time. To wit, at
the 1992 Republican National Convention, right-wing candidate Patrick
Buchanan seemed eager to marshal forces when he declared that the people
of the United States were "in a culture war for the soul of America."[92]
Buchanan's choice of metaphor underscored one political and cultural legacy
of the shared beliefs hypothesis: the concern that if the American people
shared no ideas, then the result would be a nation that had lost its very soul.

But had it? In value analysis studies conducted in the 1980s and 1990s, the
American people reported allegiance to many of the same types of traditional
values that they always had.[93] Likewise, from a historical perspective, James
Morone and Rogers Smith offered policy analyses during these decades that
seemed to suggest that the United States was both as liberal and as illiberal as
it had ever been.[94] In fact, Seymour Martin Lipset's 1996 account of American political culture suggested that the liberal tradition, especially as manifested through individualism, was alive and well in the United States.[95]

To some readers, these more optimistic accounts may appear to conflict
with other cultural indicators and may thus seem unsatisfactory. Yet perhaps
this contrast is not because the optimistic accounts are inaccurate but instead
because they only tell part of the story. It may be possible, for example, that
Americans' shared beliefs may be simultaneously more complex and more
functional than the traditional accounts have implied. Likewise, it may be that
there still exists a *rhetoric* of shared beliefs that can help the American people
feel united even when their daily experiences tell them that they are not. In
order to explore this latter possibility, we might first need to briefly consider
what such an alternative approach might entail.

THINKING RHETORICALLY ABOUT SHARED BELIEFS

In the preceding pages, I have classified much of the previous research on
shared beliefs as ontological. To consider the need for an alternative approach,
we might recall the five terms Seymour Martin Lipset used to describe the

American creed in his book *American Exceptionalism:* liberty, egalitarianism, individualism, populism, and laissez-faire.[96] This list is comprehensive and explanatory, to be sure, and Lipset's argument about how such beliefs both embolden and bedevil the American people is persuasive. Yet Lipset and others who write ontologically about these "terms" sometimes seem to forget that they are, after all, just that: terms.

Viewed as such, these words are signifiers for abstract concepts that, although clearly politically potent, can change in meaning across time, circumstance, or audiences. Liberty, egalitarianism, individualism, populism, and laissez-faire may therefore be important ideological concepts within American political culture, but they are also ideographs, and this latter characteristic is no less important than the first two.

An ideograph, according to Celeste Condit and John Louis Lucaites, is a "culturally biased, abstract word or phrase, drawn from ordinary language, which serves as a constitutional value for a historically situated collectivity." Ideographs thus can "represent, in condensed form, the normative, collective commitments of the members of a public."[97] Surely this sense of "normative, collective commitments" in American life is what Lipset and other scholars have tried to capture in studying Americans' shared beliefs. But as Condit and Lucaites have shown in their work *Crafting Equality: America's Anglo-African Word,* ideographs and the ideological commitments they represent can change in slight but significant ways over time and/or among different groups of people, even within the same nation.

For example, when Condit and Lucaites traced the usage of the word "equality" in U.S. public discourse from pre-colonial times to the 1990s, they found that the usage had shifted dramatically. The word that the Revolutionary War leaders used strategically to fight British colonialism in the late 1700s might have been the same word that civil rights leaders used just as strategically to signify uniquely American values during the 1960s, but it most certainly did not mean the same thing in both contexts, according to Condit and Lucaites's compelling analysis. These authors ask us to think epistemologically, instead of purely ontologically, about what equality is. They thus invited readers to try to grasp how Americans have come to understand this concept— and indeed, their allegedly characteristic loyalty to whatever it means—by tracing how they have used it within public discourse.

Asking how meanings change is an extremely complex question, of course. Condit and Lucaites's detailed longitudinal analysis of one term's usage within an admittedly partial set of texts is instructive as to both the methodological difficulties and argumentative compromises involved in this sort of inquiry.[98]

Furthermore, any analysis of something as ephemeral as cultural beliefs is always intrinsically incomplete, as Clifford Geertz pointed out long ago.[99] Although my analysis involves finding constitutive themes of American nationalism rather than focusing on individual words, here I will not argue that any one type of approach, mine included, can solve the many riddles of American political culture. Still, asking epistemological rather than ontological questions about Americans' allegedly shared beliefs can add at least two important dimensions to this discussion, both of which might help us understand their functions as well as the nature of these ideals.

First, thinking epistemologically about shared beliefs enables us to ask initial questions about how American citizens have been encouraged to understand these ideals. Posing these questions may reveal insights into the puzzling endurance of the contradictions that have been so jarring to Myrdal and others. As I have already discussed, very few accounts of shared beliefs have been able to explain the widespread existence of contradictory practices. Rogers Smith comes closest, perhaps, in explaining how citizenship laws that were theoretically put in place to exalt the citizenry were also imprinted with the more prejudiced impulses of the American people. Likewise, Condit and Lucaites's analysis suggests that egalitarian ideals and inegalitarian practices might not seem all that dissonant if one defines equality in particular ways.

Given this latter possibility especially, analyzing public discourse about Americans' shared beliefs might help us understand how tensions between conflicting "deeds and creed" have been assuaged in the past. One of the primary functions of public rhetoric is to smooth over exactly such contradictions, Roderick P. Hart has argued. According to Hart, "One of the most important functions rhetoric can serve is that of assimilating the diverse and competing 'goods' of a society. Because of its catholic nature, rhetoric can envelop rival axiologies, distill their essences, and transmute the products into something else. This resulting hybrid can become something around which diverse persons may rally." Perhaps because of their own diverse constitution, "Americans have a special fancy for this amalgamating function," Hart suggests.[100] If we want to know how Americans make sense of their national contradictions, we might find clues within rhetoric designed to appeal to the entire nation. Presidents' inaugural addresses and state of the union messages certainly fit this bill.

Second, thinking epistemologically about shared beliefs emphasizes the role of human agency within this discussion. Some of the literature on American ideals attributes their unique characteristics to all manner of inanimate and systemic features, including the nation's geography, its agrarian roots, or its capitalistic economy, as I have discussed. While there can be little doubt that these factors have greatly impacted the ways in which Americans might think, such analyses sometimes fail to recognize that people themselves have to articulate these beliefs in order for them to exist and be influential.

Certainly the topography of the American frontier, for instance, could have encouraged a type of national mentality, but even this mentality had to be spoken and reified to exist. Ideals, beliefs, and attitudes do not simply fall from the sky (or in the former example, rise up from the ground); they are a product of human interaction. And humans, as thinkers from Aristotle to Kenneth Burke have so patiently reminded us, have motives. Thinking epistemologically about shared beliefs allows us to ask whose interests a rhetoric of shared beliefs might serve and why.

The above criticisms and correctives notwithstanding, it is not my intention here to suggest that we must abandon the shared beliefs hypothesis altogether. After all, the United States does continue to endure as the world's most hearty and functional democracy, somehow able to balance the demands of its increasingly diverse citizens against more abstract but still powerful notions of a common good. For the American people to persist, there must be *something* that they think they have in common, and in the absence of any shared race, religion, heritage, or even (sometimes) language, the only things that would seem to be left are indeed ideas and the rhetoric used to explain them. Perhaps, then, instead of continuing to ask only *what* Americans' shared beliefs are, we might also ask *how* they are—how and when they come into being, how they are defined and understood, and how they thus constitute the "knowledge culture" that is assumed to accompany American national identity.[101] These are the same questions that this study has sought to answer. In the following four chapters, I offer an account of what I found when I searched for versions of the shared beliefs hypothesis within presidents' inaugural addresses and state of the union messages given from 1885 to 2000.

CHAPTER 2

A Presidential Rhetoric
of Shared Beliefs

I n the preceding chapter I noted that, despite the many factors that could
ostensibly pull the American people apart, for centuries scholars and
other observers have agreed that the people of the United States are somehow bound together by ideational models of national identity. The working
hypothesis behind most explanations of American nationalism has therefore
been what I have referred to as the shared beliefs hypothesis, the notion that
Americans are Americans because they share certain ways of thinking, even if
there has been debate about exactly what these ways of thinking are.

In this chapter I argue that U.S. presidents have also promoted the shared
beliefs hypothesis of American nationalism. By itself, this claim is hardly surprising. As I have already noted, chief executives clearly have a great interest
in making sure that the American people *feel* united, even if citizens' actual
demographic, economic, and psychological conditions would suggest otherwise. Likewise, supposing that U.S. presidents have tried to promote shared
beliefs through ritualistic discourses such as inaugural addresses and state of
the union messages is probably not all that surprising either. Scholars as dissimilar as political theorists and linguistic anthropologists have suggested that
such discursive moments are of extreme importance within a culture, as they
reinforce notions of identity and community.[1] But which version of the shared
beliefs hypothesis have U.S. presidents been most likely to favor on these
occasions? Which versions of American national identity have they most often promoted within these two genres? In this chapter I will suggest that presidents, unlike scholars, seem to be largely in agreement about the types of
beliefs that constitute American identity. Although chief executives sometimes
draw upon Tocquevillian themes of equality, Lockean themes of liberalism,
and some of the other popular themes discussed in chapter 1, my reading

suggests that they most commonly associate American national identity with Puritan notions of an American civil religion.

The American people are uniquely united, presidents have repeatedly argued, by nothing less than providence; as God's chosen people, Americans have a collective identity based on shared beliefs that are both sacred and sanctified.[2] This version is, of course, the same account of American identity once offered by John Winthrop, who asked an audience of pilgrims to remember God's need for their community to represent a "city on a hill" and thus a beacon for all other nations. And it is also the same explanation of American nationalism that, according to Sacvan Bercovitch, has been used repeatedly throughout U.S. history to control Americans' impulses by manufacturing a sense of ideological consensus.

When presidents speak of the American people as "one nation under God," then, perhaps they are doing nothing more than we would expect them to do. They are using the words and symbols of the historic Puritan errand to rhetorically enact another "rite of assent," to use Bercovitch's celebrated phrasing, and thus to envelop the American people into the rhetorical folds of a particular mythos. Yet to say only that U.S. presidents' rhetorical promotion of shared beliefs in this manner is unsurprising is to miss an important part of the story. Specifically, as I will argue throughout this chapter, when we take a closer look at how presidents have used these themes in the inaugural addresses and state of the union messages studied here, we can get a sense of at least two critical and interrelated findings.

First, U.S. presidents can use these themes in order to manage a diverse democracy. This usage is a function of civil religious rhetoric that has largely gone unnoticed by scholars of U.S. political communication, and it is also a feature of presidential rhetoric that may make this discourse different from other social leaders' responses to Americans' diversity. For reasons I will detail in this chapter, civil religious themes can be an especially efficient way for presidents to accommodate difference within a democratic nation. Second, U.S. presidents can use these themes not only to speak about allegedly constitutive American ideals, the backbone of the shared beliefs hypothesis, but also to promote more specific attitudinal postures that these ideals necessitate. In other words, presidents can use these themes to describe American identity in terms of both *principle* and *pose,* a combination that allows their particular rhetoric of American national identity to be more complicated than we might have expected.

To underscore the nature and functions of this discourse, I begin this chapter by describing presidents' rhetoric of shared beliefs in greater detail through a discussion of multiple textual examples. I conclude by considering both positive and negative implications of this rhetoric. Although this particular discourse might have been helpful and perhaps even necessary for the U.S. presidency, it may have some more worrisome implications for American democracy.

HOW PRESIDENTS HAVE DEFINED
AMERICAN NATIONAL IDENTITY

It is now perhaps taken for granted that when George Washington concluded his first inaugural address by noting that God "has been pleased to favor the American people," he also inaugurated a rhetorical tradition.[3] In inaugural addresses especially, this religious theme has persisted through time and circumstance; the great majority of Washington's successors similarly described Americans as "God's chosen people."[4]

In his first inaugural address, for example, Grover Cleveland noted that "Almighty God" had "at all times been revealed in our country's history."[5] His successor Benjamin Harrison would be even more specific in his 1889 inaugural address: "God has placed upon our head a diadem and has laid at our feet power and wealth beyond definition or calculation. But we must not forget that we take these gifts upon the condition that justice and mercy shall be the reins of power and that the upward avenues of hope shall be free to all the people."[6] Likewise, Woodrow Wilson offered a similar characterization in his 1920 annual message. After invoking Abraham Lincoln's acknowledgment of the "essential faith of the nation," President Wilson went on to paint a very vivid picture of the American people and their collective mission:

> With that faith and the birth of a nation founded upon it came the hope into the world that a new order would prevail throughout the affairs of mankind, an order in which reason and right would take precedence over covetousness and force; and I believe that I express the wish and purpose of every thoughtful American when I say that this sentence marks for us in the plainest manner the part we should play alike in the arrangement of our domestic affairs and in our exercise of influence upon the affairs of the world. By this faith, and by this faith alone, can the world be lifted out of its present confusion and despair.[7]

Like Wilson, Franklin Roosevelt also spoke of the nation's constitutive faith when he described the United States as a "temple of our ancient faith" in his second inaugural.[8] Almost fifty years later, Ronald Reagan would similarly use his second inaugural address to ask the American people, "with heart in hand," to rededicate themselves to this ancient faith and "stand as one today: One people under God determined that our future shall be worthy of our past."[9]

If even these brief examples of civil religious rhetoric seem familiar to the reader, it is presumably because much has been written about the use of this characterization of the American people in political rhetoric and other set pieces of Americana.[10] Although there are multiple definitions and interpretations of American civil religion, here I am using the concept as set forth by Robert Bellah in his influential essay "Civil Religion in America," first published in *Daedalus* in 1967. There, Bellah noted that although the phrase "civil religion" itself comes from Rousseau, the civil religious idea in the United States has revolved around the notion of a God "with a special concern for America." Bellah points out that the American civil religion is "not antithetical to and indeed shar[es] much in common with Christianity."[11] He argues, however, that it is "not itself Christianity. The God of the civil religion is not only rather 'unitarian,' he is also on the austere side, much more related to order, law, and right than to salvation and love." Within the American civil religion, then, God is both disciplined and disciplining, governed by principle more than compassion. According to Bellah, this god views the American people as nothing less than the New Israelites: "Europe is Egypt; America, the promised land. God has led his people to establish a new sort of social order that shall be a light unto all nations."[12]

Thus, the civil religion, made manifest through a "collection of beliefs, symbols, and rituals with respect to sacred things and institutionalized in a collectivity," according to Bellah, has direct implications for American national identity.[13] As we saw in the above examples from Presidents Cleveland, Benjamin Harrison, Wilson, Franklin Roosevelt, and Reagan, this theme suggests that the American people are God's chosen people, and that as such, they have a special relationship with each other as well as a clear responsibility to the rest of the world. In other words, the civil religion encourages the American people to associate themselves with the spiritual significance and grandeur of America's history. As Robert Jewett has observed, this association can at times be problematic, especially if it promotes "zealous nationalism" about the country's self-perceived role as a "light to the nations."[14] In spite of, or perhaps because of, this potential, this theme has often been used by presidents to justify their own policies, especially those concerning foreign policy. In his 1905 inaugural address, for example, Theodore Roosevelt linked his "big stick" philosophy of foreign affairs to the civil religion with these simple yet clearly

spiritual words: "Much has been given us, and much will rightfully be expected from us. We have duties to others and duties to ourselves, and we can
shirk neither."[15]

Apart from promoting their individual policy objectives, presidents may
have many other good reasons to associate American national identity with
civil religious beliefs. First, as Bercovitch has argued, the larger rhetoric of the
Puritan errand upon which much civil religious discourse depends lends itself easily to the support of many other allegedly shared values in the United
States, including capitalism and personal freedom.[16] In this sense it is not
necessarily opposed to any of the other beliefs or principles, especially egalitarianism or individualism, believed by many to be central to Americans' alleged ideological consensus. Indeed, civil religious rhetoric may simply be an
efficient, if banal, way to bolster these nationalistic ideals symbolically. Second, and more to the point within this discussion, this use of religious-themed
rhetoric would seem to be especially appropriate given the United States' history of ethnic and cultural diversity. Regardless of an immigrant's foreign
heritage or the nation's history of slavery, a constitutive rhetoric based on
American civil religion offers its subjects the same promises that most religions
do: rebirth, redemption, and renewal—the ability to overcome the past by
becoming part of *Novo Ordus Seclorum*. It does not matter what your past
beliefs were, this rhetoric says, as long as you cast them off in order to take
on these new beliefs. "As long as our dreams outweigh our memories," as Bill
Clinton put it as he concluded his final state of the union address in 2000,
"America will be forever young. That is our destiny."[17]

If invoking this God-given "destiny" can help presidents manage the
United States' diverse democracy, then it may be important to pay more attention to such platitudes than we might otherwise do, especially considering that this function has been typically neglected in other commentaries on
political uses of civil religious discourse.[18] For example, it may be that civil
religious rhetoric enables presidents to offer norms for proper citizenship even
as they articulate the United States' global mission; in other words, they can
unite the American people by providing a global, un-American "them" against
which the citizenry can feel like a distinctive, unified "us." If so, then the ways
in which presidents talk about such feelings of imagined community are very
important. To wit, I will argue that presidents have repeatedly used civil religious themes in inaugural and state of the union messages to associate American national identity not just with a certain set of shared beliefs but also with
a particular type of shared feelings. In other words, instead of merely articulating a set of principles upon which American national identity is based, chief

executives can use civil religious themes to promote a particular attitudinal pose as similarly constitutive.

Consider, for example, one of the texts already quoted: Wilson's eighth annual message, given in 1920. There, as the president spoke plainly of the "essential faith" of the United States, he also took care to define it as the basis for a "new order" in which "reason and right would take precedence over covetousness and force." The contrast offered here—"reason and right" versus "covetousness and force"—would have clearly made sense to his audience, painfully aware of the unprecedented international chaos caused by World War I. However meaningful its historical context, this contrast is also instructive because of the types of attitudinal postures it suggests as being constitutive of American identity. Here "reason" is positioned as the necessarily self-restrained companion to the moral good ("right"), for example, as both of these terms, and thus American character itself, are defined oppositionally in contrast to the more emotional and unchecked impulses of "covetousness" (which is also, it should be noted, a sin within the Judeo-Christian tradition) and the equally unintellectual "force." Even within this brief sample of Wilson's remarks, then, we can gain a sense of the ways in which the civil religion may be used to suggest that American people should comport themselves with self-restraint and moral certainty.

Yet how, specifically, might these qualities be relevant to the American people's diversity? What might make such a rhetoric seem to be a good way to soothe tensions within a diverse democracy? In order to answer this question, it might be helpful first to turn our attention momentarily away from presidential rhetoric and toward the Bible. Although I agree with Bellah's contention that the civil religion is not the same thing as Christianity, it is worth noting that biblical accounts of early Christianity suggested that the first believers were encouraged to reject distinction itself as the enemy of the faithful. The apostle Paul, for instance, explained their new religion to the earliest Christians as follows:

> Before faith came, we were imprisoned and guarded under the law until faith would be revealed. Therefore the law was our disciplinarian until Christ came, so that we might be justified by faith. But now that faith has come, we are no longer subject to a disciplinarian, for in Christ Jesus you are all children of God through faith. As many of you were baptized into Christ have clothed yourself with Christ. There is no longer Jew nor Greek, there is no longer slave nor free, there is no longer male nor female; for all of you are one in Christ Jesus. And if you belong to Christ, then you are Abraham's offspring; heirs to the promise.[19]

By inserting the word "America" in place of Christ's name in this passage, one can get an idea of how religious rhetoric and, specifically, this Christian logic might help the American people see themselves not just as God's favorite children but also as uniquely bound together through a new identity marked by a new feeling state: "But now that faith has come, we are no longer subject to a disciplinarian, for in America you are all children of God through faith. As many of you were baptized into America have clothed yourself with America. There is no longer Jew nor Greek, there is no longer slave nor free, there is no longer male nor female; for all of you are one in America. And if you belong to America, then you are Abraham's offspring; heirs to the promise."

"All of you are one in America"—these are powerful words, full of promise indeed, and not very far from what Gerald Ford suggested in his 1976 state of the union message when he explained that although Americans "came from many roots, and we have many branches, . . . all Americans across the eight generations that separate us from the stirring deeds of 1776, those who know no other homeland and those who just found refuge among our shores, [can] say in unison: I am proud of America, and I am proud to be an American. Life will be a little better here for my children than for me."[20] Just as Paul asked the earliest Christians to see themselves as God's children rather than in terms of their previous identifiers of ethnicity, class, or gender, Ford states that Americans are similarly bound together and can "find refuge" in this union. Regardless of their origins or "roots" (whether they "know no other homeland" or have just come to America) or their current differences or "branches," Americans are all part of one core (or tree trunk, to extend the metaphor), which is in fact both a core belief in civil religious principle *and* a core feeling of renewal and faithful restraint. Such a logic invites the American people to cast off the weight of their original identities and unite in one conviction: All individuals are equally "heirs to the promise" of both God and the United States.

If faith in a civil religion as well as the self-restraint assumed to be necessary for such faith are themselves quintessentially American characteristics, then the citizenry's greatest enemies would be those who would reject them by drawing attention to difference. Some of the best examples of this dynamic occur in presidential discussions of international affairs. On these occasions presidents can cite the unrest stemming from other nations' ancient tribal societies to warn their own citizens about the tragedies of overidentification with difference. Such primitive and divisive passions, chief executives may suggest, are the ultimate temptations that Americans must resist. As "God's chosen people," their enemy is the rest of the world indeed—not necessarily the individual citizens of other nations but rather the atavistic and irrational passions that drive them.

At times certain presidents have explicitly contrasted these "irrational" feelings from those appropriate to the true American character, suggesting that identification with difference is unpatriotic and sacrilegious and thus dangerous. Even during times of war, the "other" in presidential discourse is typically not described in terms of nationality but instead as an alien, illogical impulse. As Woodrow Wilson entered his second presidential term, for example, the world was ripped into factions by international allegiances and unprecedented aggressions resulting in World War I. In his 1917 inaugural address the president explained why the United States must inevitably enter the war against Germany:

> Although we have centered counsel and action with such unusual concentration and success upon the great problems of domestic legislation . . . other matters have more and more forced themselves upon our attention—matters lying outside our own life as a nation and over which we had no control, but which, despite our wish to keep free of them, have drawn us more and more irresistibly into their own current and influence. It has been impossible to avoid them. They have affected the life of the whole world. They have shaken men everywhere with a passion and an apprehension they never knew before. It has been hard to preserve calm counsel while the thought of our own people swayed this way and that under their influence. We are a composite and cosmopolitan people. We are of the blood of all the nations that are at war. The currents of our thoughts as well as the currents of trade run quick at all seasons back and forth between us and them. The war inevitably sets its mark from the first alike upon our minds, our industries, our commerce, our politics and our social action. To be indifferent to it, or independent of it, was out of the question.[21]

Wilson's language suggested jarring physical motion and an attendant psychic agitation. The United States, having been "drawn . . . irresistibly" and "forced" to attend to the war, suddenly finds itself "shaken" and "affected" like the rest of the world. In a sense, then, Wilson was portraying the country as relatively passive or almost powerless, a curious way to represent a nation on the verge of involvement in world war.

Yet the real enemy in this discourse was not necessarily the country's actual military foes but instead the "passions" and "apprehensions" that might "sway" "our own people." With the exception of trade considerations, the elements Wilson cites as leading America into the war are atavistic and emotional: the

"currents of our thoughts" that "run quick" among the "composite and cos-
mopolitan people" of the United States who are, after all, "of the blood of all
the nations that are at war."

Given Wilson's efforts to keep the United States out of the war during his
previous term, his explanation suggests that the negative forces of foreign
nationalism now gave him no other choice. His motion-oriented language
illustrates the notion that such passions were profoundly disruptive to the
"calm counsel" necessary to American life. In other words, Wilson was asking his culturally diverse audience of former slaves and immigrants to repudiate any allegiance they might have to their countries or cultures or origins
in favor of a more reasoned and restrained dedication to the United States. To
wit, as the president explained how the conflict itself might unite the country, he spoke of the importance of stability for the American people's collective mental state:

> And yet all of the while we have been conscious that we were not part of it. In
> that consciousness, despite many divisions, we have drawn closer together. We
> have been deeply wronged upon the seas, but we have not wished to wrong or
> injure in return; we have retained throughout the consciousness of standing in
> some sort apart, intent upon an interest that transcended the immediate issues
> of the war itself. . . . We are provincials no longer. The tragic events of the thirty
> months of vital turmoil through which we have just passed have made us citi-
> zens of the world. There can be no turning back. Our own fortunes as a nation
> are involved whether we would have it so or not. And yet we are not the less
> Americans on that account. We shall be the more American if we but remain
> true to the principles in which we have been bred.[22]

Although the American people have been pulled into the war by "tragic
events," Wilson's rhetoric defines their nationalistic impulses not in terms of
action or aggression; the righteous Americans seek no revenge for themselves,
even though they have been "deeply wronged." Instead, the American people
are described here as sharing a constitutive posture of intellectualized self-restraint, a "consciousness of standing in some sort apart" from the evil pull of
tribalism at work in the rest of the world.

This detached stance draws Americans "closer together," Wilson suggested,
enabling them to stay united; their continued union will presumably allow
them to remain rational and principled. Thus, in this rhetoric a mental state—
the ability to "remain true to principles in which we have been bred"—defines
the American people, and it is part of the people's "natural" defense against

the irrational pull of tribalism. "I need not argue these principles to you, my fellow countrymen," the president said, and then he argued them further:

> They are your own, part and parcel of your own thinking and your own motives in affairs. They spring up native amongst us. Upon this as a platform of purpose and action we can stand together. And it is imperative that we should stand together. We are being forged into a new unity amidst the fires that now blaze throughout the world. In their ardent heat, we shall, in God's providence, let us hope, be purged of faction and division, purified of the errant humors of party and private interest, and shall stand forth in the days to come with a new dignity of national pride and spirit. Let each man see to it that the dedication is in his own heart, the high purpose of the nation in his own mind, ruler of his own will and desire.[23]

Thus, although citizens of other countries may be stirred to action by emotions and irrational forms of nationalism, principle "springs up native amongst" Americans, according to President Wilson.

Nevertheless, Wilson warned, the citizenry's union is not guaranteed. It must be created and recreated by an internal commitment to "stand together" as well as by external forces ("the fires that now blaze throughout the world") that necessitate a shared vigilance against potential disruptions. Giving in to unprincipled impulses of "faction" and "division" is harmful to such a union and, therefore, anti-American, according to Wilson, for the quintessential American posture is both intellectual and restrained. Such a position is a habit of mind that all Americans must share—a "platform of purpose and action [upon which] we can stand together"—to ensure that the nation is "purified of the errant humors of party and private interest." Thus, in preparing the citizenry for international involvement Wilson also instructs the people on how to "stand forth . . . with a new dignity of national pride and spirit" in a country that ironically, yet necessarily, condemns nationalism in others.

There is a sadness in Wilson's speech about the American people becoming "citizens of the world." In general, U.S. presidents seem loath to associate American identity with the characteristics of anyone else, thereby ensuring that Americans at least discursively "stand apart" from the rest of the world. Keeping American identity distinct facilitates the citizenry's ability to see itself as uniquely united by these shared beliefs, while also keeping the American people "pure" of any other influences. Unlike the biological or hereditary characteristics appealed to in other nationalistic rhetorics, then, the purity of the American people depends not on race or ethnicity but upon a clarity of conviction.

Indeed, fifty years after Wilson's speech and one world war later, the United States had progressed from being merely a "citizen of the world" to a super-power, a leadership role prophesied in so much of the civil religious rhetoric of its leaders.[24] Despite its unquestionable military superiority, the country still needed to remain true to its original principles (habits of mind making the American suspicious of non-American ways of thinking) in order to combat potential divisions on the domestic front. In his 1965 inaugural address, Lyndon B. Johnson reminded the citizenry that the best way to contend with the global unrest of the 1960s was to look beyond the potential conflicts of diversity and instead focus on unity:

> Ours is a time of change—rapid and fantastic change—bearing the secrets of nature, multiplying the nations, placing in uncertain hands new weapons for mastery and destruction, shaking old values and uprooting old ways. Our des-tiny in the midst of change will rest on the unchanged character of our people and on their faith. They came here—the exile and the stranger, brave but fright-ened—to find a place where a man could be his own man. They made a cov-enant with this land. Conceived in justice, written in liberty, bound in union, it was meant one day to inspire the hopes of all mankind. And it binds us still. If we keep its terms we shall flourish. First, justice was the promise that all who made the journey would share in the fruits of the land. . . . Justice requires us to remember: when any citizen denies his fellow, saying: "His color is not mine or his beliefs are strange and different," in that moment he betrays America, though his forebears created this nation.[25]

Much like Wilson did, Johnson suggested that in a world of dizzying move-ment ("rapid and fantastic change," "shaking old values and uprooting old ways") the safety of the United States lies in its people's ability to overlook difference and unite in civil religious belief. What is essential to the Ameri-can people (their "unchanged character") is in fact a characteristic "faith," a set of principles and attitudinal poses that would empower them to resist pri-mary allegiances to ethnic groups or classes.

To stray from this belief system by using racist or otherwise prejudicial language, as Johnson suggests in his example, is thus to "betray" America and its promise that "a man could be his own man." Anyone who thinks differ-ently is the citizenry's foe, regardless of his or her own origins, and even if "his forebears created this country." The enemy of the American people is there-fore again indicated to be distinction. Other countries may lock their citizens into social classes or age-old ethnic hatreds, Johnson argues, but America requires only that its people have a resolute conviction that such tribalistic forces have no power in God's country.

To differentiate further between the United States and the rest of the world, Johnson associates the young country's mission with a universal good. "Our nation's course is abundantly clear," he states. "We aspire to nothing that belongs to others. . . . We seek no domination over our fellow man, but man's domination over tyranny and misery." Just as Wilson reiterated that the American people stood "in some sort apart" from the rest of the world, Johnson reminded them of their essential difference from other nations. In addition to being so moral and self-sufficient as to "aspire to nothing that belongs to others," they alone are beneficent enough to stand together for "man's domination over tyranny and misery." How might this global triumph over evil be accomplished? Through the internal rejection of painful differences, says the president: "So let us reject any among us who seek to reopen old wounds and rekindle old hatreds. They stand in the way of a seeking nation. Let us now join reason to faith and action to experience, to transform our unity in interest into a unity of purpose. For the hour and the day and the time are here to achieve progress without strife, to achieve change without hatred, not without difference of opinion but without the deep and abiding divisions which scar the union for generations."[26] Here Johnson suggests that the American people's own differences ("old wounds" and "old hatreds") will ultimately "stand in the way" of their shared spiritual growth as a "seeking nation."

Lest the citizenry be uncertain of the nature of its "unity of purpose," Johnson differentiates between the conversational or ephemeral (e.g., rational "differences of opinion") and the insurmountable and essential (e.g., the irrational "deep and dividing divisions which scar the union for generations"). It is acceptable for Americans to disagree with each other about school bonds and property taxes, for example; such discussions would in fact further signify their quintessential nature as rational, intellectual, and thus faithful servants of their country. But it is not acceptable for them to disagree about each other's character. Such judgments would mean that they have succumbed to the irrational "hatred" that has produced lasting scars at home and around the world.

As Paul told the Galatians and U.S. presidents repeatedly tell Americans, the way to overcome such pain is through belief and conviction. For President Johnson, this transcendence is made possible by joining "reason to faith and action to experience." Although such faith is itself essential to Americans, it must be constantly regenerated and actualized through hard work, according to Johnson: "In each generation, with toil and tears, we have had to earn our heritage again. If we fail now, then we will have forgotten in abundance what we learned in hardship; that democracy rests on faith, that freedom asks more than it gives, and the judgment of God is harshest on those who are most favored."[27] Here the president suggests that American nationalism, unlike any other country's nationalism or ethnic pride, is not static. It must be "earned" by the "toil and tears" of "each new generation." This toil, the work of remaining true to an American ideal that pays no mind to difference, is what will unite the American people, according to this discourse.

Presidents also promote such models of principled-and-posed national character during times of relative peace. In the years following World War I, for example, the United States enjoyed a revived appreciation for isolationist foreign policies. But things were far from well at home. African American soldiers came back to a country that valued them enough to let them fight its war but not enough to treat them as full-fledged citizens. Between 1917 and 1919, racial violence claimed lives in Saint Louis, Houston, Philadelphia, Washington, D.C., and Chicago. In 1920, reports that two robbers of a shoe factory "looked Italian" led to the executions of immigrants Nicola Sacco and Bartolomeo Vanzetti. Other newcomers were suspect due to increasing concerns about communism in Russia, while record deportations and Wobbly-inspired suspicions hurt labor unions and the working class in general. The war abroad may have been over, but at home, battles raged.

In his 1921 inaugural address, however, Warren Harding did not mention such undeniable civil unrest. Instead, he chose to speak of "a maintained America, the proven Republic, the unshaken temple of representative democracy . . . an inspiration and example . . . the highest agency of strengthening good will and promoting accord on both continents."[28] The president also said that

> when one surveys the world around him after the great storm, noting the marks of destruction and yet rejoicing in the ruggedness of the things which withstood it, if he is an American, he breathes the clarified atmosphere with a strange mingling of regret and new hope. We have seen a world passion spend its fury, but we contemplate our Republic unshaken, and hold our civilization secure. Liberty—liberty under the law—and civilization are inseparable, and though both were threatened we find them now secure, and there comes to Americans the profound assurance that our representative government is the highest expression and guaranty of both. Surely there must have been God's intent in the making of this new-world Republic.[29]

In addition to omitting any references to domestic strife, Harding in fact contradicts its existence. In his speech, the United States is "unshaken," with its "civilization secure." The world's "passion" may have "spent its fury," but Americans breathe in the "clarified atmosphere" with "regret," true, but also "new hope," secure that their civilization is protected by God (via the United States' civil religion). Although Harding was ostensibly speaking of the nation's solid standing in global affairs in the war's aftermath, his specific references to the United States emphasize its own internal order (a "Republic" with a "representative government"), leading one to wonder why the president offered no response to the multiple domestic tensions of the day.

Perhaps Harding did not see those problems as the responsibility of the federal government. Perhaps he viewed them as merely a temporary, self-correcting unpleasantness, a topic unworthy of mention during such an auspicious occasion as his inauguration. Or perhaps he was speaking about them by reifying a shared national mission and mentality in order to teach Americans how they should act. Why else would he have noted that the United States' duties to the rest of the world continued after the war's end?

> Perhaps we can make no more helpful contribution by example than prove a Republic's capacity to emerge from the wreckage of war. . . . While [the war] uncovered our portion of hateful selfishness at home, it also revealed the heart of America as sound and fearless, and beating in confidence unfailing. . . . Our supreme task is the resumption of our onward, normal way. Reconstruction, readjustment, restoration—all of these must follow. . . . If it will lighten the spirit and add to the resolution with which we take up the task, let me repeat for our Nation, we shall give no people just cause to make war upon us, we hold no national prejudices, we entertain no spirit of revenge, we do not hate, we do not covet, we dream of no conquest, nor boast of armed prowess.[30]

"Disturbed relationships" and "hateful selfishness" notwithstanding—and indeed, the president suggests that these are in fact just temporary products of the war—"the heart of America" remains emotionally strong in this speech ("sound and fearless" with "confidence unfailing"). To move forward in "our onward, normal way," the president suggests seven prescriptions (beginning with "we shall give no people just cause") that will help the American people "readjust" and presumably realign themselves to their normal collective state. When Harding says he is repeating these injunctions "for our Nation," his meaning is perhaps twofold: The president was articulating these values on behalf of the United States *and* he is issuing instructions for the proper mentality necessary for citizenship.

If so, Harding's rhetoric was not necessarily effective at the latter goal. By some measures, the American people's "disturbed relationships" among themselves had worsened by 1924.[31] By that year the Ku Klux Klan had more than 4 million members, a new record, and membership was increasing outside the South. Yet Harding's successor, Calvin Coolidge, and every president after him would define the American people in terms of this same mental profile, one characterized primarily by a reasoned yet messianic faithfulness to American ideals rather than to any biological, behavioral, or ethnic identification.

America was a savior to the rest of the world, Coolidge would testify in his 1925 inaugural address, and the American people needed only to remain true to the idea of a uniquely united citizenry to thrive at home and fulfill the nation's mission. President Coolidge continued,

> Because of what America is and America has done, a firmer image, a higher hope, inspires the heart of all humanity. . . . The old sentiment of detached and dependent colonies disappeared in the new sentiment of a united and independent nation. Men began to discard the narrow confines of a local charter for the broader opportunities of a national constitution. Under the eternal urge of freedom we became an independent nation. . . . Throughout all these experiences we have enlarged our freedom, and strengthened our independence. We have been, and propose to be, more and more American. We believe that we can best serve our own country, and most successfully discharge our obligations to humanity by continuing to be openly and candidly, intensely and scrupulously, American. If we have any heritage, it has been that. If we have any destiny, we have found it in that direction.[32]

America's example is exactly this, said Coolidge: Give up your differences, your primitive allegiances and ancient hatreds, the "narrow confines of a local charter," and your freedom will be "enlarged," "strengthened," and aligned with a universal good ("an eternal urge"). Deny your own individual needs and identifications by becoming part of something larger, says this rhetoric, drawing upon a very Christian logic indeed, and one that promises ultimate salvation, according to Coolidge: "Peace will come when there is realization that only under a reign of law, based on righteousness and supported by the religious conviction of the brotherhood of man, can there be any hope of a complete and satisfying life. Parchment will fail, the sword will fail, it is only the spiritual nature of man that can be triumphant."[33] Coolidge's prophetic tone suggested that, since all comers are one under God and America, in the end, differences themselves will not matter at all, if only Americans *believe*. It is, the presidential voice intoned, "only the spiritual nature of man that can be triumphant."

Faith and belief may seem odd solutions to the problems caused by difference. Faith did not necessarily decrease the pain felt by both black and white southerners in the 1960s, and belief will not keep women from being sexually harassed in the workplace. Yet the fairly religious notions of faith and belief have long been part of the way Americans have dealt with racism in particular and oppression in general.[34] The idea of combating life's often meaningless and sometimes painful events through spirituality is central to both Christian and non-Christian religious thought in the United States. As Roderick Hart has stated, such "religio-political" discourse can indeed tap into myths that "allow the American audience to transcend the mundanities of day-to-day existence, making them part of a larger and more satisfying social enterprise."[35]

Surely this transcendence is exactly what Ronald Reagan sought to offer the American people at the conclusion of his second inaugural address. Even in a "world that's lit by lightning" with so much that is "changing and will change," what "endures and transcends time," according to the president, is a distinctly "American sound":

> It is hopeful, big-hearted, idealistic, daring, decent and fair. That's our heritage, that's our song. We sing it still. For all our problems, for all our differences, we are together as of old. We raise our voices to God who is the author of the most tender music. And may He continue to hold us close as we fill the world with our sound—in unity, affection, and love—one people under God, dedicated to the dream of freedom that He has placed in the human heart, called upon now to pass that dream on to a waiting and hopeful world.[36]

As Reagan's words so clearly show, presidential discourse tries to makes it easier for the American people to believe that their differences matter less than their shared spiritual calling and global responsibility. This argument may be sorely tested, as indeed it has been, by specific crises throughout the nation's history, and it may not create bonds strong enough to prevent future strife. But across time and party, from 1885 to 2000 presidents have refused to acknowledge that differences among Americans could have a larger impact on the imagined national community than the country's civil religion does.

To promote this pseudo-religious version of nationalism, chief executives name reasoned and restrained habits of mind, most notably faith, loyalty, and calm detachment, as the essential characteristics of American national identity. At times they have contrasted these characteristics with more common and quintessentially human reactions: the irrational impulses of nationalism, the stubborn suspicions of racism, self-involved victimhood, and so on. True Americans control these urges, presidents often proclaim, and prefer instead to cultivate more noble ideals.

This ideationally based model of identity can reinforce the American people's self-image as "God's chosen people," making them truly unique and, in fact, an example for the rest of the world. Herbert Hoover told his constituents that their unprecedented "faith in government by the people" itself constituted "a new race . . . great in its attainments."[37] John Kennedy told the American people that they were "heirs of that first revolution" who must "pay any price, bear any burden, meet any hardship, support any friend, oppose any foe to assure the survival and the success of liberty."[38] Jimmy Carter told them that "freedom and peace in the world depend on the state of our Union."[39] Given these grave obligations, the American people owe it to themselves, the rest of the world, and even God to overlook their own problems of difference.

However noble this obligation may seem, the construction of an ideational model of national identity is not without problems. Like any rhetoric, it has both strengths and weaknesses in the Burkean sense that it invites participants to think about the world through a terministic screen, making some visions possible even as it necessarily occludes other. To conclude this chapter, I will discuss some of these advantages and limitations.

SHARED BELIEFS, SHARED FEELINGS:
SOME POTENTIAL CONSEQUENCES

James David Fairbanks has written that "all organized political societies operate from what is essentially a religious base and all political leadership has a religious dimension."[40] If this is true, then perhaps we have heard nothing very exceptional in these pages. The United States, many observers have concurred, is based on a shared civil religion, so maybe it is not surprising to hear American presidents repeatedly define American national character in its terms. Yet here I have argued that this type of characterization may have an important role in helping presidents manage a diverse democracy.

To that end I have offered various textual examples to show how some presidents have used civil religious themes to imply that different backgrounds or biologies do not matter in the United States, as long as its citizens remain committed to a generalized yet consistent set of civil religious beliefs. Indeed, in some case I have suggested that some presidents have urged their listeners to repudiate their diverse cultural backgrounds in order to join "God's chosen people." By creating an American identity based on such abstractions, presidents have been able to offer their diverse constituents ways of viewing themselves as a united group while also suggesting that their individual differences are largely insignificant relative to their larger calling. Paradoxically, then, in a country that purports to value individualism, specific markers of individual difference have been largely *verboten* in this type of presidential rhetoric of national identity.

Whatever the implications of this particular paradox, this discourse could be interpreted as promoting a functional model of national identity in the United States. For one thing, this rhetoric of national identity is overtly inclusive, as it theoretically invites all comers into the fold of national community. If, as John Miller has reasoned, the American people's "very sense of peoplehood derives not from a common lineage but from their adherence to a set of core principles," then "immigrants from all over the world can assimilate, so long as they, too, dedicate themselves to the proposition."[41] By repeatedly articulating these principles in terms of a civil religion, presidents can promote a particular type of ideological consensus as the hallmark of American democracy and offer what Edwin Black has termed an "idiom of social identity" that equates citizenship with faith-driven commitment.[42] This rhetoric thus locates American national identity not within skin color or pedigree but instead within the heart and the brain, making it theoretically available to anyone.

Likewise, the notion that this ideational rhetoric is infused with religious overtones can also be viewed as contributing to its ability to promote social cohesion. Writing about the relationship between religion and American political culture, Kenneth Wald has suggested that "in what social scientists call 'legitimation,' or its 'priestly aspect,' civil religion helps cement loyalty to the nation. So long as the nation conducts its affairs according to some higher purpose, it warrants allegiance from its citizens on grounds other than mere self-interest."[43] Allegiance to such a "higher purpose" evokes the classical Greek ideal of republicanism, in which citizenship is only the right of individuals who were willing to put the needs of the *demos* ahead of their own personal concerns.

If classical republican philosophy seems an unlikely one to capture the hearts and minds of an American people known for their individualism and competitiveness, then perhaps that is why U.S. presidents must, across time and party, draw upon the themes discussed here in order to manage a diverse democracy. Indeed, one wonders if there are other themes that recur with such predictable regularity within more than one hundred years of presidential rhetoric; I certainly found no other theme as hardy as civil religion in the inaugural and state of the union messages. Furthermore, presidents seem unwilling or perhaps even unable to talk about the American people's diversity without simultaneously invoking the civil religion. Although I have already provided examples of how various presidents have made direct and indirect linkages between the two topics, it is worth noting that even William J. Clinton, who had famously pledged to lead frank and open discussions on the American people's racial diversity, found it difficult to talk about this topic in his inaugural addresses or state of the union messages without also talking about the nation's shared beliefs. Near the end of his 1996 state of the union message, for example, President Clinton remarked, "There have always been things we could do together—dreams we could make real—which we could never have done on our own. We Americans have forged our identity, our very union, from every point of view and every point on the planet, every different opinion. But we must be bound together by a faith more powerful than any doctrine that divides us—by our belief in progress, our love of liberty, and our relentless search for a common ground."[44] Even as this president was speaking self-consciously about the fact that the identity of "we Americans" had been "forged" from multiple elements and diverse heritages, he reminded his listeners that the thing that ultimately held "us" together was faith, "a faith more powerful than any doctrine that divides us."

While some may dismiss Clinton's and other presidents' similar comments in these two genres of speeches as merely platitudinous, I would argue that platitudes persist because they are useful. Indeed, in the case of the United States' diverse democracy, this discourse might even be beneficial. Given Americans' rich multicultural heritage as well as perennial problems with their own diversity, presidential inaugurals and state of the union messages may be a sorely needed ritual of national unity. Similarly, given the themes of individualism of in U.S. culture and politics, these occasions for presidential speech-making may represent to the American people rare reminders of their own collectivity. In other words, in order for them to remain a unified people, Americans may need to believe in their abiding, secret similarities, whether or not they really have any. In fact, the less the citizenry actually shares, the more we might expect its leaders to argue that their constituents' similarities are present indeed but that they merely manifest themselves in ways that are intangible or invisible, such as shared beliefs and shared feelings. If, as Kenneth Burke has suggested, rhetoric is a prayer, then presidents may use inaugural addresses and state of the union messages to pray that such unseen, mythic common bonds seem real enough to the citizenry to keep it from simply disintegrating, a fate that haunts all reifications.

Whatever its potential benefits, however, the presidential rhetoric of shared beliefs that we have heard here is not without its problems, even in theory. I will suggest four.

First, such discourse relies heavily on a strong moral component, reminding listeners of their constitutive characteristics of faith, dedication to principle, and self-restraint. This level of emotional fortitude requires a somewhat detached stance from one's own experiences—the disciplined turning of the other cheek, perhaps, rather than an impassioned obscene gesture. Maybe this is why the contradictions between American "deeds and creed" are so easily elided by this discourse. In calling for citizens to view themselves as part of something far beyond the "worldly" realm of everyday practices, such rhetoric may actually reinforce the logic used by some religious denominations that espouse the idea that deeds matter far less than creed, that good works count for less than good faith.

The second potential problem is also related to the first and more specifically to the overall restrained and detached posture that this rhetoric associates with American national identity. By their very nature, restraint and detachment require some ability to transcend one's immediate circumstances and/or concerns. Clearly, there are times when this ability can be helpful to a democracy's citizens, who, while in a deliberative forum, for example, might benefit from the perspective-taking involved in thinking about other citizens' needs and viewpoints. Yet one has to wonder if this same state of detachment, when taken to extremes, might not also license a more troubling form of transcendence, something closer to disengagement. For example, if Americans truly are God's chosen people and their fates are guided and protected by divine providence, then why should they vote? Likewise, if their obligation as citizens is to remain principled and calm and "unshaken" by the passions of others, why should they go to city council meetings, where decisions are informed by lively, impassioned debate? Although such questions may seem farfetched, they do beg questions about the possibility that a constitutive rhetoric of civil religion might discourage democratic engagement even as it attempts to stir the souls of its citizens.[45]

Third, this rhetoric desperately needs a specific type of opposition in order to survive. To claim that Americans are emotionally detached from and intellectually superior to the rest of the world's "tribes," for example, it needs world wars and Auschwitzes and Sarajevos and other examples as evidence of the kinds of un-American events that passionate tribalism can lead to. It needs hungry and tired immigrants, willing to face life-threatening conditions just to land on American shores. It needs constant, fresh evidence to support country singer Lee Greenwood's proclamation, "I'm proud to be an American, where at least I know I'm free," implying that the United States is a pretty good place to live when one considers the alternatives. Ironically, then, the more peaceful and prosperous the rest of the world becomes, the less compelling this particular rhetoric of allegedly unique American ideals may seem.

Fourth, although this rhetoric may seem to be inclusive by offering an ideational model of national identity, it could actually inhibit the possibility of good-faith discussions of diversity among the American people. By establishing the passionate identification with distinction as an un-American trait, such a rhetoric may keep individuals from being able to talk about their own differences without seeming somewhat unpatriotic or, worse, menacing. In short, because this rhetoric conflates American ideals with a particular feeling or state of detachment, it can make people who care about their cultural heritage seem suspect. Women in veils, Sikhs in turbans, African Americans in tribal robes—these are some of the people this rhetoric can teach others to mistrust and perhaps reject on the grounds that they might comport themselves differently, both physically and mentally, than "real" Americans do. While it does offer such comers redemption via faithfulness to a specific set of beliefs, this discourse may risk making any cultural difference seem somehow un-American.

Because of the troubling nature of some of these potential consequences, presidential efforts at promoting a sense of shared beliefs via civil religious themes warrant further investigation. It may be that U.S. citizens as well as their presidents desperately need this rhetoric of ideological consensus, whatever its consequences. As evidence of how abiding this need may be, in this chapter I have suggested that, from 1885 through 2000 at least, and regardless of party affiliation or personal circumstances, chief executives have largely avoided explicitly discussing Americans' differences in the texts studied here. Instead, they have preferred to speak of the American people as being united by their shared beliefs, with some of them even making the suggestion that to be an American is to be adamantly opposed to such distinctions.

Yet there have been times in the nation's history when the American people were not content to follow this advice. In these moments, such as when immigration and racial crises or the campaign for female suffrage became prominent issues, the American people appeared unconvinced that either civil religious principles or the intellectual, detached postures they necessitated would be sufficient responses to their own diversity. Likewise, in these moments of strife and civil unrest, presidents' more abstract rhetoric of shared beliefs has not been able to quell the nativist and racial fears of the American people. In the next three chapters, I will examine how presidents have responded to specific problems of immigration, race relations, and gender issues in inaugural addresses and state of the union messages from 1885 to 2000. In these speeches, I have looked for what presidents have said about problems related to immigration, civil rights, and women's roles when they could not avoid talking about them. At these times, I will argue, we can hear continual references to the ideational, inclusive models of citizenship discussed here, but we can also hear more subtle yet insidious messages of exclusion as well—messages that suggest that perhaps not everyone can be an American after all.

CHAPTER 3

Immigration and Presidents' Rhetoric of Shared Beliefs

One can hardly think about the United States' diverse democracy without also thinking about Frédéric Auguste Bartholdi and Emma Lazarus. Bartholdi's copper Statue of Liberty, one of the few uncontested icons in the United States, symbolizes the nation's great invitation to the rest of the world, captured so eloquently in Lazarus's poem, "The New Colossus." Carved into the base of his sculpture are her words, the most famous of which are still recognizable to many Americans today:

> *Give me your tired, your poor,*
> *Your huddled masses yearning to breathe free,*
> *The wretched refuse of your teeming shore,*
> *Send these, the homeless, tempest-tost to me,*
> *I lift my lamp beside the golden door!*

However powerful these words may seem now, they received "merely polite applause" when read at the statue's dedication in 1886, according to historian Alan Kraut. The rest of the day's orations hardly concerned immigration at all, as speaker after speaker thanked France for its monumental gift of the statue and then expounded on democratic philosophy. Kraut has even suggested that the notion "Liberty might be raising her torch in welcome to the immigrants did not occur to most of those who addressed the crowd."[1]

In later years, both Liberty's raised torch and Lazarus's poem would be closely associated with the symbolic "golden door" to the American dream. Time after time, even U.S. presidents would invoke the statue's tacit promise, reiterating that their country was a "place where a man could be his own man."[2] Over time, such assurances may have become trite, but they remain central to the quintessential image of the United States as a New World where individuals, freed from ancient constraints, can make their fortunes according to their own spirit, determination, and belief in an American dream.

Indeed, in much presidential rhetoric, as we have seen, qualities like "spirit," "determination," and especially "belief" are commonly featured as the hallmarks of American national identity. Like the Statue of Liberty, presidents have thus also ostensibly invited all comers into the citizenry by invoking a constitutive rhetoric of shared beliefs. Nationalism may be based on heredity, ethnicity, or other traits elsewhere, but in the United States, as chief executives have maintained across time and party, it is defined ideationally. Whatever this logic's shortcomings, it has enabled presidential rhetoric to sound inclusive, emphasizing likemindedness rather than diversity.

Yet the American people themselves have had difficulty ignoring their own ethnic differences at times. Like the first audience of Lazarus's poem, they have never wholly welcomed foreigners. Nativist social movements date back to colonial times.[3] As the population has expanded, such anti-immigrant feelings have ostensibly grown too, especially during times of economic scarcity. Even a brief history of some of the major landmarks of the hundred years or so of immigration restrictions shows the interrelationship of public fears, public opinion, and public policy on immigration to the United States.

Historians report a marked increase of nativism when immigration to the United States peaked during the late nineteenth century.[4] Organizations such as the Ku Klux Klan and the American Protective Association appealed to the "millions of Americans . . . intimidated by the size and diversity of the foreign intrusion."[5] By 1882, public concern was strong enough to ensure the passage of the Chinese Exclusion Act, the nation's first immigration restrictions limiting entry based on national origin, even though this legislation had been met with repeated presidential vetoes just a few years earlier. New laws were not enough to abate nativist fears, however. An increasingly troubled citizenry worried about the "alien menace" and the biological threat of "race mixing" as the nineteenth century closed.[6] Even the American intelligentsia endorsed these suspicions. When MIT president Francis Walker described immigrants as "beaten men from beaten races," the clear implication was that newcomers were both physically and psychologically different from U.S. citizens.[7] Scientists routinely documented the dangers of "alien blood," and many scholars agreed that immigrants would harm the "purity of the Anglo-Saxon American stock" by contributing to the production of a "hybrid race" of a "more ancient, generalized, and lower type."[8] Such arguments were persuasive to many Americans, including a prominent group of Harvard graduates who formed the Immigration Restriction League (IRL) to lobby for firmer restrictions.[9]

In 1891, in response to the growing demand to "protect Americans from potentially dangerous elements in the immigration population," the federal government established the Bureau of Immigration.[10] For the next thirty years, both public resentments and federal restrictions would increase rapidly. In 1924 Congress passed the Johnson-Reed Act, which "permanently crippled the new immigration" of the late nineteenth and early twentieth centuries by establishing a "national origins system" linking quotas for new arrivals to percentages of immigrants already in the country.[11] Roger Daniels, who suggests that the study used to obtain these percentages was "closer to mysticism than social science," quotes the arguments of one of the law's authors, Albert Johnson, a Republican member of the House from Washington state:

> Today, instead of a well-knit citizenry, we have a body politic made up of all and every diverse element. Today, instead of a nation descended from generations of freemen bred to a knowledge of the principles and practices of self-government, of liberty under the law, we have a heterogenous population no small proportion of which is sprung from races that, throughout the centuries, have known no liberty at all. In other words, our capacity to maintain our cherished institutions stands diluted by a stream of alien blood, with all its inherited misconceptions respecting the relationship of the governing power to the governed. It is out of appreciation of this fundamental fact that the American people have come to sanction—indeed demand—reform of our immigration laws.[12]

According to Johnson, then, one of the main forces driving the need for heightened immigration reform was growing public concern that new immigrants simply did not—and could not—understand American democracy.

Daniels suggests that as immigration to the United States slowed down somewhat in the early 1930s, the scarcity of jobs during the Great Depression paradoxically made immigration less attractive to foreigners even as it made U.S. citizens more fearful of immigrants.[13] Although the Franklin Roosevelt administration made great changes to most other areas of federal policy via New Deal legislation, there was no similar revolution in immigration law. In fact, Daniels argues that Roosevelt was reluctant to use even the existing laws and unmet quotas to help German Jews fleeing the Nazi regime.[14] (So small was public support for helping the Jewish refugees that Roosevelt reportedly "told his wife, in February 1939, that 'it is all right for you to support the child refugee bill, but it is best for me to say nothing [now].'"[15]) With the United

States' increasing involvement in World War II came more changes to immigration policies, including the Alien Registration Act, as well as the internment of Japanese Americans.

By the 1950s, however, public demand for immigration restrictions seemed to decrease slightly. Both legal and illegal immigration from Mexico increased, for example, partially due to the popular *bracero* program for manual laborers. Likewise, in 1952, all "purely racial" barriers to naturalization and immigration ended with the passage of the McCarran-Walter Act. Although this latter legislation eased many restrictions that had been in place since 1924, it passed only after Congress overrode the veto of President Truman, who argued that it was still too discriminatory, especially to immigrants from southern and eastern Europe, home to the United States' assumed enemies during the Cold War.[16] President Johnson lifted such prohibitions by signing the Immigration and Naturalization Act of 1965, which allowed for the entry of "refugees from communist or communist-dominated countries" as well as for family members of already naturalized citizens and resident aliens.[17]

Although there was some public concern about immigration from China and Cuba in the late 1960s and throughout the 1970s, nothing would come close to the "turn against immigration" that would take place in the 1980s, almost exactly one century after the previous triumph of nativism in the United States.[18] According to Daniels, the Mariel Crisis of the 1980s was perhaps the key event fueling public fears of immigrants, mainly because it "connected immigration intimately with two major fears of most Americans at that time: crime and AIDS."[19] Whether this crisis itself marked a clear turning point for public opinion or not, the poor economic conditions during the Carter administration and early Reagan presidency also made the American people nervous—and, more to the point, made them more likely to fear new immigrants. By some accounts, anti-immigrant sentiment grew throughout the 1990s. A 1993 *Newsweek* poll reported that roughly 60 percent of the American people agreed that immigration "was a bad thing for this country in the past" and was still harmful.[20] Likewise, Otis Graham has noted that opinion polls throughout the 1990s found "Americans in general opposed to the high volumes" of recent immigration, but "when asked for details, they were uninformed on immigration, unable to comprehend demographic facts or trends, restrictionists without deep convictions or knowledge."[21]

These more recent concerns have often been framed a bit differently than were their predecessors. In general, in the 1980s and 1990s arguments for increasing immigration restrictions have been focused more explicitly on economics than biology, as they were in the nineteenth century, with contemporary public concerns ranging from newcomers' proclivity to "steal American jobs" to their perceived dependence on taxpayer-funded social services.[22] Since 1986, bipartisan federal commissions have made increasingly urgent pleas for limited entry from Mexico and South American countries. State governments have also taken action. In California, for example, voters passed Proposition 187 in 1994 to eliminate social services for illegal immigrants, while legislators in other states, notably Texas and Florida, voiced their support for similar restrictions.

As we have seen, then, no matter how inclusive and welcoming presidents may sound in their inaugural and state of the union messages, the American people themselves have frequently engaged in exclusionary and restrictive thinking on the topic of immigration. Undeniably aware of the ideal that U.S. citizenship can be available to almost all seekers, Americans have nonetheless sought to limit this invitation at times. This contradiction between presidential rhetoric and psycho-sociological reality certainly mirrors the "American Dilemma" of racial differences that Gunnar Myrdal wrote about. He observed that in the United States popular feelings of prejudice and even bigotry belied the nation's more official philosophy of egalitarianism and tolerance.

Yet American dissonance on the topic of immigration is slightly different. For example, almost no one in the United States can speak of his or her own American identity without invoking forebears' arrival from elsewhere; thus, to repudiate even the symbolic ideal of the United States as a "golden door" is also to impugn the facts of one's own heritage. While it may be relatively easy to justify one's views of racial difference based on one's parents' feelings, it would seem far more difficult to be "anti-immigrant" if you are the child, grandchild, or even great-grandchild of an immigrant. Likewise, in a nation in which citizenship is defined ideationally, arguments for restricting citizenship on nonideational grounds, such as economics, seem to somehow challenge the very heart of the shared beliefs hypothesis. Shared beliefs may have been enough to unite an ethnically diverse nation before, such protestations imply, but they alone will not work anymore. To some, the United States simply does not have enough jobs, land, or other resources left to be run solely on shared beliefs.

If the shared beliefs notion of American identity seems irrelevant or even unconvincing to the American people during immigration crises, what happens to this theme in presidential rhetoric during these times? One might expect that presidents might have responded in one of two very different ways. On one hand, given their inclusive rhetoric of citizenship, we might expect that they would simply amplify these appeals in such moments: The greater the outcry against immigration, the louder the presidential insistence on shared beliefs, the more adamant the chief executive's invocation of civil religion. Similarly, we might also expect that presidents forced to attend to such problems would do so impatiently, reprimanding the American people for their ignoble fears and prejudices. If this is so, then presidential discourse about shared beliefs could possibly inhibit popular campaigns against newcomers, keeping crises of immigration from happening as frequently or violently as they might have in an ethnically diverse nation. Presidents, after all, may provide the only clear and consistent message of unity available to an otherwise fractured polity. Perhaps they have responded to immigration crises by providing this message more loudly and steadfastly than they do at other times.

On the other hand, chief executives might also have downplayed the shared beliefs hypothesis in such moments. Presidents are politicians, after all, and they are presumably reluctant to ignore the concerns of their constituents, especially when recently naturalized immigrants may or may not be expected to vote. Ignoring popular worries altogether might thus jeopardize their own political careers. What, then, have they said on such occasions? In 1885 or 1985, when the American people have called for legislation to curb the "alien menace," how have their presidents responded?

My analysis suggests that while presidents have both emphasized and downplayed civil religion and shared beliefs, they have also discussed immigration conflicts in a third and slightly different way. In several of the speeches studied here, presidents simultaneously reinforced the shared beliefs hypothesis while echoing their constituents' fears and prejudices. Although such moves may seem mutually exclusive, in the pages that follow I discuss numerous actual instances of this mixed message. Overall, when discussing immigration during times of increased anti-immigrant sentiment among the American people, presidents often seem to imply that although American citizenship is in fact based on shared civil religious beliefs, some immigrants simply may not be capable of understanding them.

In this chapter I will discuss the nature and recurrence of this executive suggestion, using examples from speeches from 1885 to more recent times to illustrate its various discursive manifestations. In less recent presidential rhetoric, particularly in the late 1800s and early 1900s, immigrants are more likely to be portrayed as hopelessly alien and dangerous to the citizenry specifically because they cannot or are unwilling to understand American beliefs and the laws that manifest them. While more recent speech-writing is less likely to feature such harsh generalizations, it still shows traces of essentialist assumptions about immigrants' capacity for participating in the American people's alleged ideological consensus.

Overall, then, we might say that an oddly exclusive logic about immigrants recurs throughout presidential discourse. That this happens within a nation originally composed of immigrants is odd, but it is perhaps even more curious still that it happens so regularly within genres of presidential rhetoric that are presumably designed to build national political community rather than fracture it. Nevertheless, when one considers how some presidents described immigrants in inaugural addresses and state of the union messages during the late nineteenth and early twentieth centuries, it is hard to imagine how these individuals could be welcomed by anyone. During this time period, certain chief executives implied that foreign newcomers were ignorant, vicious, and dangerous, unflattering characterizations all, but especially so in a nation whose union is allegedly predicated on the stability of shared beliefs.

IGNORANT, VICIOUS, AND DANGEROUS: 1880S–1920S

In 1889 the United States was divided by multiple internal tensions. Deep resentments lingered after the Civil War, particularly in the South. In the North, industry was booming, creating greater discrepancies between the existing classes as well as a demand for a new underclass of laborers. Seemingly eager to meet this need, immigrants arrived daily at unprecedented rates.[23] Despite this unstable union and a rapidly expanding population, Benjamin Harrison spoke mainly of a calm and united citizenry at his March 4 inauguration:

> Surely I do not misinterpret the spirit of the occasion when I assume that the whole body of the people covenant with me and with each other today to support and defend the Constitution and the Union of the States, to yield willing obedience to all the laws and each to every other citizen his equal civil and political rights. Entering thus solemnly into covenant with each other, we may reverently invoke and confidently expect the favor and help of Almighty God—that He will to give me wisdom, strength, and fidelity, and to our people a spirit of fraternity and a love of righteousness and peace.[24]

Like all presidents, Harrison spoke of an American citizenry bound by ideas and faith. His constituents are depicted here as supportive, solemn, and obedient defenders of the Constitution, joined in covenant with each other and favored by God. Such a portrayal is consistent with the ideational rhetoric of American identity, the favored way for presidents to describe their people.

Minutes after reassuring his listeners, however, the president hinted that not all was perfect within his bountiful community. The strife, Harrison reported, did not stem from the understandable "sectional" divisions engendered by the war but from the widespread "systematic violation of laws."[25] The problem was so serious that Harrison abandoned his appeals to a monolithic united citizenry and began blaming individual groups of citizens by name. He first chastised the "educated and influential classes," noting that if they "either practice or connive at the systematic violation of laws . . . what can they expect when [that] lesson . . . has been learned by the ignorant classes?" But the president castigated the upper class not so much for its unlawful actions as for the bad examples they set for the rest of the citizenry. It was the "ignorant classes" who were the real culprits, and Harrison's accusations grew more pointed as he explained the true cost of their crimes: "A community where law is the rule of conduct and where courts, not mobs, execute its penalties is the only attractive field for business investments and honest labor. Our naturalization laws should be so amended as to make the inquiry into the character and good disposition of persons applying for citizenship more careful and searching." Given the harm done to "business investments and honest labor," Harrison asserted that the best way to solve this problem was to amend the naturalization laws. Thus, immigrants were the real problem; their growing numbers constituted the United States' most ignorant class of all. "We accept the man as a citizen without any knowledge of his fitness," Harrison explained, "and he assumes the duties of citizenship without any knowledge as to what they are."[26]

If increased lawlessness was merely the result of immigrants' ignorance of American ways, the president might have advocated better public education or social services. Instead, Harrison advocated a more draconian approach: "We should not cease to be hospitable to immigration, but we should cease to be careless about the character of it. There are men of all races, even the best, whose coming is necessarily a burden upon our public revenues or a threat to social order. These should be identified and excluded."[27] Rather than educating or policing immigrants, Harrison called for a more searching inquiry into an immigrant's "character." Such a plea might seem oddly subjective since immigration is, after all, a legal matter, but its use here points to a subtle yet important distinction. The problem of "lawless mobs" was not merely a consequence of immigrants' ignorance of the law, but, more importantly, the result of a deficiency of "character" leading them to become mobs, "burden . . . our public revenues," and "threaten [the] social order." Harrison thus spoke of disregard for the law as an essential characteristic of immigrants, who were presumably not capable of adhering to the rules in their new home. If this was true, then there could be no better solution than the president's; such comers must be "identified and excluded."

Whatever the president's proposed policy, its underlying logic here is more significant, for it both reflected and encouraged nativist sentiments. Try as he might to speak mainly of the ideational "covenant" that transcended individual differences, Harrison repeatedly reinforced a variety of nativist essentialisms. Even his presumably well-intentioned disclaimers ("There are men of all races, even the best, whose coming is necessarily a burden") supported a perceived hierarchy among citizens, one that would have been especially salient during times of widespread fear of "race mixing."[28] According to this way of thinking, some immigrants were more acceptable than others simply because of their racial or ethnic backgrounds.[29] Such a sentiment would also have been consistent with the scholarly biological arguments popular at the time, particularly those concerned about how immigrants' "racial characteristics" would taint the citizenry's "pure American" bloodline. To be a member of a "race," it would seem, was essentially un-American, a perception that President Harrison supported by singling out the "lawless mobs" from the rest of the presumably white and presumably law-abiding population. Immigrants were both of a race *and* incorrigible, according to this logic, which subtly implied a natural correlation between the two conditions.

In addition to reinforcing racially and biologically essentialist assumptions, the president suggested another reason to be wary of newcomers, especially those who would be a "burden upon our public revenues or a threat to the social order." Although people who need such services may be the most likely to immigrate to the United States in the first place, Harrison suggested that these seemingly "foreign" states of being (e.g., poverty and/or unfamiliarity with democracy) were so alien to the essentially American condition that their presence alone within the citizenry would compromise the nation. Thus, even a material condition like poverty can be attributed to a basic ignorance of American life, according to Harrison's logic.

In Harrison's inaugural address, then, a foreign state of mind is ultimately more debilitating than sheer newness itself, presumably because it threatens the preeminence of Americans' shared beliefs. Even though this lack of cultural knowledge is itself easily changed through education, such "ignorance" is treated here as the immigrant's most immutable trait. Interestingly, Harrison's predecessor, Grover Cleveland, painted a similar picture of how stubbornly immigrants were likely to cling to their native ways. In his 1885 inaugural address, President Cleveland offered ostensible praise for the newly passed Chinese Exclusion Act by noting that the U.S. should "prohibit the immigration of a servile class to compete with American labor, with no intention of acquiring citizenship, and bringing with them and retaining habits and customs repugnant to our civilization."[30] Worse than immigrants' ignorance alone, then, was their lack of concern for it. The immigrants in Cleveland's discourse had "no intention" of learning American beliefs and chose instead to "retain" their "repugnant" customs and habits. In Cleveland's inaugural address, as in Harrison's, immigrants were portrayed in ways that would have simultaneously reinforced popular perceptions of immigrants' biological inferiority while also suggesting a new, more generalized reason to be suspicious of them. Immigrants either could not or did not want to understand American ways, these two presidents implied, and they were therefore a serious threat to the United States' shared beliefs.

In his 1897 inaugural address, Cleveland's successor William McKinley introduced his remarks by embracing the entire citizenry and its ideational bonds, just as most presidents do. According to the president, he had been called to this "high trust" by his fellow Americans, and, with the help of God ("who has so singularly favored the American people in every national trial"), he would walk "humbly in His footsteps" to assume the "arduous and responsible duties" of the presidency. Like other presidents, McKinley also demonstrated his readiness to face the special challenges of his day. He discussed the need for better international trade policies and then turned to domestic concerns.[31] As Harrison had, he called specifically for greater obedience to the nation's laws: "The great essential to our happiness and prosperity is that we adhere to the principles upon which the Government was established and insist upon their faithful observance. Equality of rights must prevail, and our laws be always and everywhere respected and obeyed. . . . Courts, not mobs, must execute the penalties of law."[32] Because "the citizens of the United States are both law-respecting and law-abiding people, not easily swerved from the path of patriotism and honor," McKinley stated, he implied that the threats to American happiness and prosperity were coming from external forces. Accordingly, to protect "greater love for law and order in the future," he advocated tougher immigration restrictions: "Our naturalization and immigration laws should be further improved to the constant promotion of a safer, a better, and a higher citizenship. A grave peril to the Republic would be a citizenship too ignorant to understand or too vicious to appreciate the great value and beneficence of our institutions and laws, and against all who come here to make war upon them our gates must be promptly and tightly closed."[33] Like Cleveland and Harrison had, McKinley called for greater restrictions because of immigrants' unfamiliarity with American life. But this president suggested something more sinister at work here: Immigrants were not only "too ignorant" to understand "our institutions and laws" but also "too vicious to appreciate [their] great value." Just as Harrison's subjects were assumed to lack the appropriate "character" necessary for citizenship, McKinley's were irredeemably deficient as well due to their inherently hostile natures.[34]

Instead of suggesting how governmental institutions might rehabilitate such individuals, the president spoke mainly of the federal government's interest in excluding them altogether. He implied, for example, that stricter laws would facilitate a Darwinian selection of only the best immigrant stock to promote a "safer, better, higher" citizenry. Because he failed to specify just who these "best" immigrants might be, however, his talk cast all newcomers as part of the "grave peril to the Republic."

"Ignorance" and "maliciousness," of course, are hardly qualities foreign to the United States. Yet McKinley's discussion of how to deal with them also reveals much about the significant distinctions being made between the immigrant and the American. While laws and regulations should be used to keep out such newcomers, education should be used to edify "our own citizens," according to the president: "Nor must we be unmindful of the need for improvement among our own citizens, but with the zeal of our forefathers encourage the spread of knowledge and free education. Illiteracy must be banished from the land if we shall attain that high destiny as the foremost of the enlightened nations of the world which, under Providence, we ought to achieve."[35] The American people should restrict the entry of those who arrive in the United States without an education but "encourage the spread of knowledge and free education" among themselves. Native-born Americans are somehow blessed with an innate love of freedom and can be taught everything else, this logic implies, but newcomers are not capable of such rehabilitation, presumably because of the same cognitive shortcomings suggested by Harrison. Although immigrants may have represented a biological or economic threat to some, McKinley was most troubled by their suspiciously foreign attitudes, their irredeemably "vicious nature[s]."

The three presidents discussed so far advocated immigration restrictions because they believed that immigrants had foreign and dangerous habits of mind. In doing so, the presidents gave voice to the same impulses motivating the nativist groups of the late 1800s who worried about the "alien menace" of "foreign blood."[36] But in these examples of presidential rhetoric, alien *thoughts* are the menace, with foreign *dispositions,* not "blood," necessitating stricter immigration laws. Given the fervent pitch of the popular campaigns against immigrants during those years, why did these presidents choose to alter the existing arguments in this particular way?

The most obvious reasons might have been practical and political. The Immigration Restriction League might have been able to rank nationalities of newcomers in terms of their "worthiness" to become citizens, but presidents could not be so specific. By the late 1800s, many of their constituents were themselves recent immigrants who continued to take pride in their nationality of origin. If presidents were to restrict anyone from the citizenry prima facie, they had to justify this exclusion by speaking only of general traits that could not necessarily be associated with one ethnicity more than another. As Harrison put it, there were "men from even the best races" who could not be allowed into the citizenry.

Discussing new immigrants' unfamiliarity with American ways in terms of an essentialized ignorance was thus perhaps a politically expedient way to argue for the restriction of new arrivals without offending their predecessors. Indeed, such portrayals may have helped assimilated immigrants feel even more "American" by enabling them to distinguish themselves from more recent comers by participating in the very nativistic logic once used to disparage them. Like many popular anti-immigrant arguments of this era, then, presidential rhetoric was less likely to dwell on past immigration than it was to focus instead on limiting the "next wave."

These presidents' criteria for excluding immigrants were not limited to merely intellectual points, however. They also warned of new immigrants' "characters" or "dispositions" and thus portrayed attitude as chief among immigrants' most dangerous traits. Yet describing newcomers in this way was the ultimate indictment against them because of the logic established by the ideational rhetoric of American national identity (as discussed in chapter 2). As I pointed out there, because this nationalistic rhetoric is closely related to the nation's civil religion, it requires citizens to be true believers above all else. Because of this logic's emphasis on faith and a uniquely American covenant with a perhaps uniquely American God, the mind and soul are perceived as being more important than the body, meaning that biological differences would not be as significant as attitudinal ones.[37] In fact, the originators of this logic, the Puritans, reserved their harshest punishments for people who thought differently, rather than those who looked different.[38]

To speak of different ways of thinking is to move beyond external signifiers of ethnicity (e.g., skin color, dress, etc.) to a more interior realm of thoughts and motives. Anyone who looked foreign may also have been suspected of thinking in "foreign" or "dangerous" ways. Those patterns of thought might carry the imprint of a "foreign" deity, such as Allah, or perhaps be driven by ancient loyalties rather than the practical logic of the New World. Despite presidential efforts at maintaining an inviting rhetoric of citizenship, then, the nature of the civil religion is such that it almost necessarily excludes immigrants. Ideational rhetorics are not intrinsically inclusive; they only offer refuge for believers. All presidents had to do was hint at the possibility of non-believers among the faithful to justify their derision and exclusion. Citizens, meanwhile, could continue to feel good about their own beliefs, viewing the immigrant's weakness of mind and character as proof of their own God-given blessings.

Given this logic, it is perhaps surprising that at least one of the presidents of this era did not take an evangelical stance toward immigration, encouraging the citizenry to help newcomers "save" themselves by embracing American beliefs.[39] Yet these beliefs themselves seem to have essentialist properties suitable only to native-born minds. Indeed, once immigrants had been labeled as cognitively or attitudinally different from the rest of the American people, the perception that they were thus inherently dangerous and irredeemable could persist for generations. (Consider, for example, the Immigration and Naturalization Service's "roundups" of immigrants of Arabic descent after September 11.)

Presidents may not have necessarily created this logic, but their use of its rhetoric may have both sanitized and sanctioned more general anti-immigrant feelings among the American people. While many popular campaigns "documented" their anti-immigrant arguments through scholarly studies of the "alien menace," presidents were not obliged to offer similar evidence. In fact, over time some presidents' arguments against immigrants would become increasingly terse and simplistic. To wit, by the 1920s Calvin Coolidge was able to speak as if new immigrants were inherently dangerous to the country without ever elaborating on the exact nature of the threat, making distinctions among types of newcomers, or explaining why foreignness alone implied an immutably contrary state of mind.

Although immigration historians often designate 1920 as the end of the peak immigration years that began in the nineteenth century, newcomers were still settling into American life long after their arrivals stopped setting records. Likewise, ongoing nativistic campaigns continued to provide evidence of resentment at the "foreign intrusion." President Coolidge may have helped citizens justify such fears in his 1923 state of the union message, in which he used the following language to characterize immigration's ultimate harm: "American institutions rest solely on good citizenship. They were created by people who had a background of self-government. New arrivals should be limited to our capacity to absorb them into the ranks of good citizenship. America must be kept American."[40] In just four simple sentences, Coolidge had made an exclusive argument that sounded inclusive indeed. He refers first to the participatory nature of the United States' democracy, the health of which "rest[s] solely on good citizenship." Yet in alluding to the country's creators and the "background[s]" that made them capable of self-government, the president makes a subtle yet important distinction that could set already established citizens apart from the "new arrivals" introduced in the third sentence. Because newcomers may not have this familiarity with "self-government," their entry "should be limited" to those who understand democracy, this increasingly exclusivist voice argues. Such intellectual criteria alone would ensure that "America [can] be kept American," the ultimate goal of an ideational rhetoric that had both inclusive and exclusive undertones.

Thus, in crisp language, and without pointing to any specific nationality or race of people, Coolidge could use this rhetoric to articulate a specious argument against immigrants, an argument that persists to this day. Because immigrants are, by definition, foreign, they are unfamiliar with American democracy. Because they do not understand American democracy, they are unfit for citizenship. Because they are unfit for citizenship, they are inherently dangerous to America. Because they are dangerous, they must be regulated and restricted. As Coolidge himself said a few sentences later, "We should find additional safety in a law requiring the immediate registration of all aliens. Those who do not want to be partakers of the American spirit ought not to settle in America."[41]

This argument is, of course, fallacious for several reasons.[42] Yet Coolidge's simple reasoning provides an excellent example of how a necessarily foreign mindset is conflated with an inability to uphold or even understand American shared beliefs. Coolidge, like McKinley, even implied that immigrants are actively opposed to the idea of America. His reference to an "American spirit" that can be "partaken of" suggests the ideational nature of the American character that is so well established in presidential discourse. Those who cannot join together in a union based on shared beliefs—because, presumably, of an essential nature rendering them incapable of appreciating certain ideas— should be kept from "settling in America." Rhetoric like this makes it almost impossible for immigrants to partake in the American spirit, however. Like his predecessors, Coolidge portrayed all immigrants as alien to the world of American ideas, relegating them to the status of perennial outsiders.

Presidents cannot always make such sweeping generalizations, to be sure. At times they have to be more charitable toward the concept of immigration. After all, the United States' popularity with foreigners has long been considered strong evidence of the nation's global superiority. Even Benjamin Harrison, speaking during a time of heightened anti-immigrant sentiments, could not suggest that immigration be ended altogether. "We should not cease to be hospitable to immigration," the president proclaimed, "but we should cease to be careless as to the character of it."[43] In the years that followed, presidents would not as boldly impugn the "character" of immigrants. Still, whether they were using their inaugural addresses and state of the union messages to call for decreased or increased restrictions, presidents' discourse still featured some noteworthy statements, many of which were implicitly based on the notion that immigrants think differently than "real" Americans do.

IMMIGRANTS AS REFUGEES: 1930S–1960S

In the years since the great wave of immigration at the end of the nineteenth century, presidents seem to have spoken less explicitly of the "immigrant threat" of foreign dispositions. At the beginning of the twentieth century, this trend may have merely reflected changing public preoccupations. By the end of the 1920s, Kraut writes, "a calm [had] settled over the country as the harassment of new-comers subsided and Americans were distracted by a new source of entertainment, the radio."[44] In addition, Daniels suggests that the strict federal quota system mandated by the Johnson-Reed Immigration Reform Act of 1924 may have been something of a red herring. Although Congress and the public may have assumed that immigration rates would decrease dramatically to totals at or below quota rates, that did not happen.[45]

Whatever the actual versus perceived rates of new arrivals in the late 1920s, it would take the Great Depression to get public attention refocused on immigration as a national problem. Although no major immigration laws were passed during Herbert Hoover's administration, the president used his 1930 annual message to argue that immigration ought to be "more limited and more selective" given the "conditions of greater unemployment."[46] Missing from Hoover's discourse, then, were the moral indictments of immigrants and aspersions on their collective "character" that figured so prominently in the previous examples; in this text at least, his argument was based instead on economic considerations. It would seem fitting, then, that under Hoover's guidance federal immigration officials applied the "LPC" clause of immigration law more stridently than in the past.[47] (LPC stood for "likely to become a public charge.") The LPC clause had been part of the law since 1882. Under this provision, officials could deny entry to anyone who seemed incapable of supporting himself or herself, such as the ill, the elderly, or the physically disabled. During the Hoover administration, the clause was used to bar entry to all but the most affluent, and Daniels notes that it was a "policy that would later have murderous consequences for many attempting to flee Nazi Germany."[48]

President Hoover did not mention his use of the LPC clause in his inaugural or state of the union speeches, of course, nor did his successor, Franklin Roosevelt, who also did not propose any significant changes to immigration law as part of his New Deal.[49] Although the issue of what to do with Jewish refugees became quite public while FDR was in office, the president did not use the bully pulpit afforded by his annual messages to address it. Given that Roosevelt was otherwise known as a skilled orator who famously proclaimed that the role of the president was to provide "moral leadership" to the American people, his silence was odd. The president did make some "nonpublic directives" that enabled refugees on tourist and other short-term visas to remain in the country, and in 1939 he penned a repentant note for inclusion in the 1938 volume of his public papers.[50]

Roosevelt's successor was not as silent. In his 1947 state of the union message, Harry Truman argued that the United States could and should do more for political refugees:

> The United States can be proud of its part in caring for the peoples reduced to want by the ravages of war, and in aiding nations to restore their national economies. We have shipped more supplies to the hungry peoples of the world since the end of the war than all other countries combined! However, insofar as admitting displaced persons is concerned, I do not feel that the United States has done its part. Only about 5,000 of them have entered this country since May, 1946. The fact is that the executive agencies are now doing all that is reasonably possible under the limitation of the existing law and established quotas. Congressional assistance in the form of new legislation is needed. I urge Congress to turn its attention to this world problem, in an effort to find ways whereby we can fulfill our responsibilities to these thousands of homeless and suffering refugees of all faiths.[51]

Compared to the words of his predecessors, as highlighted here, Truman's rhetoric sounds more charitable toward immigrants. Indeed, although Otis Graham has written about some of the political calculations that might have motivated Truman's public rhetoric on immigration, this president's words represent something of a turning point in the discourse studied here.[52] Rather than suggesting that immigrants might be inherently incapable of understanding and/or performing democratic citizenship, Truman's rhetoric portrayed them as more helpless, if not more benign—the "thousands of homeless and suffering" to whom the United States had "responsibilities." Using language that more obviously embraced the civil religious idea that the United States had a God-given charge to help the rest of the world, Truman thus "staked out the new liberal position," in Graham's words, that linked immigration restriction with discrimination.[53]

Yet even this new type of rhetoric was ripe with noteworthy distinctions between Americans and new arrivals. Consider Dwight Eisenhower's 1961 state of the union message, for example. As Truman had, Dwight Eisenhower also spoke of the United States' ongoing responsibility to "assist refugees from tyranny," especially from, presumably, communism. To this end, the president said, "The Administration has also made legislative recommendations to liberalize existing restrictions upon immigration while still safeguarding the national interest. It is imperative that our immigration policy be in the finest American tradition of providing a haven for oppressed peoples and fully in accord with our obligation as leader of the free world."[54] Seventy-five years after the unveiling of the Statue of Liberty, Eisenhower spoke about immigration in ways that recalled the inclusive promise of Emma Lazarus's poem. Lazarus's weary subjects, "yearning to be free," seemed Eisenhower's also, especially as he urged his audience to continue that "finest American tradition of providing a haven for oppressed peoples."

Like the poem, however, Eisenhower's talk showed signs of subtle but important distinctions between its subject and its audience. The president spoke of a need to "liberalize existing conditions" but quickly reassured his listeners that the modified legislation would still "safeguard the national interest." Here Eisenhower may have subtly reinforced the idea that immigrants continued to pose some sort of threat to the United States. Indeed, the abstract yet menacing nature of this threat is emphasized by the vagueness of the term used to describe that which must be protected ("the national interest"). Are immigrants likely to steal state secrets? Are they likely to become an economic burden? Are they, as suggested in previous presidential speeches, likely to cause domestic insurrections? This president neither clarifies nor rebuts such assumptions. In fact, the most positive conclusion one can draw about immigrants from his rhetoric is that they are simply the necessary charges of the United States, the "leader of the free world." *They* need *us,* this logic says, echoing nativist notions that people from nondemocratic backgrounds are essentially weaker than "true" American citizens are.

Furthermore, Eisenhower's use of the term "oppressed" here may evoke some of the turn-of-the-century beliefs about perceived inherent mental or attitudinal differences between immigrants and American citizens. The American people have a special responsibility to "oppressed peoples," he argued, pointing to the broken spirit of potential immigrants, not their race or nationality, as their most salient characteristic as a collectivity. Sounding a bit like prior presidential rhetoric suggesting that immigrants could not be taught to love or even understand democracy, Eisenhower suggests that the United States has no greater responsibility to these newcomers than to offer merely temporary shelter. America can be their "haven," in the president's words, but perhaps not their home.

Following Eisenhower, John Kennedy also called for changes in immigration policy. Kennedy had argued in the book *A Nation of Immigrants* that immigration was an untapped source of national strength, and two years after his election in 1960 he sent a proposal for legislative reforms to Congress. Because no significant congressional action had been taken at the time of his assassination, most of Kennedy's suggestions would not be enacted as laws until 1965, under the signature of his successor, Lyndon Johnson.[55]

To garner public support for these relaxed restrictions, Johnson spoke plainly of the existing system's discriminatory nature:

> We must also lift by legislation the bars of discrimination against those who seek entry into our country, particularly those with much needed skills and those joining their families. In establishing preferences, a nation that was built by the immigrants of all lands can ask those who now seek admission: "What can you do for our country?" But we should not be asking: "In what country were you born?" For our ultimate goal is a world without war, a world made safe for diversity, in which all men, goods and ideas can freely move across every border and every boundary.[56]

Unlike many of his predecessors, Johnson directly acknowledged the existing citizenry's immigrant roots as well as its obligation to admit more newcomers. More specifically, in this 1964 state of the union message and through its proposed legislation Johnson rebutted decades of admissions criteria based solely on national origin. Despite this departure from long-standing policy, however, his rhetoric was still haunted by the logic of a previous era.

In discussing how the United States might still "establish preferences," Johnson echoed negative ideational judgments about immigrants that had been stated more bluntly by past presidents. Indeed, his criteria were not necessarily any more inclusive than Harrison's or Coolidge's had been. Rather than being based on whether or not immigrants revere American beliefs, the eligibility of Johnson's new arrivals could be determined by the more tangible benefits they might offer: in short, what *they* can do for "*our* country" (emphasis added).

Such commodified criteria imply a one-sided, nonreciprocal transaction, especially since Johnson neither asked nor answered questions of what "we" can do for "them." Indeed, this president seems to disregard immigrants' intellectual properties or desires, framing newcomers instead as service providers to the existing citizenry. Even in the presumably well-intentioned talk of Johnson and other presidents during this era, then, important boundaries remained, signaling basic differences among people: Americans are idealistic thinkers, attracted to a "world made safe for diversity, in which all men, goods and ideas can freely move across every border and every boundary," but immigrants are only eager doers, forced to demonstrate their worth before they can move across the very real "borders" that persist.

Arguments about immigration framed in terms of restrictions, differences, and tradeoffs may be completely justifiable and even inevitable, given the limited resources available to a growing population. Yet the blending of some of the ideational criteria implied in presidential rhetoric makes much of it appear far more nativist than numbers-driven. As presented in the textual examples offered throughout this chapter, much of the logic in presidential discourse repeatedly suggests that foreign-born people have "characters," "dispositions," and "spirits" that are essentially different from those of native-born Americans. Over time, these characteristics, not scarce resources, can become excuses for the exclusion of immigrants. Arguments like Johnson's may seem to focus more on actions than beliefs, but even this talk suggests that foreigners have unique responsibilities and obligations to the United States. In fact, such talk may portray immigrants as so different from the American people that they might only be expected to *do* for the American people rather than to *think,* and thus be, like them.

A KINDER, GENTLER RHETORIC
OF DISTINCTION: 1970S–2000

After Johnson, the next chief executive to preside over changes in federal immigration legislation was Ronald Reagan. That does not mean that Presidents Nixon, Ford, and Carter did not have to worry about immigration. In 1972, for example, Richard Nixon received a report from the National Commission on Population Growth encouraging the federal government to "plan for a stabilized population" with stricter controls on illegal immigration.[57] Likewise, during the Carter administration there was public concern over immigration from Asia in particular. Nevertheless, as Roger Daniels has written,

> During the 1980s, for the first time since the mid-1920s, immigration took up a central position on the American social agenda. While both the volume and the incidence of immigration continued the steady increase that had begun just after World War II, anti-immigration attitudes . . . again emerged. These nativistic attitudes had been largely quiescent during the fifteen years between the enactment of the Immigration Act of 1965 and the Mariel boatlift, a period in which the United States as a whole moved from the euphoric confidence of the Great Society to the resentful feelings of impotence best typified by the Iranian hostage crisis, whose denouement, at the moment of Ronald Reagan's assumption of the presidency, seemed to symbolize a sea change in American life.[58]

Viewed historically, this resurgence in nativism represented not so much a "sea change" in American attitudes as a simple and perhaps cyclical return to previous fears and suspicions. Nevertheless, the passing of one hundred years since immigration's last peak did result in some changes, at least rhetorically. Grover Cleveland might have been able to complain about immigrants' "habits and customs repugnant to our civilization" in 1885, but Reagan could use no such tone in 1985. Indeed, in his state of the union message that year he spoke of the nation's need for more inclusive ways of thinking. "Let us begin by challenging our conventional wisdom. There are no constraints on the human mind," he offered, "no walls around the human spirit, no barriers to our progress except those we ourselves erect."[59]

In fact, however, more restrictive immigration legislation was being drafted by the time Reagan gave this speech. The laws that would later become known as the Immigration Act of 1986 made distinctions between "legal" and "illegal" immigrants more salient to business owners than ever before, with employers facing stiff penalties for hiring "ineligible" workers, for example. Clarifying such differences among immigrants meant that the American citizenry, too, might be able to shift its resentments from all foreign newcomers to merely those who resided or worked in the United States unlawfully (never mind the economic benefits provided by their tax-free labor).

For his part, Reagan may have contributed indirectly to such public impressions of immigration by sharing the story of one legal newcomer's success:

> Ten years ago a young girl left Vietnam with her family, part of the exodus that followed the fall of Saigon. They came to the United States with no possessions and not knowing a word of English. Ten years ago—the young girl studied hard, learned English, and finished high school in the top of her class. And this May, May 22nd to be exact, is a big date on her calendar. Just ten years from the time she left Vietnam, she will graduate from the United States Military Academy at West Point. I thought you might like to meet an American hero named Jean Nguyen.[60]

Reagan did not use this anecdote to argue specifically for any particular policy, although one might argue that he was making a plea for more inclusive thinking by featuring a non-native-born citizen as "an American hero." Whatever his reasons for relating Nguyen's story, this discussion is noteworthy for at least two reasons. First, it marks the first occasion among the texts studied here that an immigrant is portrayed both individually and positively in presidential rhetoric. Like much of Reagan's characteristically narrative-driven discourse, this discussion takes the focus off "groups" of people, placing it instead on individuals and their achievements. Reagan's story thus features the refutation of the previous presidential tendency to discuss immigrants primarily as "masses" or "mobs." Second, the positive nature of this portrayal shows that the ability to "make dreams come true" (as he defines American heroism elsewhere) is not merely the birthright of the native-born. Other races and nationalities can also participate in the American dream, according to Ronald Reagan, displaying a rhetorical generosity seldom matched by his predecessors.

However revolutionary Reagan's remarks are, this speech still bears traces of the exclusivist logics discussed previously. Consider, for example, the fact that Reagan does not even utter the word "immigrant" in this account, perhaps because of the word's association with inherent "non-Americanness." To call Nguyen an "immigrant" might be to label her as essentially and irredeemably different, a label that even a presidential pronouncement of heroism could not transcend. Because Reagan's is a story of redemption, he cannot use such a term, preferring instead to frame her, à la Eisenhower, as a refugee, although he does not use this term either.

In addition, it is perhaps no coincidence that this story centers around Nguyen's education—or, perhaps more accurately, her re-education. This tale is one of hard work, to be sure, but it is also a tale of the U.S. educational system's ability to teach "Americanness" and transmit shared beliefs. Indeed, in Nguyen's case, her training was so successful that she ended up in one of the most American institutions of all: the United States Military Academy at West Point. Given how previous presidents had focused so heavily on foreigners' perceived essential differences and undemocratic ways of thinking, Nguyen's graduation from West Point can be read as testament to American institutions' ability to do the impossible, to redeem the irredeemable.

Thus, even though the American people may have been offered a strikingly positive depiction of a non-native-born citizen in Reagan's 1985 state of the union message, this rhetoric takes on additional meaning when read against the backdrop of previous presidents' more suspicious discourse. As I have noted, even this portrayal can be read as more of a testament to the nation's strength than to Jean Nguyen's, and hence it may signal a more subtle voice of exclusion. In the 1980s and 1990s, when public figures could no longer speak openly about ethnicity, especially differences among ethnic groups, nativism may have needed a new guise. No longer can presidents publicly disparage immigrants' "character" or chastise them for "viciousness." In the absence of the ability to openly label the "other" as inferior, nativist rhetoric must work harder at the opposite end of the spectrum: labeling the collectivity and its beliefs as increasingly superior *and* somehow unattainable to all but a noteworthy few, such as Jean Nguyen. Such talk can incorporate now-unspoken but still salient prejudices of the past into more subtle recognitions of the rhetorical boundaries remaining between "us" and "them."

Intentionally or not, George H. W. Bush may have reinforced exactly these types of distinctions in his 1990 state of the union message. Ironically, he was speaking of immigration in one of the most positive and seemingly inclusive ways yet: "America, not just the nation but an idea, is alive in the minds of people everywhere. As this new world takes shape, America stands at the center of a widening circle of freedom—today, tomorrow, and into the next century. Our nation is the enduring dream of every immigrant who ever set foot on these shores, and the millions still struggling to be free. This nation, this idea called America, was and always will be a new world—our new world."[61] In keeping with the ideational logic of American exceptionalism, Bush reiterated the fundamental American belief that opportunity is constantly available in the United States, making the nation both the envy of and an example to the rest of the world. Using a familiar page from the hymn book of American civil religion, the president described the United States as "the enduring dream of every immigrant who ever set foot on these shores, and the millions still struggling to be free."

Bush's words may have provided hope to inhabitants of other countries, but they were perhaps also useful in soothing the fears of American citizens, the same impulse inspiring the other presidential rhetoric on immigration I have described in this chapter. To this end, the president concluded his remarks with a clear distinction, one marked by a simple pronoun: "This nation, this idea called America, was and always will be a new world—*our* new world" (emphasis added). Read by itself, this sentence might seem innocuous enough. Read within the larger context of the presidential rhetoric of shared beliefs, however, Bush's words seem to echo the exclusivist tone articulated more plainly by some of his nineteenth-century predecessors: Americans discovered this idea, they claimed land for it, and it will always be expressly theirs. They alone understand the idea of America, and they alone are thus entitled to its rewards.

In spite of its centrality to U.S. history, immigration has always engendered prejudice among the American people. At times some of their presidents may have reinforced these fears in more or less obvious ways. In the first set of examples discussed in this chapter, U.S. presidents portrayed immigrants as essentially different from the true American citizenry, usually due to foreign habits of mind presumed to derive from their foreign heritages. In the second set, we heard presidents use some of their most public moments in the bully pulpit to focus on immigrants as refugees—needy masses who would benefit from U.S. aid while also, and perhaps more importantly, offering aid to the United States itself via their labor and services. However mythic and outdated, such clear distinctions between "immigrant" and "American," between "them" and "us," still persist in presidential talk, much as they do within the public sphere. In fact, such sentiments may be strong enough now as to need no elaboration. Indeed, in the two instances discussed so far in this third set of examples, Presidents Reagan and Bush were not ostensibly speaking negatively of immigrants at all. Yet by the time Bush spoke in 1990, perhaps it took only three simple words, "our new world," to signal the same sorts of distinctions made more explicit by his executive forebears. Viewed as the elegant legacy of previous presidential rhetoric on immigration, these three words may signal the gradual and rhetorical closing of the golden door once opened for Lazarus's "huddled masses." One suspects that the audience who first heard her poem in 1886, like Bush's in 1990, would almost certainly approve.

The audience for Bill Clinton's 1995 state of the union message would presumably have agreed. In this speech Clinton noted that "all Americans, not only in the states most heavily affected, but in every place in this country are rightly disturbed by the large numbers of illegal aliens entering *our* country" (emphasis added). As if his pronoun choice, like Bush's, were not enough to signal the distinction at the heart of his rhetoric, Clinton made his point even more directly:

> The jobs they hold might otherwise be held by citizens or legal immigrants. The public services they use impose burdens on our taxpayers. That's why our Administration has moved aggressively to secure our borders more, by hiring a record number of new border guards, by deporting twice as many criminal aliens as ever before, by cracking down on illegal hiring, by barring welfare benefits to illegal aliens. We are a nation of immigrants, but we are also a nation of laws. It is wrong and ultimately self-defeating for a nation of immigrants to permit the kind of abuse of our immigration laws we have seen in recent years, and we must do more to stop it.[62]

To some, President Clinton may have simply seemed to be responding to the demands of his worried constituents, who presumably wanted guarded borders, deported criminals, and the like. In juxtaposing immigrants and the law, however, Clinton's discourse may have also done something else.

By declaring that "we are a nation of immigrants, but we are also a nation of laws," the president may have evoked the logic of previous generations, one suggesting that immigrants could not possibly understand U.S. laws and would therefore almost necessarily represent a threat to the United States. In this passage the president discusses immigration almost exclusively in terms of its unlawfulness (using phrases such as "criminal aliens," "illegal hiring," and "illegal aliens") and its presumed "burden" to taxpayers. Similarly, the descendants of immigrants are told that the federal government would preserve their American destiny by designing and enforcing laws that keep unworthy newcomers out. To do anything else, according to the president, would be "wrong and ultimately self-defeating for a nation of immigrants," a kind of "abuse" of the American dream and the shared beliefs it rests upon.

In a sense, then, this section of Clinton's 1995 state of the union message directly recalled the tone of Benjamin Harrison's 1889 inaugural address. Ultimately, both presidents reassured their audiences that "the law" would protect them against immigrants, with Clinton's promise that his administration would "move aggressively" to secure borders and deport illegal aliens strongly

echoing Harrison's concern about those "whose coming is necessarily a burden upon our public revenues or a threat to the social order."[63] Viewed within
the rhetorical context established here, this similarity points to an important
discursive continuity in how certain presidents have talked about immigration
in their inaugural and state of the union speeches. Even though we might
expect these genres of presidential speech to be inclusive to the point of being platitudinous, in this chapter I have argued that when certain presidents
spoke of immigrants on these important occasions, their rhetoric could not
help but reflect and perhaps even encourage some of the American people's
more exclusivist impulses. In addition, I have suggested that earlier presidential
rhetoric may have even added another type of negative characteristic, one
based on perceived cognitive and/or attitudinal shortcomings, to the list of
those traits already presumed to set immigrants apart. More recent examples
suggested that the belief that immigrants think differently from American citizens may be a very enduring notion, perhaps even displacing ethnicity as the
most salient difference between current citizens and new arrivals.

CHAPTER 4

Race and Presidents' Rhetoric of Shared Beliefs

A lthough many pundits of the mid-1990s declared O. J. Simpson's murder trial to be the "trial of the century," future historians may wonder whether this event deserved such a title. What could possibly make the Simpson trial more important than, say, the 1925 Scopes "monkey trial," 1953's *Brown v. Board of Education,* or 1973's *Roe v. Wade?*

The most obvious answer is also the most democratic: public interest. In the O. J. Simpson trial's early days, television networks abandoned their daily schedules to make room for gavel-to-gavel coverage. As entertainment, this trial had everything: a fallen hero, misguided love, innocent bystanders, unscrupulous lawyers (as well as some who rhymed), and even intermittent comic relief. Because it took place in the "politically correct" 1990s, however, the case was entertainment with a social conscience, as the trial invigorated campaigns against spousal abuse and for legal reform. For others, though, the trial also seemed like a referendum on something else, something much larger than the guilt or innocence of an individual man: race. The trial's outcome, these observers thought, would reveal something important about race relations in the United States. Eager for the resolution to this real-life cliffhanger, they watched.

The media reinforced this perception. Weeks before a jury was selected, reporters interviewed legal consultants about the ideal racial composition for a Simpson jury. Would having a majority of whites hurt or help the former football star? Would the prosecution have to change tactics to present its case to an all-black jury? During the trial itself, these discussions heightened as the "race card" became increasingly significant to the proceedings. Even the lawyers fought about it: Should the jury hear testimony containing the "n-word?" Should an allegedly racist police officer be forced to testify? Was Simpson a murderer or merely another victim of the Los Angeles Police Department's bigotry?

On October 3, 1995, the trial ended with Simpson's acquittal, but it seemed as if something else had begun. The next morning the *New York Times* reported that "the reactions to the verdict parallel the racial divide in every opinion poll taken since the trial began. Separated by a constant gap of about 40 percentage points, many whites tend to hold fast to the belief that Simpson was guilty, while blacks believed as adamantly in his innocence. Several polls indicate that behind [this response] is a deep suspicion of the police and the criminal justice system."[1] Reporters from all over the nation cited uniform disparity among the reactions of black and white citizens, discrediting the notion that blacks' suspicions were directed at the Los Angeles legal system alone. In Manhattan's Pasqua Coffee Bar, Dallas's Texas Bar-B-Q, and Jocks N Jills Sports Bar in Atlanta, patrons reportedly rejoiced or became enraged at the O.J. verdict, depending on their skin color.[2]

The Los Angeles Police Department had prepared for riots following the decision, but no one could have anticipated such a deep division of opinion. Instead of creating public mayhem, the American people voiced more private resentments—of police officers or lawyers or celebrities, perhaps, but also of each other. How could whites be so blind to the justice system's institutional racism? Conversely, how could blacks ignore such brutal slayings? A few observers, including President Bill Clinton, ignored the specifics of the case to worry aloud about why black people and white people "saw the same things so differently."[3] Thus, a crisis of interpretation, not a police conspiracy or a double homicide, seemed to be the country's main racial problem, according to the president. How could there be such a tremendous psychological split among the citizenry?

People who lamented this divide assumed that it was new or at least unprecedented in its intensity. The American people, though demographically diverse, are supposed to share the same thoughts and dispositions; in terms of the phrasing I have used throughout this book, they were assumed to have "shared beliefs." Even their presidents say so, describing citizenship in ideational terms so as to avoid racially or ethnically essential ones, as I have shown. To speak of a division of *ideas* among the American people is thus to speak of a very serious problem, making Clinton's question an important one indeed.

Actually, it was a president's admission of such a division rather than the division itself that was unprecedented in American history. The nation has always been deeply split on racial matters. Slavery was initially illegal in some of the American colonies, for example, until colonists overturned the law in order to acquire an additional labor force.[4] By the late 1800s, African slaves made up almost one-eighth of the population, at least by Abraham Lincoln's estimate, with the majority living in southern states. In the North, reformers made moral and economic arguments against slavery for decades before its abolition. Long after its end, slavery left an indelible mark on American people of all races and colors. Indeed, Judith Shklar has argued that American citizenship has historically been defined as what it meant *not* to be slave.[5] Likewise, Ralph Ellison once wrote that without slaves, there could be no American national identity at all:

> Since the beginning of the nation, white Americans have suffered from a deep inner uncertainty as to who they really are. One of the ways that has been used to simplify the answer has been to seize upon the presence of black Americans and use them as a marker, a symbol of limits, a metaphor for the "outsider." Many whites could look at the social position of blacks and feel that color formed an easy and reliable gauge for determining to what extent one was or was not American. Perhaps that is why one of the first epithets that many European immigrants learned when they got off the boat was the term "nigger"—it made them feel instantly American.[6]

Ellison's words underscore a troubling reality of American life: To be American is to be acutely aware of "outsiders," those who somehow seem less American than one's self.

Despite the American people's ongoing obsession with racial difference, U.S. presidents perennially use their inaugural addresses and state of the union messages to espouse an ideational model of national identity that attempts to minimize its significance, as I have shown in previous chapters. Such a contradiction between American rhetoric and American reality may itself be quintessentially American, as many have argued.[7] Yet racial problems make it a particularly difficult problem to ignore. In a country founded on principles of equality, race-related problems signal systematic and recurring inequities. In a country that promises social mobility, race-related problems remind us of ancient but enduring hierarchies. In a country based on freedom, race-related problems attest to oppression. "To engage in a serious discussion of race in America," Cornel West has suggested, we must also talk about these contradictions: "We must begin not with the problems of black people but with the flaws of American society—flaws rooted in historic inequalities and long-standing cultural stereotypes. How we set up the terms for discussing racial issues shapes our perception and response to these issues."[8] If West is correct, and if racial problems constitute compelling evidence of major American "flaws," why do they resist correction? And if racial problems themselves have always been present in American society, why did so many Americans express such shock upon learning of them after the Simpson murder trial in 1995 or the deadly riots that erupted in Los Angeles in 1992 after an all-white jury acquitted white police officers on charges of beating a black man named Rodney King?

In this chapter I will suggest that we may get a better understanding of why certain racial problems persist by looking at the ways in which U.S. presidents have talked about them. Specifically, I will argue that, when viewed against the backdrop of the shared beliefs hypothesis of American nationalism, numerous instances of presidential rhetoric on race can be read as contributing to the perception that African Americans are outside this world of shared beliefs. The purpose of this chapter is therefore not to claim that chief executives cause racial crises or even that they explicitly condone racism. I will argue, however, that in certain inaugural addresses and state of the union messages from 1885 to 2000, some U.S. presidents have subtly sanctioned the continued exclusion of African Americans even as they have demanded greater inclusion of them. In other words, various presidents of this period have dealt with race and not dealt with it at the same time. Using three particular rhetorics, I will claim here that chief executives have *sounded* inclusive without actually advocating inclusion. By presenting such talk to the American people, they have perhaps encouraged their constituents to share its logic. To answer Cornel West's question, then, about "how we [as a society] set up the terms for discussing racial issues," this chapter asks questions about how these terms are set up for us as citizens within some of the nation's most public instances of ceremonial discourse.

To be sure, U.S. presidents would probably prefer not to deal with racial problems at all. Chief executives from 1885 to 2000 have dedicated relatively little time in their inaugural and state of the union addresses to these matters, a recurring omission that may itself shed some light on why such problems persist. When they have discussed racial differences within these genres of rhetoric, they have typically done so in response to specific problems, such as lynchings or riots. This tendency suggests that, over time, presidents have been much more likely to discuss race as a problem rather than as a fact. Rather than framing the citizenry's racial differences as one of its constitutive parts, this logic implies that the commingling of different skin colors will necessarily result in civil unrest.

If presidents have repeatedly spoken of race itself as a problem, the most frequent victims and/or perceived causes of such difficulties have been African Americans. Despite the citizenry's diverse heritage, the term "race" seems almost synonymous with the terms "Afro American," "black," or, later, "African American" in the discourse studied here. This pattern itself might be telling, for it shows that most presidents have spoken of skin color itself as an essentialism, a rhetorical shorthand that may have enabled them to make sweeping distinctions between African Americans', European Americans', and other "hyphenated" Americans' perceived shared characters.

Indeed, perhaps the most effective way to sound inclusive without actually being so is to hint at inherent differences between one's self and another. Within essentialist theories of identity, "they" cannot be part of "us" because of "their" fundamentally different and immutable natures. Not surprisingly, then, racial essentialisms lurk within all three rhetorical strategies found in this reading. Just as some presidents suggested that immigrants could never fully understand American ways of thinking, certain presidents have repeatedly implied that Native and African Americans were essentially different from the "true" U.S. citizenry in important ways, most of which also involved their aptitude for participating in the nation's allegedly shared beliefs. Despite these distinctions, however, presidents argued that these latter groups, unlike immigrants, could be gradually transformed into American citizens.

Some might suppose that such notions about the problematic relationship between race and American national identity originated in the Reconstruction era. However, in this chapter I will explore such ideas via a few examples of presidential discourse on Native Americans, noting later how rhetoric and logic used in the late 1800s to frame Native Americans as wards of the state reappears decades later in presidential rhetoric on civil rights. As one might expect, both Native Americans and African Americans receive more sympathy from presidents over time. Nevertheless, in several of the speeches studied here chief executives have frequently portrayed these groups as needing help en route to citizenship. Given their descriptions of why Indians and black Americans warrant assistance, however, one wonders why the existing citizenry would want to include them at all.

EXCLUSIVIST INCLUSION: "IT'S THEIR PROBLEM"

I have suggested that when presidents have spoken of race in the national addresses studied here, they have done so only in response to a perceived problem.

It is thus perhaps redundant to refer to an "Indian problem" at all, since observers from Christopher Columbus to Theodore Roosevelt portrayed Native Americans mainly as irritating impediments to conquest. In 1831, after European settlers and American citizens had fought with Native Americans for almost three centuries, President Andrew Jackson proposed a solution: The United States government would simply remove the remaining tribes from the frontier. Over the next seven years, Indians were systematically executed or relocated. Even those who had shown they could assimilate into white culture by adopting European dress and American customs were shown no mercy.[9]

By 1885 most Native Americans lived on reservations, segregated from the citizenry by government order. In his message to Congress that year, however, President Cleveland still spoke of them as a pressing domestic problem. If Indians were to become civilized enough to live among the American people, he argued, the government would have to intervene, for Native Americans themselves possessed no aptitude for citizenship. Thus, even in what was ostensibly an appeal to include Native Americans in the citizenry, this president used an exclusivist logic to explain how and why they needed help.

Consider this passage from Cleveland's 1885 message, for example, in which the president urged the government to do more regarding "this most intricate and difficult subject":

> There is a lack of a fixed purpose or policy on this subject, which should be supplied. It is useless to dilate upon the wrongs of the Indians, and as useless to divulge the heartless belief that, because their wrongs are revenged in their own atrocious manner, therefore they should be exterminated. They are properly enough called the wards of the government; and it should be borne in mind that this guardianship involves, on our part, efforts for the improvement of their condition and the enforcement of their rights.[10]

In asking Congress to overlook the "the wrongs of the Indians," Cleveland sounded surprisingly progressive. As his speech continued, however, it became evident that the "conditions" he sought to improve were neither material nor physical but attitudinal and perhaps even cognitive. Indians deserved assistance, he suggested, not because they had lost their homelands or been ravaged by war and disease. They needed government help because of their "heartless beliefs" and "atrocious manner[s]," dispositional qualities that stood in the way of their becoming American citizens.

To Cleveland, Indians simply lacked the habits of mind necessary for "civilization and citizenship." This handicap was why it was "useless" to dwell on their "wrongs"; they knew no better than to commit them. Even those who had presumably already become more "civilized" had struggled to overcome the "savagery of their natural state":

> Among the Indians . . . there exist the most marked differences in natural traits and disposition and in their progress toward civilization. While some are lazy, vicious and stupid, others are industrious, peaceful, and intelligent; while a portion of them are self-supporting and independent, and have so far advanced in civilization that they make their own laws, and educate their children in schools of their own establishment and maintenance, others still retain, in squalor and dependence, almost the savagery of their natural state.[11]

The president acknowledged "marked differences" among the Indians; not all were "lazy, vicious and stupid" and not all lived in "squalor and dependence." Yet Cleveland still emphasized how fundamentally different the Indians were from the American citizenry at large. European Americans were born civilized, his logic suggested, but Indians first had to transcend their natural state and make painstaking efforts in their "progress toward civilization."

Even the "portion" of them that were "self-supporting and independent" had achieved this success in separation from American society at large, "mak[ing] their own laws, and educat[ing] their children in schools of their own establishment and maintenance." The boundary between Indian and American institutions further underscored these groups' substantially different natures. "Their inclination, long fostered by a defective system of control, is to cling to the habits and customs of their ancestors and struggle with persistence against the change of life which their altered circumstances press upon them," the president explained.[12] Yet the ways in which he chose to characterize these "inclinations" contrasted sharply with the habits of mind demanded by the United States' civil religion. Unlike the American people, who were presumably liberated from ancient tribalisms of the Old World, Indians "cling to the habits and customs of their ancestors." Assisted by God, American citizens actively create their own circumstances, but Indians "struggle with persistence" against the "altered circumstances press[ed] upon them." Up until now, the president seemed to worry, the U.S. government had perhaps driven Indians even further into such wrong habits, using a "defective system of control" that "fostered" this regression.

It is not my intention to label Cleveland a xenophobe or to apply contemporary standards to his discourse. Instead, I mean to draw attention to the logic at work in his rhetoric and, more specifically, the ways in which it contrasts with the logic driving the rhetoric of shared beliefs. When confronted with evidence of difference among Americans, the presidents discussed so far in this chapter and the preceding one have been quick to describe the "Other" in ways that directly clash with (and can thus threaten) those characteristics seen as being shared by a monolithic American public. In Cleveland's discussion of the "Indian problem," as in the presidential discourse on immigrants discussed in chapter 3, this un-American otherness is attributed to essentially different ways of thinking. With respect to Native Americans more than immigrants, however, Cleveland seemed to argue that the United States has a special responsibility to include these "Others" in the citizenry. Over time, then, the "Indian problem" gets cast in such rhetoric as an educational challenge, the problem of helping Indians overcome their natural states. But exactly *whose* problem was this?

At first Cleveland seemed to argue that helping the Indians transform themselves was the U.S. government's responsibility:

> Barbarism and civilization cannot live together. . . . [but] they are a portion of our people, are under the authority of our government, and have a peculiar claim upon, and are entitled to, the fostering care and protection of the nation. The government cannot relieve itself of this responsibility until they are so far trained and civilized as to be able wholly to manage and care for themselves. The paths in which they should walk must be clearly marked out for them, and they must be led or guided until they are familiar with the way and competent to assume the duties and responsibilities of our citizenship.[13]

Here the president insisted that Indians must be "led" out of their essentially "barbaric" mindset. The government would provide the training, he promised, but by using educational terms such as "training" and "guidance" he also implied that Indians, like students, were themselves ultimately responsible for their progress. Although the "paths in which they should walk" would be "clearly marked out for them," the Indians would have to decide to walk in them, presumably by giving up their old beliefs and accepting American ones. Only then would they be able to "assume the duties and responsibilities of our citizenship."

Benjamin Harrison, who became president after Cleveland's first term in office, provided a more concrete example of how such a transformation might occur. In his 1891 message to Congress, Harrison recommended that Indian men be enlisted into the army and "organiz[ed] . . . into separate companies." The secretary of war had already tested such a plan with great success, the president reported:

The men are readily brought into discipline, acquire the drill with facility, and show great pride in the right of discharge of their duty and perfect loyalty to their officers, who declare that they would take them into action with confidence. The discipline, order, and cleanliness of the military posts will have a wholesome and elevating influence upon the men enlisted, and through them upon their tribes, while a friendly feeling for the whites and a greater respect for the government will certainly be promoted.[14]

Harrison detailed exactly the type of training necessary for the Indians' rehabilitation. They must be taught "discipline," "pride," "duty," and "loyalty," attitudinal qualities alien to their own "naturally savage" states. Once they have learned these new dispositions, they will take them back to their tribes, Harrison reasoned, promoting within the larger Native American population a "friendly feeling for the whites and a greater respect for the government."

If Indians had to alter their dispositions in order to be citizens, and the government was responsible for facilitating this transformation, what should citizens do? Upon his return to the presidency after Harrison's administration had ended, Cleveland suggested in his 1893 inaugural address that the American people need not do very much at all. In order to be more inclusive for both Native Americans and the newly freed African Americans, the citizenry needed only to renew its commitment to that quintessentially American characteristic, "loyalty to principle": "Loyalty to the principles upon which our Government rests positively demands that the equality before the law which it guarantees to every citizen should be justly and in good faith conceded in all parts of the land. The enjoyment of this right follows the badge of citizenship wherever found, and, unimpaired by race or color, it appeals for recognition to American manliness and fairness."[15] Even as their society was becoming more racially diverse, then, the American people did not need to alter their own beliefs in any way. In fact, Cleveland argued that they should become even more committed to them, as American ideas would ultimately eradicate difference itself, presumably via shared allegiance to the civil religion. Never mind that this same belief system was used just a few years earlier to justify the exclusion and extermination of the Indians as well as the institution of slavery. In one of the relatively few instances where a president of this era spoke directly of ethnic diversity, Cleveland did so to lionize American habits of mind ("manliness and fairness") that would presumably make diversity irrelevant to the "badge of citizenship wherever found."

Later in the speech, when Cleveland did ask his audience for some help, even then he called mainly for civic understanding as the government educated its charges:

> Our relations with the Indians located within our borders impose upon us responsibilities that we cannot escape. Humanity and consistency require us to treat them with forbearance and in our dealings with them to honestly and considerately regard their rights and interests. Every effort should be made to lead them, through the paths of civilization and education, to self-supporting and independent citizenship. In the meantime, as the nation's wards, they should be promptly defended against the cupidity of designing men and shielded from every influence or temptation that retards their advancement.[16]

If this is how the president encouraged the citizenry to include Indians, one would hate to hear him argue against them. The president hinted at Indians' essential unworthiness in every sentence. He suggested, for instance, that the government was only trying to help them because they are a "responsibility . . . we cannot escape." Similarly, he advocated "treat[ing] them with forbearance," as if including them was an unpleasant but necessary chore. Even his pronouns reinforced a great divide between things American and Indian. He spoke almost grudgingly of "*our* relations with the Indians located within *our* borders" (emphasis added), and he reiterated that "they," as the "nation's wards," deserved "our" assistance. At the same time he was asking the citizenry to be understanding, then, Cleveland offered additional evidence of the Indians' perceived inferiority, evidence that would seem to justify their continued exclusion.

Given this president's rhetoric, why should his constituents welcome Indians at all? Cleveland suggested that such action was merely the nation's duty, and his logic suggested that U.S. citizens should respond with civic pity. In short, the special consideration he advocated was somehow related to the "Other's" inferiority. Native Americans must not have the same God-given rights or capacities as the true citizenry does, this logic suggests, so they need extra help to become the type of person that true Americans already are by dint of something more like predestination. Note that Cleveland did not ask for public understanding while the Indians recovered from government-inflicted poverty and disease. Instead, both his call for national sympathy and his justification for federal aid seem warranted by the Native Americans' perceived shortcomings.

While Cleveland's request appealed for pity for the Indians, William McKinley's first annual message focused on a different target for sympathy:

"United States citizens residing in the [Indian] territory." Issued on December 6, 1897, the president's message contained this report on their well-being:

> The present area of the Indian Territory contains 25,694,564 acres, much of which is very fertile land. The United States citizens residing in the territory, most of whom have gone there by invitation or with the consent of tribal authorities, have made permanent homes for themselves. Numerous towns have been built in which from 500 to 5,000 white people now reside. Valuable residences and business houses have been erected in many of them. Large business enterprises are carried on in which vast sums of money are employed, and yet these people, who have invested their capital in the development of the productive resources of the country, are without title to the land they occupy, and have no voice whatever in the government of either of the Nations or the Tribes. Thousands of their children who were born in the Territory are of school age, but the doors of the schools of the Nations are shut against them, and what education they get is by private contribution. No provision for the protection of the life or property of these white citizens is made by the Tribal Governments and Courts.[17]

Here the Native Americans, while still portrayed as being un-American in ways that would have made sense during this era, are not discussed as being inferior, just exclusive. They have shut the doors of their own schools to the children of the white citizens, for example, and allowed these settlers "no voice" in their government. Indeed, it is the growing power of the Indians that really seems to concern McKinley.

He continues by referring to the secretary of the interior's report that "leading Indians have absorbed great tracts of land to the exclusion of the common people, and government by an Indian aristocracy has been practically established, to the detriment of the people." This un-American government, the president explains, has hurt white citizens as well as the Indians themselves, as it has been impossible for the "Tribal Governments to secure to each individual Indian his full enjoyment in common with other Indians of the common property of the Nations." The solution to this problem? "Friends of the Indians have long believed," noted the president, "that the best interests of the Indians of the Five Civilized Tribes would be found in American citizenship, with all the rights and privileges which belong to that condition."[18] Again, then, even without suggesting that the Indians deserved or even needed Americans' pity, this president advocated that Native Americans be transformed into U.S. citizens. Although this change may be a laudable goal, note how McKinley's argument for their inclusion depended on the perceived harms done by their independent governance. Here the Indians are not portrayed as savages who cannot take care of themselves but instead as a self-governing people who might in fact be too capable of looking out for their best interests. Granting them U.S. citizenship would compromise their own systems of self-government as well as their rights to tribal lands, a result that could conceivably bring them closer to the depiction of them as "wards of the state" offered by Cleveland.[19]

In his 1901 message to Congress, McKinley's successor, Theodore Roosevelt, furthered this argument. In demanding a decrease in government assistance, he used language that suggested that the "Indian problem" would perhaps become even more of a problem for the Indians themselves: "In my judgment the time has arrived when we should definitely make up our minds to recognize the Indian as an individual and not as a member of a tribe. The General Allotment Act is a mighty pulverizing engine to break up the tribal mass. . . . Under its provisions some sixty thousand Indians have already become citizens of the United States."[20] Roosevelt sought an end to the "gradual guidance" favored by Cleveland and Harrison. Instead, in rhetoric that seemed closer to McKinley's, he advocated the "pulverization" of the "tribal mass" and the repudiation of the Indians' ancient heritage. If the Indian wanted to be a citizen of the United States, he or she should be treated like one, according to the president:

> The effort should be steadily to make the Indian work like any other man on his own ground. The marriage laws of the Indians should be made the same as those of the whites. In the schools the education should be elementary and largely industrial. The need for higher education among the Indians is very, very limited. . . . The ration system, which is merely the corral and the reservation system, is highly detrimental to the Indians. It promotes beggary, perpetuates pauperism, and stifles industry. It is an effectual barrier to progress. . . . The Indians should be treated as an individual—like the white man.[21]

Ironically, in arguing for the immediate inclusion of Indians into the citizenry, this president may have reinforced their perceived inferiority even more than his predecessors had. He relied on essentialist assumptions regarding Indians' intellect and dispositions, for example, by suggesting that they were inherently unintelligent or nonindustrious. (Interestingly, in his second annual message Roosevelt noted that Indians were industrious, at least at certain tasks, yet even here his language incorporated essentialist tones. "Every effort should be made to develop the Indian along the lines of natural aptitude, and to encourage the existing native industries peculiar to certain tribes," he noted, "such as the various kinds of basket weaving, canoe building, smith work, and blanket work."[22]) Furthermore, his insistence that the "Indians should be treated as an individual—like the white man" hinted at presidential resentment over previous governmental assistance.

Whether these presidents sought to guide or force Native Americans into citizenship, their public appeals for inclusion relied heavily on exclusivist logic. They repeatedly implied that Indians were somehow essentially different from U.S. citizens even as they instructed the citizenry that Native Americans were now "part of our people." In general, they explained how and why Indians would become American citizens but failed to indicate what the American people might do to facilitate this transformation. Indeed, given these presidents' descriptions of Native Americans' shortcomings, their appeals seem odd: Why would anyone want to include someone who was both dissimilar and inferior?

Despite its internal contradictions, the rhetoric of exclusivist inclusion persists in discussions of American diversity because it allows users to sidestep issues of responsibility and to disregard evidence of inequity. If Native Americans complain of not feeling fully included, for example, citizens can blame them rather than the government or themselves, arguing that "we gave you a chance to join us." Similarly, such a logic can be used to explain current inequities by "blaming the victim," asserting that perhaps Native Americans did not work hard enough to become American or that they clung to their tribal ways rather than embracing American individuality. Ultimately, this rhetoric promotes neither charity nor compassion but instead disinterest, making it a very uninclusive form of inclusion.

EXEMPTIVE INCLUSION: "IT'S NOT OUR PROBLEM"

If presidential rhetoric about Native Americans helped the largely European American citizenry to think about inclusion using exclusive logic, it may have encouraged them to care even less about the societal status of African Americans. While the former slaves were adapting to freedom in the late 1800s, several presidents made careful distinctions about what kind of assistance the government and the existing citizenry should provide. The federal government was committed to the former slaves' equality in principle, its leaders often said, but it must be more careful when intervening in practical matters. Citizens,

too, should keep to themselves, some of these presidents implied, letting blacks
achieve as much as they could on their own. The institution of slavery may
have officially ended with the ratification of the Thirteenth Amendment in
1865, but the logic that blacks were an altogether separate type of people persisted long after. In a sense, this logic might have been bolstered by some of
the rhetoric used by presidents in their inaugural addresses and state of the
union messages during this era.

We might expect that presidents, as defenders of the Constitution, would
have rebutted this logic vehemently in their national addresses. Many times
they did, typically using an ideational rhetoric to remind citizens of the
nation's commitment to equality, as I have discussed previously. Yet even when
presidents demanded allegiance to these ideals, they sometimes also suggested
that citizens did not necessarily need to *act* on them.

To be clear, inclusion of African Americans was apparently so far removed
from the domestic agenda at the end of the nineteenth century that Presidents
Cleveland, Harrison, and McKinley hardly addressed the matter in their state
of the union messages. In his third annual message, Cleveland made a passing reference to the failed "scheme for the colonization in Mexico of
negroes."[23] And McKinley discussed the consideration that the United States
must give to the "history and racial peculiarities" of Puerto Ricans when it
devised an educational system to serve the island's population.[24] Overall, however, these three presidents devoted surprisingly little time in the discourse
studied here to the subject of the nation's newest citizens. Instead, they repeatedly reminded the existing citizenry of its ideational commitments. "The love
of the law and the sense of obedience and submission to the lawfully constituted judicial tribunals are embedded in the hearts of our people," McKinley
said in 1899, adding that

> any violation of these sentiments and disregard of their obligations justly arouses
> public condemnation. The guaranties of life, liberty, and of civil rights should
> be faithfully upheld; the right of trial by jury respected and defended. . . . What
> I said in my inaugural address of March 4, 1897, I now repeat: The constituted
> authorities must be cheerfully and vigorously upheld. Lynchings must not be
> tolerated in a great and civilized country like the United States. Courts, not
> mobs, must execute the penalties of the laws.[25]

Although lynchings were becoming increasingly common in the South,
McKinley did not refer here to the lynching of African Americans but instead
to the killing of eleven Italian immigrants in New Orleans eight years earlier.[26]

Nevertheless, the president used a rhetorical strategy of exemptive inclusion that was common in discussions of African Americans' status during this era.

First, he affirmed the theoretical principles of inclusion. Even though the president was delivering a state of the union message, which at that time would generally include specific policies and plans, McKinley mentioned the abstract concepts that would guarantee "life, liberty, and . . . civil rights" for all. He offered no plan other than to rely upon "the love of the law and the sense of obedience and submission" so deeply "embedded in the hearts of our people." Indeed, "loving the law" seems to be the most specific thing the citizenry might do to ensure inclusion, an *in*action that suggests the second element of this rhetoric: its implicit yet important argument against more specific practices.

Although McKinley stated that "violation of these sentiments" may "arouse . . . public condemnation," for example, he also implied that any public response to them would be unnecessary. According to this logic, citizens were not really expected to be outraged over inequality because as long as they remained law-abiding citizens, such matters were simply not their problem. Even when McKinley spoke of a terrible multiple murder, he did so to demand that "the constituted authorities . . . be cheerfully and vigorously upheld." In other words, citizens themselves should, cheerfully and vigorously, keep out of racial problems.

By appealing to the law to adjudicate such matters, McKinley started a trend that would recur in other presidents' discussions of race and may even exist today in American cultural logic. He framed "the law" as the foremost agent in the inclusion process—indeed, perhaps as the only real actor here. In this logic neither the president nor the government nor the American people are directly responsible for facilitating inclusion, as the "constituted authorities" will settle any unpleasantries that arise during this transition. While we might assume that the "constituted authorities" are actual people and/or governmental agencies, they are portrayed here as merely the embodiment of the legal system. To this way of thinking, individuals are not ultimately responsible for solving racial problems; problems must be adjudicated through the courts.

Not surprisingly, then, presidents frequently appeal to "the law" when discussing racial diversity and its discontents.[27] They do so not merely to keep themselves from appearing personally accountable but also to prevent the American people from feeling responsible or even invested in such matters. The law is impersonal and unprejudiced—the same characteristics presidents challenge the citizenry to share in their ideational rhetoric of American identity. By letting "the law" take care of racial problems, the American people are thus being better citizens, overcoming their own "earthly" fears and impulses to let a "higher power" exercise its will. In the rhetoric of exemptive inclusion, then, presidents use the civil religion to urge apathy rather than zealotry and indifference over advocacy.

This tendency is especially evident when presidents of this era made explicit public appeals for restraint. In 1906, for example, in his sixth state of the union message, Theodore Roosevelt warned of an "epidemic of lynching and mob violence that springs up, now in one part of our country, now in another." The president explained that "a great many white men are lynched, but the crime is peculiarly frequent in respect to black men. The greatest existing cause of lynching is the perpetration, especially by black men, of the hideous crime of rape—the most abominable in all the category of crimes, even worse than murder. Mobs frequently avenge the commission of this crime by themselves torturing to death the man committing it; thus avenging in bestial fashion a bestial deed, and reducing themselves to a level with the criminal."[28] Roosevelt was indignant, to be sure, but which crime did he actually present here as the greater? The "hideous crime of rape," "the most abominal in all the category of crimes"? Or the "avenging in [a] bestial fashion [of] a bestial deed"? Although Roosevelt said that both were inexcusable, he also implied that the lawless activity of lynching "reduces" its white perpetrators, while rape might just be an impulse native to black men.

To make his point about the *real* danger of lynching, Roosevelt quoted Bishop Charles B. Galloway of Mississippi, who had been a fiery preacher in the Methodist Episcopal church during the late nineteenth century: "'The mob which lynches the Negro charged with rape will in a little while lynch a white man suspected of crime. Every Christian patriot in American needs to lift up his voice in loud and eternal protest against the mob spirit that is threatening the integrity of this Republic.'"[29] Roosevelt thus spoke to the separatist sentiments of his day. Lynchings of blacks were not necessarily egregious on their own; indeed, the president seems to commiserate with those who sought to avenge the "perpetration, especially by black men, of the hideous crime of rape." Instead, lynchings are wrong because they will lead to unrest among white people, thereby "threatening the integrity of this Republic"—*this* is why "every Christian patriot" should denounce them, not because of the frenzied acts of violence directed largely at African Americans.

To be sure, there were more inclusive moments in Roosevelt's message, as there are in all other presidents' national addresses. At one point, Roosevelt even acknowledged that "there is but one safe rule in dealing with black men as with white men": "to treat each man, whatever his color, his creed, or his social position, with even handed justice on his real worth as a man."[30] Yet even in progressive moments like these, the president could not overcome the essentialisms embedded in his earlier remarks, where he implied that different "colors" of men had inherently different amounts of "real worth," signified through different motivations and different capacities for lawfulness. Whites should not stoop to blacks' level, his logic implied; each group should keep to itself, stay out of the other's problems, and let the law exercise its "even-handed justice."

Roosevelt's successor, William Taft, also asserted that different ethnicities had fundamentally separate natures, but he used "the law" (the Constitution) to advance rather than settle this argument. Shortly after advocating "an increase in the tolerance of political views of all kinds" in his 1909 inaugural address, he reminded his audience of blacks' constitutional rights: "The thirteenth amendment secured them freedom; the fourteenth amendment due process of law, protection of property, and the pursuit of happiness; and the fifteenth amendment attempted to secure the negro against any deprivation of the privilege to vote because he was a negro."[31] While Taft might have made such comments to support the idea of full inclusion of African Americans, he might have also used them to show just how different blacks and whites truly were. After all, amendments to the Constitution have been written to grant blacks the rights that whites had simply been born with, and government had had to enact laws to include blacks in the (mostly white) citizenry. African Americans did not even have the right to pursue happiness until 1868, the president reminded his audience. Given the fact that these laws had been part of the Constitution for more than forty years, why was the president using precious moments in his inaugural address to point out a long-standing legal reality?

Taft did so, by his own admission, to appeal to disgruntled southerners, suggesting that the president was arguing for something other than inclusion here. "I look forward with hope to the already good feeling between the South and the other sections of the country," he stated, adding that he also wanted to ensure that "all the people in the South [feel] that this Government is their Government." Perhaps to minimize southerners' alienation, then, Taft suggested that problems of inclusion would solve themselves "in time," with governmental involvement being limited to "fair and just enforcement." More urgent, the president argued, were additional voting laws: "Hence it is clear to all that the domination of an ignorant, irresponsible element can be prevented by constitutional laws which shall exclude from voting both negroes and whites not having education or the qualifications thought to be necessary for a proper electorate."[32] Taft admitted that the voters he sought to exclude were "both negroes and whites."[33] His underlying message was clear, however:

If voting were limited to educated citizens, whites would do most of the voting. Southern fears thus allayed, Taft reasoned that the "interest . . . the Southern white citizens take in the welfare of the negroes" would surely increase over time. Inclusion would suddenly materialize, Taft seemed to argue, especially if some members of the citizenry were excluded from voting.

Taft may have been genuinely concerned about "the welfare of the negroes," and he may have truly wanted the rest of the American people to share this concern. Yet this interpretation of his inaugural address reveals just how difficult it must have been for presidents to talk about inclusion in the decades after the Civil War. Like other presidents, Taft was trapped by his own rhetoric's exclusivist impulses, especially those inherited from past presidents and maintained by popular fears of difference. Using language almost identical to Cleveland's on the "Indian problem," for example, Taft concluded these remarks by reminding his audience that "the Negroes are now Americans. . . . We are charged with the sacred duty of making their path as smooth and easy as we can."[34] Instead of talking about African American inclusion as an educational problem, however, Taft and other presidents during this era suggested that it would simply take place on its own—not as a function of presidential action or even citizens' sense of duty, but merely as a matter of time. In this exemptive rhetoric of inclusion, "making their path as smooth and easy as we can" meant standing out of the way.

One wonders, perhaps, why this shift occurred. Why did presidents choose not to speak about former slaves in the same ways they had about Native Americans? Although presidential discussions of both groups focused on what *we* should do about *them,* presidents argued for far less practical assistance for African Americans than they had for Native Americans. Chief executives did not speak of where and how blacks should live, for example, or how they might be taught American ways but instead about why it was important for whites to respect the law and to have patience. The underlying suggestion was that African Americans could not easily overcome their essential natures, so the European American people would have to brace themselves for the inevitable changes that would occur as blacks began to live and work around them.

Indeed, this sentiment explains why presidents of this era would choose to use an exemptive rhetoric over a merely exclusive one. In addition to telling the citizenry that inclusion was "not our problem," this rhetoric may have allowed presidents to sound as if they were saying that the problems created by inclusion were not their responsibilities. Obviously, the notion of inclusion itself was extremely controversial for decades after the Civil War ended. In national addresses presidents could not simply demand that inclusion take place (lest they deeply offend southerners) nor could they take responsibility for it themselves (lest they affront northerners and others impatient with its slow progress). To speak to such a divided citizenry, the only rhetorically feasible solution was to advocate *principled inaction.* In other words, speaking exemptively about inclusion may have allowed presidents to adjust the largely white American citizenry to the *idea* of inclusion without actually demanding that they change their own attitudes or behaviors at all.

INSTITUTIONAL INCLUSION: "SOMEONE ELSE WILL FIX IT"

Presidential discussions of how to guide former slaves into citizenship left a tremendous rhetorical legacy. Chief executives after Taft did not need to speak of specific or essential differences between African Americans and the rest of the citizenry. Using an exemptive inclusivism, their predecessors had shown that blacks, even if theoretically equal to white citizens, were indeed separate from them.[35]

Taft's assurances notwithstanding, inclusion did not become any easier over time. If racial problems appear to have subsided temporarily after his presidency, it is only because the citizenry was increasingly focused on foreign events leading up to World War I.[36] In fact, the United States' racial problems worsened, particularly during and after the war. After record numbers of blacks migrated north to fill wartime jobs, for example, many whites voiced newfound resentment over what became known as the "Negro invasion."[37] In the South, black war veterans returned home to prejudice and racism, phenomena they had dealt with before but of which they were now less tolerant. Southern whites, it seemed, were also less tolerant; between 1914 and 1920 they lynched at least 382 blacks, some still in their military uniforms.[38]

Perhaps the worst racial problems of the early 1900s occurred in the "red summer" of 1919. Race riots erupted in more than two dozen cities, killing scores of people and injuring hundreds. "For some white Americans," historian Mary Beth Norton and colleagues have noted, "this sad record meant that the nation should redirect its missionary zeal at the reform not of foreign societies but of its own."[39] For their part, presidents seem to have acted on exactly this impulse around this particular time. After World War I, they started to attack problems of inclusion as they might a foreign enemy: through programmatic involvement. The government will eradicate racial discrimination, they argued, thereby teaching the American people to think institutionally about inclusion.

At first presidents did not talk specifically about how this intervention would occur. Before they could present a plan or program to the American people, they needed to explain why it was necessary. After all, quite a few former presidents had spoken against specific governmental involvement for decades after the Civil War. The first president to speak regularly and specifically in inaugural addresses and state of the union messages about the government's need to assist "the Negro race" was Calvin Coolidge. Coolidge discussed the nation's racial problems with much more candor than his predecessors had; in his inaugural address, for example, he lamented the "false and ignorant prejudice" too often directed at African Americans.[40] In addition to admitting that blacks were systematically discriminated against, however, the president also suggested that they could not overcome such an obstacle on their own. Blacks' need for help did not exist because of any weakness on their part, Coolidge argued.[41] As President Coolidge explained in his third annual message to Congress, they needed help because they were truly handicapped by the biases of their fellow citizens:

> Nearly one-tenth of our population consists of the Negro race. The progress which they have made in all the arts of civilization in the last 60 years is almost beyond belief. Our country has no more loyal citizens. But they do still need sympathy, kindness, and helpfulness. They need reassurance that the requirements of the Government and society to deal out to them even-handed justice will be met. They should be protected from all violence and supported in the peaceable enjoyment of the fruits of their labor. Those who do violence to them should be punished for their crimes.[42]

The president was thus "sympathetic, kind, and helpful" indeed. Perhaps, though, his rhetoric was *too* helpful—not toward African Americans necessarily but instead toward white citizens. Although Coolidge implied that other Americans were the cause of the problem, he did not condemn those who would act violently or deny justice to "our most loyal citizens." He asserted instead that the government merely needed to do a better job of shielding African Americans from such elements. In this logic, prejudice and violence are not unexpected crises but instead normal functions of the population's diverse constitution, with governmental institutions, not the American people, ultimately responsible for "managing" such matters. In a way, then, this Republican president initiated the thinking that would set the stage for future Democratic civil rights reforms by suggesting that the citizenry needed to be protected against its own base impulses.

The president did ask the citizenry to do something about these problems, calling for some serious introspection at one point in this speech. Full equality, Coolidge argued, "cannot be granted to others, or enjoyed by ourselves, except by the application of the principle of broadest tolerance. Bigotry is only another name for slavery. It reduces to serfdom not only those against whom it is directed, but also those who seek to apply it. An enlarged freedom can only be secured by the application of the golden rule. No other utterance ever presented such a practical rule of life."[43] If bigotry enslaves American minds, "reducing to serfdom" its perpetrators as well as its victims, why did the president advocate no stronger solution than "the application of the golden rule"? One answer: because he could not escape the rhetoric of his executive forebears. Previous presidents had encouraged the American people to think of inclusion in particular ways, by using essentialist logics of exclusion or exempting themselves from its difficulties, meaning that most citizens still had no reason to think of blacks' problems as theirs as well.

Try as he might to suggest that inclusion was every citizen's concern, Coolidge could only appeal to a time-honored platitude that actually undermined his own argument by emphasizing essentialism ("Do unto others," not "Do unto each other") and reactivity (by advocating that individuals choose how to behave based on the perceived consequences rather than the inherent value of their behaviors). More important, perhaps, was Coolidge's message that a "rule" would facilitate inclusion. Citizens used to thinking exemptively about inclusion could easily follow the rules of this new kind of inclusion by avoiding interaction with blacks altogether, for example; citizens who could not follow the rules would be punished.

To his credit, Coolidge tried to associate inclusion with positive ideals rather than merely negative reinforcement. At one point, he suggests that successfully dealing with the population's diversity is necessary to the nation's success: "Our country has many elements in its population, many different modes of thinking and living, all of which are striving in their own way to be loyal to the high ideals worthy of the crown of American citizenship. It is fundamental of our institutions that they seek to guarantee to all our inhabitants the right to live their own lives under the protection of the public law."[44] Finally, an observer might note, a president spoke freely and without judgment of the population's "many different modes of thinking and living." Yet even this acknowledgment did not necessarily commend diversity for its own merits. Recognizing "different modes of *thinking* and *living*" (emphasis added) might just have been another way of reinforcing the cognitive essentialisms central to previous descriptions of immigrants, Native Americans, and former slaves, the same perceptions that made some citizens see others as inherently "less American" than themselves. If all these different types of people were now "striving in their own way" to become citizens, then Coolidge's plan was long overdue.

Although he was ostensibly arguing against racial discrimination, then, President Coolidge was also partially contributing to it by reinforcing the notion of perceived and historically significant differences between the races. Perhaps he had no choice. (Celeste Condit and John Louis Lucaites have argued that the post-*Plessy* ideology of separatism would dominate American conceptions of racial equality until the 1960s.) Or perhaps Coolidge's explicit rhetoric on race was something of a historical anomaly. His successor Herbert Hoover used his state of the union messages to express his administration's growing interest in immigration reform. Likewise, Franklin D. Roosevelt's inaugural addresses and state of the union messages included little discussion of race-related issues. FDR, whose "program on race was neither dynamic or sustained," according to Garth E. Pauley, did speak out against lynching in his first annual message, mentioned the nation's history of "enslavement" in his seventh, and talked about the dangers of "divisions among ourselves," including "racial discrimination," in his ninth.[45] Still, even after the Truman administration helped *Brown v. Board of Education* overturn *Plessy* in 1954, presidents sometimes still spoke of African Americans as being somehow removed from the "true" citizenry. Even those who leaders who consciously sought to challenge a separatist ideology through specific federal programs and initiatives could not expunge its presence in some of their discourse. By explaining inclusion as a program that would be regulated by the federal government, presidents in the 1950s and 1960s at times implied that blacks' problems were not those of the entire citizenry. Institutional inclusion meant that "minority problems" were minorities' problems—and the federal government's—alone.

In his 1956 state of the union address, for example, Dwight Eisenhower spoke in earnest about "the progress our people have made in the field of civil rights":

> In executive branch operations throughout the Nation, elimination of discrimination and segregation is all but completed. Progress is also being made among contractors engaged in furnishing Government services and requirements. Every citizen now has the opportunity to fit himself for and to hold a responsibility in the service of his country. . . . It is disturbing that in some localities allegations persist that Negro citizens are being deprived of their right to vote

and are likewise being subjected to unwarranted economic pressures. I recommend that the substance of these charges be thoroughly examined by a bipartisan commission created by Congress. It is hoped that such a commission will be established promptly so that it may arrive at findings which can receive early consideration.[46]

In light of his military background, the president's metaphorical choices are perhaps unremarkable. Here Eisenhower seems to approach civil rights as a military campaign, with the goal of eliminating "discrimination and segregation" through "operations" in the "field." Given this already belligerent style, however, one might have expected the president to have spoken even more vehemently against racial intolerance. He could have shown how discrimination, like communism, is anathema to democratic philosophy. Or he could have reminded his constituents of their calling as Christian soldiers, associating efforts against racism with the civil religion. The president made neither of these arguments. He did not trouble the American people with philosophical matters but only reported on the campaign's success, even referring any unfinished business back to committee ("I recommend that the substance of these charges be thoroughly examined by a bipartisan commission created by Congress").

Many of Eisenhower's successors would seek to minimize problems of difference by trying to promote a "color-blind" society where advancement or reward would be based on merit alone. Some of these presidents spoke more than Eisenhower did about why this was the right thing to do; they used the ideational rhetoric of American essentialism to remind the citizenry of its spiritual bonds. Yet even these chief executives occasionally slipped back into more exclusive voices, maintaining that they would eradicate racism themselves (or with congressional assistance), thereby using the bully pulpit to bureaucratize the issue of racism instead of democratize it. John Kennedy told his audience in 1962 that "a strong America requires the assurance of full and equal rights to all its citizens, of any race or of any color," but he did not invite the citizenry to join him in ensuring these rights. He told them instead that this would be accomplished through "the full use of Executive powers . . . through persuasion, negotiation, and litigation to secure the constitutional rights of all."[47] Lyndon Johnson argued passionately that "we must abolish not some, but all racial discrimination . . . [for] it is a moral issue," and in the same breath he talked about how this moral imperative would be "met by the passage this session of the bill now pending in the House."[48] Richard Nixon declared that the United States had a clear responsibility to "promote equal

opportunity for members of minorities and others who have been left behind" and then implied that he could accomplish this through "an extensive
written message to Congress."[49] Needless to say, executive powers cannot ensure full and equal rights, the House of Representatives cannot abolish racial
discrimination, and a written message to Congress cannot by itself promote
equal opportunity. Yet presidents of this era, wise men all, still preferred
to offer institutional solutions to the problems of the United States' racial
diversity.

Perhaps they could not speak in any other way. After all, my reading suggests that U.S. presidents, undeniably some of the most powerful individuals
in the world, did not have power over their own words when discussing diversity. Like the other presidents studied here, chief executives of this era inherited from their predecessors not only racial problems but also a particular logic
for dealing with them. By refining an institutional rhetoric of inclusion, modern presidents may have extended their forebears' exemptive logic of inclusion
in at least two important ways. First, they could have reinforced the assumption that race itself was a *problem* rather than just an individual characteristic,
something to be solved rather than merely acknowledged. Framing racial distinctions in this way allowed those who appeared to be "non-racial" (i.e., European Americans) to distance themselves from the whole issue of race and from
the victims of racism (except when majority privilege seemed threatened by race
matters, with affirmative action, for example). More importantly, such rhetoric also implied that racial dilemmas are temporary conditions that will, upon
being solved, simply go away. Perhaps this belief partly explains why the American people appear to profess shock each time there is a reminder that severe discrepancies still exist, as in the O. J. Simpson or Rodney King cases, for example.

Second, and more significantly, this institutional rhetoric transformed racial problems into the government's problem. This logic may therefore have
changed the nature of presidential talk on race in national addresses, adding
a new requirement for particularity to a discourse that had historically ignored
it. No longer could chief executives speak only of ideationally bound and
heavenly blessed constituents; now they had to speak specifically of black
Americans and brown Americans. While such acknowledgments might have
been long overdue, they also may have shattered the fragile reification of a
"united citizenry" so well protected in previous presidents' discourse. Although
reifications may literally be immaterial, they are not unimportant, and as the
American people grow increasingly preoccupied with each others' differences
perhaps we will see a reactionary demand for the return of this one in
particular.

Or perhaps we have already seen it. Ronald Reagan, credited by many with reinvigorating the nation's economy in the early 1980s, may also have rejuvenated its favored self-image. In his first inaugural address, he spoke of how "all of us together, in and out of government, must bear the burden" of governing.[50] Although he was clearly making one of his characteristic arguments against big government, he may have also been doing something else. He continued,

> We hear much of special interest groups. Well, our concern must be for a special interest group that has been too long neglected. It knows no sectional boundaries or ethnic or racial divisions, and it crosses political party lines. It is made up of men and women who raise our food, patrol our shores, man our mines and factories, teach our children, clean our homes, and heal us when we're sick—professionals, industrialists, shopkeepers, clerks, cabbies, and truck-drivers. They are, in short, "We the people," this breed called Americans.[51]

Here Ronald Reagan inclusively rejects his predecessors' rhetoric about inclusion. The citizenry in this passage "knows nothing" of exclusion (it is all one "breed" with no essentialized "boundaries or ethnic or racial divisions"), exemption (it includes everyone, from professionals to truck drivers), or institutionalism (it "crosses political party lines" and takes responsibility for itself). The citizenry is inclusive because it is American.[52]

Perhaps Reagan's approach is merely the logical outcome of the institutional rhetoric favored by other modern presidents, as if the government had been so successful at "fixing" racial problems as to have eradicated them entirely. By the time Reagan took office, then, there was no "us" or "them" anymore, at least not in this instance of his rhetoric.[53] Lamentably, however, in this view there was also no one who needed or warranted assistance, a concept that clearly distinguishes Reagan's rhetoric from his predecessors'. Many of those presidents talked about inclusion in response to racial problems, as I have shown, and whether they encouraged the American people to think exclusively, exemptively, or institutionally about race relations, they also implicitly acknowledged the systemic inequities that necessitated such responses. Native Americans or African Americans may have needed help because of their deficient "natural states," but they needed help nonetheless.

As we have seen, however, chief executives had great difficulty explaining why the European American citizenry should support such assistance. If they pointed out that the "Others" were different from the American people, they also implied that inclusion was the sole responsibility of those who wanted to be included. If they argued that the "Others" should be allowed to advance on their own, they framed inclusion as merely an inevitable and evolutionary process in which human agency was unimportant. If presidents declared that governmental programs would help the "Others," they associated inclusion with bureaucracy and paperwork, making it someone else's job rather than the average citizen's concern. And no matter how presidents explained inclusion, the logics of the past haunted their efforts, reinforcing previous distinctions between "us" and "them" long after Indians roamed the plains or slaves plowed southern fields.

Perhaps this is why Reagan renounced the past in order to call the citizenry together in his first inaugural address. Initiating what he termed "a new beginning," he announced that "this administration's objective will be a healthy, vigorous, growing economy that provides equal opportunity for all Americans, with no barriers born of bigotry or discrimination"—an admirable goal, to be sure, but also a rhetorically dubious one.[54] To announce the end of all "barriers . . . of bigotry or discrimination" is to imply that the American people need no further discussions about inclusion. By taking inclusion off the national agenda, Reagan might have pushed it into the somewhat more private realms of localized resentments over minority hiring practices and jury decision-making, for example.

The modern president who will be remembered for, among other things, trying to put race back on the national agenda was of course Bill Clinton. As Martin Carcasson and Mitchell Rice have written, Clinton, unlike previous chief executives, "sought to provoke a major change in the racial climate without an obvious national urgency."[55] To execute this change, in 1997 the president convened an advisory panel of experts who were to participate in, among other activities, town hall–style meetings throughout the United States. The president and his aides promised that such meetings were intended to promote a "national dialogue" about race, which they mentioned frequently. Also supporting the initiative was an interactive website.

As one might expect, when Clinton discussed race in his inaugural and state of the union addresses, his rhetoric was much more explicit than many of his predecessors' had been. In his second inaugural address, for example, he referred to the "divide of race" as "America's constant curse."[56] In his 1997 state of the union address a few weeks later, after naming the country's diversity as its "greatest strength," Clinton acknowledged that the American people "still see evidence of biting bigotry and intolerance in ugly words and awful violence, in burned churches and bombed buildings. We must fight against this in our country and in our hearts."[57] With these last three words, the president admitted to both the problem of racism and its location—"in our hearts"—in a way that no other president had before him. Rather than disassociating racial problems from the entire American *demos* through one of the three rhetorics previously discussed in this chapter, Clinton's discourse attempted to link such matters to every American citizen, even presumably to himself. No more was a U.S. president willing to suggest to all of the American people that race was not their problem or that someone else would fix it. In short, there seemed to be a newfound emphasis on both national and individual accountability in Clinton's rhetoric.

Viewed against the rhetorical context described throughout the rest of this chapter, such candor is admirable. Yet immediately after he made this discursive departure from the presidential rhetoric of the past, Clinton seemed to swerve quickly to get right back onto his forebears' tracks. How could the American people "fight" against racism "in our country and in our hearts?" The president continued:

> Just a few days before my second inauguration, one of the country's best known pastors, Reverend Robert Schuller, suggested that I read Isaiah 58:12. Here's what it says: "Thou shalt raise up the foundations of many generations, and thou shalt be called the repairer of the breach, the restorer of paths to dwell in." I placed my hand on that verse when I took the oath of office, on behalf of all Americans, for no matter what our differences in our faiths, our backgrounds, our politics, we must all be repairers of the breach.[58]

Given the centrality of the civil religion to presidential rhetoric in general and inaugural addresses and state of the union messages in particular, Clinton's turn to Judeo-Christian religious rhetoric here is probably not all that surprising. Yet I would like to end this chapter by suggesting that this turn was not benign.

In decades of previous discussions of immigration and race relations within these same genres of presidential rhetoric, the civil religious "idea of America" has frequently been associated with a European American tradition, as we have seen. As a result, this idea has been rhetorically racialized, suggesting that it comes more naturally to white citizens than to others. In chapter 3, for example, we heard that presidents repeatedly suggested that immigrants could not understand American ideas. Likewise, in this chapter we have seen how certain presidents have, intentionally or not, suggested that Native Americans and African Americans have to somehow be gradually led and/or facilitated into living with this idea, most often, it has been suggested, through education or legal adjudication. For President Clinton to refer specifically to a biblical verse as the foundation of the nation's new fight against racism is thus a somewhat loaded rhetorical gesture, one suggesting that even the Judeo-Christian tradition can mean different things to different people, something that African Americans have known since the days of slavery.

Clinton himself may have inadvertently invoked such a racialized distinction as he concluded this televised address. Speaking to a mostly white, mostly male audience of Congress and other invited guests, Clinton warmly embraced the presidential tradition of using the civil religion to unite all Americans. "America is more than a place: it is an idea—the most powerful idea in the history of nations," the president explained, "and all of us in this chamber, we are now the bearers of that idea, leading a great people into a new world."[59] The Congress and the president may be the "bearers" of that idea, but unless the "idea of America" can be rehabilitated from its racialized rhetorical roots, the "new world" that Clinton sought to lead the American people into may look—and sound—a lot like the old one.

Throughout this chapter I have suggested that when presidents talk about racial inclusion in their inaugural addresses and state of the union messages, they provide their audiences with a logic of why race matters and, over time, of how it might matter less. In addition to being more aware of the limitations of these past rhetorical efforts, however, perhaps we also ought to have greater appreciation for them. No matter how worrisome these efforts might seem to observers now, there is no question that presidential rhetoric on race in largely ceremonial discourse has appeared more frequently and has changed over time. Furthermore, it is reasonable to assume that these same discussions, along with other socio-political events and social movements, have also created more space within the public sphere for such discussions. The trick, I think, is to avoid the Reaganesque tendency to announce that race is irrelevant to the future of the United States and instead, to think harder about how we—and our leaders—talk about race. How can leaders, for example, speak of racial differences without falling into the traps seen (and heard) here? How can they motivate the many to care about the problems of the few? Better still, how might they enable citizens to see through such distinctions, convincing them that "minority problems" are the "majority's" as well, even as these words themselves lose statistical meaning as the nation's population changes?

CHAPTER 5

Gender and Presidents'
Rhetoric of Shared Beliefs

Woodrow Wilson did not mention American women's suffrage in his December 2, 1913, annual message to Congress. This omission was hardly unusual; almost none of his predecessors had mentioned the issue when dispatching the annual message to Congress. Yet Wilson's failure to mention women's voting rights was significant nonetheless, at least to Anna Howard Shaw. Like many other suffragists of her day, Shaw had expected Wilson to pay some rhetorical attention to the issue in this message because her cause had received a great deal of public attention during the months preceding the annual message.

Since March, 1913, the suffragists had been parading and picketing on Capitol Hill, garnering public support as their peaceful demonstrations were met with violent attacks from onlookers and the federal government. Over the summer they had even succeeded in winning the attention of the U.S. Senate, which, for the first time since 1887, had decided to debate an amendment enfranchising women. "When the amendment failed," Karlyn Kohrs Campbell has written, "a delegation of seventy-three women from Wilson's home state of New Jersey went to the White House asking the President to support passage by the next Congress of a constitutional amendment enfranchising women."[1] Yet the president made no such remarks to Congress in December, leaving Shaw and her colleagues profoundly disappointed.

The week after Wilson issued his message, Shaw and a group of delegates arranged to meet with the president. Campbell recounts their exchange as follows:

According to *The Washington Post* of December 9, Wilson told them: "I am not at liberty to urge upon Congress policies which have not had the organic consideration of those for whom I am a spokesman. . . . I have to confine myself to those things which have been embodied as promises to the people at an election." Anna Howard Shaw . . . then asked, "As women are members of no political party, to whom are they to look for a spokesman?" Wilson is supposed to have responded, "You speak very well for yourself," to which Shaw replied, "But not with authority."[2]

In Shaw's terse response was the crux of her cause's biggest problem: American women of her day were considered citizens but not voters. They were the only class of native-born adults in the United States to officially hold this second-class status since the 1868 passage of Fourteenth Amendment, and thus they were the only U.S. citizens forced to submit to the authority of the U.S. government without having any voice in it.[3] No amount of speaking well, to use Wilson's terms, could change that fact until the U.S. Constitution was itself changed.

And yet, as we all know now, Shaw and the other early feminists ultimately prevailed, and U.S. women won national suffrage in 1920. How this happened is one of American history's richest stories, one that scholars have told from a variety of perspectives.[4] In this chapter, however, I will take a slightly different approach from the activism-oriented analyses typically offered by historians, political scientists, and communication scholars.[5] Here I will provide an overview of the ways in which certain U.S. presidents have told this story, at least through their allusions to gender in inaugural addresses and state of the union messages. In this chapter, then, I ask if we can find in these texts ways that presidential discussions of American national identity might have changed as women's political roles and behaviors changed from 1885 through 2000. As in previous chapters, here I also ask what we might learn about presidents' rhetorical portrayals of American womanhood if we read this rhetoric within the larger framework of the shared beliefs hypothesis of U.S. nationalism. Are women assumed to share in quintessentially American beliefs just as men do, or are they believed to engage these beliefs differently than their male counterparts might?

As mentioned, to answer these questions I have searched through the same two genres of presidential rhetoric as I have in preceding chapters of this book. Yet the analysis in this chapter must begin differently than the previous two chapters have, for U.S. presidents have faced different types of cultural constraints, in terms of both political incentives and disincentives, when approaching the topic of American womanhood during the time period in question.

To understand this difference, it might be helpful to return first to the example of presidential rhetoric mentioned previously. Recalling the exchange between Shaw and Wilson, if we focus not on the activist's words but instead upon the president's, we might notice that Wilson referred to himself as a "spokesman," a representative not of all U.S. citizens but of all U.S. voters ("the people at an election"). Reading this rationale charitably, we can begin to understand exactly what a rhetorical dilemma the "woman question" was for U.S. presidents before, during, and even after the passage the Nineteenth Amendment in 1920.

By the time of Wilson's presidency, U.S. chief executives had routinely faced problems related to groups of people who, like some American women, wanted to be included in the nation's voting citizenry. These groups included immigrants, Native Americans, and African Americans. But presidential responses to most of these challenges were typically precipitated by perceptions of impending material and economic social crises, as I have suggested. For example, economic fears fueled the nativism of the late 1800s, just as the "Indian problem" grew out of a desire to expand the western frontier. The government's attempts to orchestrate racial integration were typically responses to instances of real or imagined civil unrest.

American women, in contrast, had been neither responsible for nor involved in any such widespread crises. To the contrary, since the early days of the Republic they had often been depicted as model citizens and were in fact routinely championed as paragons of American virtue and patriotism.[6] Functionally, then, from the perspective of most male political elites as well as the majority of their constituents, there was presumably no pressing "woman problem" in the United States when Wilson spoke, not even in 1913 after suffragists had been campaigning for years. In this sense, Wilson did not need to mention American women in his first annual message to Congress. In 1913 the stability of the nation's union demanded attention to world peace, Mexico, banking reform, farmers, mines, railroads, and sea safety—pressing issues all, as discussed in this message—but not to U.S. women.

Obviously, however, just because President Wilson did not mention women's voting rights in this particular instance does not mean that U.S. women were not politically active by then. As I have already suggested, the main reason Wilson's omission was noteworthy was the fact that early feminists had experienced some relative successes by that time. Yet if women were not present in Wilson's state of the union message in 1913, a mere seven years before the passage of the Nineteenth Amendment, when—and in what contexts—did American women finally appear in this genre of presidential discourse?

In the pages that follow I argue that the U.S. presidents studied here have regularly portrayed American women in at least one of four different and sometimes conflicting ways. Drawing upon themes that I will document here via textual examples, presidents have frequently discussed U.S. women in terms of (1) true womanhood, (2) feminized industry, (3) women-in-need of solicitous care, and (4) their equality as citizens. Although the chronological exposition of this chapter may seem to suggest that these themes are discrete and/or correspond roughly with specific historical phases, I will also argue that presidents have often blended one or more of these themes in their discussions of American womanhood. This polysemy, which is especially evident as we look comparatively at these texts over time, may suggest that presidential portrayals of U.S. women have become more complicated as women have become more integrated into U.S. politics.

These complications themselves have implications, of course. Ultimately, I will argue, hybridized depictions of U.S. women may reinforce the notion that women are simultaneously inside and outside of the world of Americans' shared beliefs. Women can be seen as embodying the highest forms of nationalistic piety, for example, while also seeming oddly incapable of enacting citizenship in highly efficacious ways. To see how such a complex vision of American womanhood could have evolved in the late twentieth century, let us first briefly recall the nature of the political and social landscape that existed for U.S. women before they won the vote in 1920.

THE LATE NINETEENTH CENTURY AND THE EMERGENCE OF THE "MODERN AMERICAN WOMAN"

Some U.S. women were seeking national suffrage before 1885, of course, but these efforts developed great momentum in the mid- to late 1800s. This period was also a time of rapid geographical expansion of the nation, of course, and this growth itself gave Grover Cleveland an opportunity to speak directly, and strategically, about American womanhood, as we shall see.

There are also some more specific and persuasive historical reasons to listen carefully to presidential depictions of American womanhood in the late 1800s and early 1900s. By most accounts this time period represented years of significant change for American women. Mary Ryan has argued that the end of the nineteenth century brought the "emergence of the Modern American Woman."[7] Similarly, Theda Skocpol has written that "American women developed the largest and most assertive 'woman movements' in the world" in the early to late 1900s.[8] Indeed, much evidence suggests that during these decades, the boundaries between the uniquely American "distinct spheres of action for the two sexes" that Alexis de Tocqueville observed in the 1840s started to become less discrete.[9]

Some of the most important gains during this period related to women's legal status and educational opportunities. Most states revised their common law doctrine during the late 1800s, for example, making more females eligible for property ownership.[10] Similarly, by the mid-1800s more and more U.S. public schools had begun to admit girls, and female educators reportedly outnumbered males by century's end. By 1900, Ryan writes, "80 percent of the colleges, universities, and professional schools in the nation admitted women."[11]

American women also increasingly participated in religious and civic associations during this time period. Although almost all denominations prohibited their ordination, women made significant contributions within the Shaker, Quaker, and other Protestant traditions.[12] Religious institutions facilitated the mobilization of women eager to fight slavery and "King Alcohol," giving rise to significant female leadership within the abolitionist and prohibitionist movements.[13] U.S. women were actively involved with agrarian and labor organizations, too, such as the Knights of Labor, the Farmers' Alliances, and the Populist Party, as well as with more local initiatives, including the "community-building" work that Gerda Lerner has acknowledged as political.[14] Certainly Populist orator Mary Elizabeth Lease was eager to make both local and national headlines as she traveled the country urging farmers to "raise less corn and more hell" in the 1890s.[15]

Female labor, vital to the economic development of the United States since colonial days, became more obviously so during these years. Census and survey figures typically underreport women's labor, but even these data sources reveal an increase in the number of women "employed away from home for wages" from about 15 percent of all U.S. females sixteen years old and older in 1870 to just over 25 percent in 1910.[16] Anecdotal evidence also suggests that women slowly gained economic influence during the late 1800s, when sisters Virginia Woodhull and Tennessee Clafin sat on the New York Stock Exchange and predicted market trends for such notable clients as Cornelius Vanderbilt.[17] Surely this literal and figurative "seat at the table" was an early sign that women would soon finally have to be recognized as equal political agents in American society. Or was it?

Theme One: Memorializing True Womanhood

As I have just suggested, as the nineteenth century was closing, women were becoming increasingly involved in almost every institution of American society. Even if presidents of this era might not have had to appeal to women for votes per se, one might expect that they would at least acknowledge their contributions. After all, long before women sought national suffrage in the United States, they were believed to influence politics by swaying the beliefs of their husbands and sons, a persuasive power illustrated most memorably by Abigail Adams's 1776 request that her husband consider the American women when developing the nation's new laws. Given women's social, cultural, and economic activity in the United States in the late 1800s, one might suppose that John Adams's successors of this era would also have had some incentive to "remember the ladies" in their national addresses.

On the other hand, these same presidents might also have had plenty of good reasons not to talk to, or even about, U.S. women. The most obvious reasons were political and cultural; although some states had granted women the vote long before 1920, most American women did not have that right or perhaps even want it, and most American men liked it that way.[18] Despite the burgeoning public activity of women, the majority of Americans viewed those seeking national suffrage "with displeasure," according to Campbell, largely due to the cultural prominence of a norm of true womanhood popular during the nineteenth century.[19]

According to these beliefs, females were not necessarily unequal to their male counterparts; indeed, they were usually perceived as being morally superior. Yet American women, especially those who were married and members of the middle class, were nonetheless strongly discouraged from entering the "cold, hard, competitive public world" of commerce and politics, which might compromise their morality.[20] Theirs instead was the "private space of the home," writes Skocpol, where they were "expected to be loving, full-time mothers, devoted to raising their children to be God-fearing, solid citizens." Over time, "formal 'politics' became strictly a male sphere as home life was a female sphere," with "True Womanhood [making] the pursuit of virtue in a separate sphere centered on the home the touchstone of feminine identity."[21]

Keeping these spheres separate apparently made sense to most Americans for much of the nineteenth century. The Fifteenth Amendment's exclusion of the word "sex" in 1870 legitimated such distinctions, and in 1875 the Supreme Court defended that exclusion by deciding that voting rights were not implicit in citizenship—a decision that held for fifty years.[22] It is reasonable to assume that this logic made sense to U.S. presidents of this era as well. While

Campbell and others have explained how such beliefs prohibited women from speaking in public, these same ideas may have kept male political leaders from speaking to and perhaps even about them. To do so would have been to violate the tacit understanding that women did not belong in the polluted world of public politics.

Yet the increasingly apparent contradiction between such exclusive ideals and the reality of women's increasing inclusion in American institutions presented a rhetorical dilemma for presidents at century's end. They could not easily ignore but also could not easily acknowledge approximately half of the people living in the United States. So what did they choose to do?

One obvious option was to remain silent on the topic of women's political rights, and, like Wilson in 1913, many presidents who served between 1885 and 1920 did not specifically discuss issues relating to American womanhood in the texts studied here. To be clear, some chief executives did use the words "woman" or "women" at certain points in these texts. Grover Cleveland certainly did in his third annual message to Congress in 1887, when he discussed the ways in which a certain tariff held a "relentless grasp . . . upon the clothing of every man, woman, and child in the land."[23] In his third annual message Theodore Roosevelt spoke of the advantages of rural free delivery of technology and other services to keep "restless young men and women" on the farms and out of the cities.[24] Yet when we look at the few instances where presidents of this era spoke on the nature of American womanhood specifically and not of women as merely a demographic fact, a trend becomes clear.

The few presidents who took on the topic of American womanhood in these years before national suffrage did so in ways that we might expect. They promoted the norms of "true womanhood" that maintained separate spheres for American men and women even as these spheres were becoming less distinct. During this period of tremendous social change, then, presidential rhetoric did not reflect newer circumstances but instead evoked the still powerful sentiments of a previous time. This finding may not be surprising, but it is not unimportant. Here presidential discourse can be interpreted as functioning conservatively and perhaps even nostalgically. That is, in the rare moments when presidents of this era did mention American womanhood in any detail, they seemed more intent on promoting previous conceptions of gender rather than on commenting, either negatively or positively, on current and/or emergent ones. As a result, in these speeches we can hear the most powerful men in the free world ignoring, and thus perhaps resisting, social changes that were already in motion all around them.

Consider Grover Cleveland's first annual message to Congress, on March 4, 1885, in which there is a plainspoken discussion of true womanhood. Yet on this occasion the president was not arguing about American women's voting rights or any other issues that would have been newsworthy at the time. His topic instead was *men's* rights and, more specifically, polygamy.

President Cleveland was against polygamy. Although he was happy to report on its ongoing "suppression" in the territory of Utah, he was still concerned. Utah's democratically elected leaders, according to the president, were largely "men who, though not actually living in the practice of polygamy, subscribe to the doctrine . . . as a divine revelation and a law unto all higher and more binding upon the conscience than any human law, local or national." Such beliefs resulted in a "strange spectacle" of dueling loyalties between a "republican form of government, to which they owe allegiance," and "a principle and belief which set at naught that obligation."[25]

As Cleveland continued, however, it became apparent that he was concerned not only with this compromised allegiance or even polygamy itself, but also with something larger. "The strength, the perpetuity, and the destiny of the nation rest upon our homes," he explained, "established by the law of God, guarded by parental care, regulated by parental authority, and sanctified by parental love. These are not the homes of polygamy." The president elaborated: "The mothers of our land, who rule the nation as they mold the characters and guide the actions of their sons, live according to God's holy ordinances, and each, secure and happy in the exclusive love of the father of her children, sheds the warm light of true womanhood, unperverted and unpolluted, upon all within her pure and wholesome family circle. These are not the cheerless, crushed, and unwomanly mothers of polygamy."[26] Although Cleveland appears to be interested in protecting Utah's women and children from a cheerless fate, his discourse points to an additional victim of polygamy: the United States. Without the "warm light of true womanhood, unperverted and unpolluted," the president warned, the nation could lose its "strength," its "perpetuity," and its "destiny."

When Cleveland spoke of "true womanhood" in this speech, then, his reference was a rallying cry against that which could threaten it. Indeed, a few sentences later, the president stated this need more explicitly by urging that "a law be passed to prevent the importation of Mormons into the country."[27] It may seem odd that Cleveland would argue that the best way to protect American womanhood was to squelch Mormonism. If his real goal was to maintain "the warm light of true womanhood, unperverted and unpolluted," it might seem more logical for him to decry women's matriculation in American universities or their paid work outside the home. These growing phenomena would eventually threaten the distinctions between separate spheres more than polygamy in Utah ever could. Yet these things were already rapidly taking hold throughout the nation; given the social, political, and economic advances women had started to make by 1885, Cleveland may have had to find a safer way of promoting traditional female roles. By focusing on the polygamous Mormons, an issue of concern for many other politicians and social leaders of his day, the president was also able to reinforce a particular paradigm of American womanhood. In the process, by associating true womanhood with the nation's stability, he offered his none-too-subtle disapproval of women's changing roles.

Most of Cleveland's immediate successors also played it safe rhetorically during this time of change. Indeed, some of their references to gender and women's political rights are so conservative and unsurprising as to almost escape notice. But they could be meaningful to today's observers, if only as a reminder of how much things have changed. American citizenship was clearly gendered in this era, at least within these genres of presidential rhetoric.

For example, William McKinley did not discuss the question of women's suffrage in his four state of the union messages. He used the word "women" only twice in all of them, once to discuss female victims of warfare in his first annual message and in his second when praising Clara Barton and the "patriotic women" of the Red Cross.[28] While this latter mention might also be read as evidence of a conservative longing for true womanhood, McKinley's texts deserve closer attention for another reason as well, for in them he repeatedly discussed citizenship in terms of the fraternity it engendered. Indeed, for McKinley, "the growing feeling of fraternal regard" was a sign of the health of the nation, evidence that "the spirit of patriotism is universal and is ever increasing in fervor" within "every earnest citizen," no matter "whatever party he belongs to or in whatever section of the country he may reside." Similarly, during the 1898 war with Spain over Cuba, McKinley reassured the American people that "military service under a common flag has strengthened the national spirit and served to cement more closely than ever the fraternal bonds between every section of the country."[29] Clearly, few American women could know such strength of spirit or bond.[30]

Theodore Roosevelt, himself no stranger to fraternal spirit and military bonds, also frequently spoke of citizenship in patently gendered terms. In his first annual message, he condemned McKinley's assassins, who were widely considered to be anarchists, by arguing that "anarchy is no more an expression of 'social discontent' than picking pockets or wife-beating," a curious analogy indeed. Later in the message, the president declared that the "rule of brotherhood" was the "indispensable prerequisite to success in the kind of national life for which we strive."[31] Likewise, in his second annual message, Roosevelt went so far as to describe the American people as being *all* male, a peculiar configuration from at least a reproductive standpoint: "Our people, the sons of the men of the Civil War, the sons of the men who had iron in their blood," the president proclaimed, "rejoice in the present and face the future high of heart and resolute of will."[32] And in his fifth annual message, Roosevelt reckoned that "the one vital factor in the permanent prosperity of the country is the high individual character of the average American worker, the average American citizen, no matter whether his work be mental or manual, whether he be farmer or wage-worker, business man or professional man."[33]

Again, I do not mention these references so as to paint TR as a misogynist but instead to show the ease with which the president, like the great majority of Americans of his day, imagined the idealized American citizen to be male.

We should, of course, probably expect nothing else from TR. Clearly he, McKinley, Cleveland, and perhaps even their predecessors were invoking true womanhood and using masculine pronouns and metaphors of citizenship in ways that merely reflected the sensibilities of the day. (Indeed, some of these sensibilities exist today, according to Dana Nelson's persuasive analysis in *National Manhood*.[34]) Yet it is precisely because U.S. presidents no longer use these terms that this rhetoric of the past deserves further attention. Overall, this group of chief executives appeared eager to cling to a rhetorical vision of American political community infused with masculinity during a time when the real American community was becoming more feminized via the suffrage movement and the influence of Progressivism. In a sense, then, these presidents' rhetoric memorialized a kind of citizenry that no longer existed and would never return.

Theme Two: Feminized Industry

If the "modern American woman" did in fact emerge at the end of the nineteenth century, as Ryan and others have argued, when, and why, did U.S. presidents finally start acknowledging her in their inaugural addresses and state of the union messages? Put differently, if chief executives of the late 1800s and early 1900s seemed content to memorialize a nostalgic view of American womanhood rather than deal with the realities of a changing order, what made their successors abandon this rhetoric?

One might suspect that such a change might be evident around the year 1920. Specifically, once women throughout the nation were granted the vote, we might expect that chief executives would have started to seek their support relatively soon thereafter. Thus, politicians would be embracing women as voters rather than mere citizens in their public discourse. Similarly, one might also suspect that presidential discussions of women's suffrage would not only increase at this time but also might reflect some of the moral, philosophical, and political arguments put forth by the suffragists themselves or, alternatively, even by their detractors.

While the first suspicion seems to be at least partially correct, the second does not. The first president to tackle the subject of women's suffrage explicitly in a state of the union or inaugural address during the period studied was Woodrow Wilson. In 1918, Wilson, the same leader who was so conspicuously silent on the subject just five years earlier, finally argued for national suffrage in his annual message to Congress. Some scholars have suggested that Wilson came to support suffrage publicly as a result of the very public demonstrations that the Women's Party held at the White House in 1917 and 1918. Christine Bolt has noted, for example, that the Women's Party members themselves believed that "their pressure had moved Wilson from anti-suffragism to support for the once hopeless-looking women's cause."[35] Indeed, as Wilson prepared to run again in 1916, the Women's Party "maintained an anti-Democratic position throughout the campaign [and] directed its principal attack against Wilson," according to Eleanor Flexner.[36] The National Suffrage Association also focused on increasing the pressure on Wilson, although it took a different approach, largely because of suffragist leader Carrie Chapman Catt's fierce determination to "win over Mr. Wilson to support a federal amendment," according to Flexner. By the fall of 1915, Catt's goal seemed to have been met; the president had stopped arguing that he "could do nothing until Congress acted" and had started saying that the matter was "solely up to the several states."[37] By September, 1916, the recently remarried president seemed to change his tune once again. Appearing at the NSA's annual convention with his bride, the former Edith Galt, Wilson proclaimed, "I have not come to fight anybody but with somebody. . . . We feel the tide; we rejoice in the strength of it, and we shall not quarrel in the long run as to the method of it."[38]

Whatever Wilson's private motivations, in his 1918 message he did not cast his support in terms of the suffragists' logical, political, and moral arguments, which by some accounts were by then hopelessly unpopular among the American people.[39] Instead, he offered the nation a wholly different rationale. Simply put, Wilson urged Congress to give women the vote as an expression of a nation's gratitude for women's service in World War I. After taking up most of his message with praise for American men's "vast achievement" in the war ("the patriotism, the unselfishness, the thoroughgoing devotion and distinguished capacity that marked their toilsome labors, day after day, month after month"), the president turned his attention in another direction:

> And what shall we say of the women—of their instant intelligence, quickening every task they touched; their capacity for organization and cooperation, which gave their action discipline and enhanced the effectiveness of everything they attempted; their aptitude at tasks which they had never before set their hands; their utter self-sacrifice in what they did and what they gave? The contribution to the great result is beyond appraisal. They have added a new lustre to the annals of American womanhood.[40]

Coming from a president whose effigy had been recently burned by members of the Women's Party, such effusive words were remarkable indeed.[41] Yet the president's remarks are as noteworthy for their specific content as for their valence.

Here the president portrayed American women in terms of their "organization" and "effectiveness," descriptions that seem better suited to the Fordist environment of the rapidly industrializing American factory than to the more genteel realm of the domestic private sphere nurtured by "true women" within American homes. In emphasizing productivity and efficiency, not only did Wilson provide good reasons why women could be viewed as good citizens during the war but he also seemed to stray from the rhetoric of true womanhood, a noteworthy departure in light of previous presidents' portrayals of American women.

Yet Wilson did not abandon the notion of true womanhood altogether. He held on to some of its themes by invoking the "discipline" and "self-sacrifice" that American women were long presumed to have as the morally superior and self-restrained helpmates to men. Thus, the president seemed to be describing an American woman who embodied the best of both worlds, combining the busy efficiency of an increasingly industrialized public world with the moral principle and quiet sacrifice more traditionally associated with the private realm of domesticity. The result, according to Wilson, was nothing less than an update to the "annals of American womanhood," in which the use of a term describing this improvement ("lustre") underscored the ways in which these contemporary women's skills could expand previous notions of U.S. women's nature and capabilities.

Having announced the arrival of the newly revised American woman, President Wilson made a specific request of Congress in her name:

> The least tribute we can pay them is to make them the equals of men in political rights as they have proved themselves equals in every field of practical work they have entered, whether for themselves or for their country. These great days of completed achievement would be sadly marred were we to omit that act of justice. Besides the immense practical services they have rendered, the women of the country have been the moving spirits in the systematic economies by which our people have voluntarily assisted to supply the suffering peoples of the world and the armies upon every front with food and everything else that might serve the common cause. The details of such a story can never be fully written, but we carry them at our hearts and thank God that we can say we are the kinsmen of such.[42]

Here the president again described women's efforts in terms of their demonstrated efficiency at public service, for example, "the immense practical services they have rendered" as the "moving spirits in the systematic economies" mobilized to assist the "suffering peoples" and "serve the common cause." He framed his support for national suffrage in nearly contractual terms, calling it a deserved "tribute" and noting how "these great days of completed achievement would be sadly marred were we to omit that act of justice." Here American women are portrayed as being worthy of "political rights" because of how well they have "prove[n] themselves equals in every field of practical work they have entered." In other words, President Wilson argued that women were now owed voting rights as the fitting, fair compensation for their good works—*not* because of any overarching democratic principles or even the arguments of the suffragists. Women's work in the war had thus finally earned them "kinsmanship" with the male electorate, and the Congress should express the nation's collective gratitude by finally granting women suffrage. Lest this proposal seem too radical, Wilson's incorporation of themes of true womanhood into his argument might have served to temper his endorsement.

To his credit, Wilson's successor Warren Harding sounded almost eager to depart from metaphors such as "kinsmanship" in his descriptions of the strength and unity of the American people. In perhaps the only achievement that feminists could ever thank President Harding for, this chief executive used decidedly gender-neutral language in his first state of the union address. "It has been the proudest claim of our American civilization," he declared, "that in dealing with human relationships it has constantly moved toward such justice in distributing the product of human energy that it has improved continuously the economic status of the mass of the people."[43] Harding was perhaps only reporting the obvious. By the time he took office, American women had increasingly begun occupying jobs that were traditionally reserved for men, largely because of economic expansion during World War I.[44] Thus, the country was in fact being driven by new sorts of "human relationships" and "human energy" that were in fact novel when compared to the clearly gendered forms of social relations that existed before World War I.

Yet there are additional reasons that the suffragists of the day might have expected more from Warren Harding than they did from Woodrow Wilson. As a presidential candidate in 1920, and apparently with some guidance from Ohio suffragist and Republican National Committee official Harriet Taylor Upton, Harding "went well beyond the Republican platform in his support of issues women had long supported," according to historian Dorothy M. Brown. The campaign strategy seemed to have worked. Harding would become the first U.S. president to be elected by women, whom Brown claims constituted approximately one-third of the national electorate in 1920.[45] Although scholars have made much of the relatively low female turnout for the presidential elections that year, Robert K. Murray has argued that "the women who did vote showed a decided preference for Harding."[46]

Perhaps it was no surprise, then, when Harding heralded the passage of the Nineteenth Amendment in his March 4, 1921, inaugural address as follows: "With the nation-wide induction of womanhood into our political life, we may count upon her intuitions, her refinements, her intelligence, and her influence to exalt the social order. We count upon her exercise of the full privileges and the performance of the duties of citizenship to speed the attainment of the highest State."[47] Here the president sounded, quite predictably, positive about the recent suffrage victory. Its impact on U.S. society would not be negative or radical, he seemed to reassure the nation, but instead beneficial, and, perhaps most important, relatively slight. According to Harding, U.S. women's most significant contributions to their country *after* suffrage would be their intuitions, refinements, intelligence, influence—the same quiet and genteel contributions that American women had been presumed to be making *before* suffrage and, in fact, since the early days of the Republic. Harding's discussion of the suffrage victory can thus be read as not necessarily reflecting the historic reality of women's newly gained legal status as voters or even his own personal stance on the issues. Instead, one might be tempted to read in even this relatively progressive discourse a great dependence upon time-worn symbolic ideals about women's clearly circumscribed political agency found within the "separate spheres" doctrine and especially in the concept of "Republican motherhood."

That themes of Republican motherhood should appear in presidential rhetoric after women gained the vote is telling for at least two reasons. First, historically, the concept of Republican motherhood rose to prominence in the United States in the eighteenth century and thus predated the cult of true womanhood. According to Linda K. Kerber, Republican motherhood was "invented [as] a definition of women's relationship to the state that sought to fill the inadequacies of inherited political theory" from the Enlightenment. She adds that "it made use of the classic formulation of the Spartan Mother who raised sons prepared to sacrifice themselves to the good of the *polis*."[48] Secondly, some aspects of the ideology of Republican motherhood suggested that American women would be most effective as political agents if they remained behind the scenes of U.S. society. For example, Republican motherhood ideology suggested that American women's chief and unique civic virtue was in fact the "disinterestedness" or "unselfish public-mindedness" that came from their standing outside of the worlds of commerce and traditional politics.[49] "Because women did not have (or were not presumed to have) a direct connection to the market or the polity as individuals," Kristi Andersen has explained, "they were not characterized by the kinds of 'interests' that since Madison's day had been seen as motivating political choices."[50] None of this presumed disinterest meant that American women did not serve an important function within U.S. society and politics, however. As Kerber has explained, "[The] Republican Mother's life was dedicated to the service of civic virtue . . . [in that] she educated her sons for it . . . [and thus] the traditional womanly virtues were endowed with political purpose."[51]

The cultural norm for American women of political efficacy being equated with propriety was strong enough to last well past the Revolutionary War era from which Republican motherhood drew its name, and the president would hardly have been alone in using such an argument to cast the suffrage victory in a positive light. During Harding's day, "the illusion that women did not have selfish interests was widespread, as can be seen in many of the arguments for suffrage," Andersen has noted.[52] In 1896, for example, Mrs. Frank O. Immler wrote a pro-suffrage editorial in the *American Magazine of Civics* in which she encouraged readers to "think of the effect when a woman, being her husband's political equal, will study social science with him and the sons no longer need to go to the beer saloon to be initiated into politics."[53] By suggesting that the suffrage victory would primarily result in clearer yet still conservative channels for female influence on U.S. society, the president thus

invoked a vision of American women's political agency that was simultaneously nostalgic and progressive in ways that would almost certainly have
resonated with his constituents.

In less explicit terms than Wilson's rhetoric had, then, Harding's words also
expressed gratitude for U.S. women and sounded optimistic about the impact
of female suffrage. By invoking the indirect influence that women had had in
the past, the president prophesied that now that U.S. women had the vote
they would use it to similarly "exalt the social order" and "speed the attainment of the highest State." Indeed, in another section of Harding's 1921 inaugural address that actually occurs before his specific mention of the suffrage
victory, the president voiced this expectation even more colorfully when en-
visioning what would need to happen if "war is again forced upon us": "I
earnestly hope a way may be found which will unify our individual and collective strength and consecrate all America, materially and spiritually, body and
soul, to national defense. I can vision the ideal republic, where every man and
woman is called under the flag for assignment to duty for whatever service,
military or civic, the individual is best fitted."[54] In this passage, women are
portrayed slightly more progressively, more as equal citizens than as helpmates,
"called under the flag" as part of the unification of "individual and collective
strength" necessary to "consecrate all America." Lest this description seem to
stray too far from norms of Republican motherhood, however, the president
ended his address with a passage that spelled out more specifically where
American women would be "best fitted" to serve their country.

In the conclusion of his inaugural address, and ostensibly within a discussion of the nation's economy, Harding stated,

> We ought to find a way to guard against the perils and penalties of unemploy-
> ment. We want an America of home, illuminated with hope and happiness,
> where mothers, freed from the necessity for long hours of toil beyond their own
> doors, may preside as befits the hearthstone of American citizenship. We want
> the cradle of American childhood rocked under conditions so wholesome and
> so hopeful that no blight may touch its development, and we want to provide
> that no selfish interest, no material necessity, no lack of opportunity shall pre-
> vent the gaining of that education so essential to best citizenship.[55]

No longer portrayed as soldier-citizens toiling under the flag, women are depicted quite literally as Republican mothers, protected from "long hours of
toil" (at least those that might take place "beyond their own doors") so that
they might "preside" over the "hearthstone of American citizenship" within

homes "illuminated with hope and happiness." In ending his inaugural address with these images, the president may have offered his solution to any anxiety that the American people might have felt about the suffrage victory. American women could work "under the flag" in new ways if necessary, but their true place was by the hearthstone, doing this same work by rocking the "cradle of American childhood."

Theme Three: Women in Need of Solicitous Care

Although Calvin "Silent Cal" Coolidge is typically not remembered today for oratorical accomplishments, he was the second president to mention women's suffrage explicitly in an inaugural address after the ratification of the Nineteenth Amendment. Having completed Harding's presidential term after his predecessor's death in 1923, Coolidge ran in his own right in 1924 and was elected by a landslide. Whereas President Harding had been more vocal in his support for women's suffrage and social reforms, and despite the fact that Coolidge had endorsed female suffrage while serving as a Massachusetts senator, President Coolidge's domestic agenda seemed to focus primarily on "business and . . . businessmen," according to Sarah Jane Deutsch.[56] The "Coolidge prosperity" of economic boom times from 1922 to 1929 meant that "America had seven biblical fat years," writes Brown, although organized laborers and farmers did not share in this plenty.[57] Against this backdrop of perceived mainstream content as well as the rapid disorganization of the suffragists themselves, the president articulated his theory of government in his first annual message to Congress, delivered on December 6, 1923:

> [The United States'] enormous material wealth, our institutions, our whole form of society, can not be considered fully successful until their benefits reach the merit of every individual. This is not a suggestion that the Government should, or could, assume for the people the inevitable burdens of existence. . . . But the government can and should always be expressive of steadfast determination, always vigilant, to maintain conditions under which these virtues are most likely to develop and secure recognition and reward. This is the American policy.[58]

Whether it would eventually be translated into American policy or not, Coolidge's philosophy sounded a lot like the goals of many of the women's organizations of the 1920s.

As Banner notes, "The formation both of the National Federation of Business and Professional Women's Clubs (BPW) and of the Women's Bureau in the federal department of Labor in 1919, as well as of the Women's Joint Congressional Committee (WJCC) and the League of Women Voters in 1920, seemed to promise further striking progress for women." Many of these groups comprised women Banner labels "social feminists." She classifies their goals as "general social reform; the elimination of state laws that discriminated against women; and the education of women to their responsibilities as citizens."[59] Especially in the case of the League of Women Voters, these women's efforts remarkably influenced local, state, and national policies, according to Banner, who recalls Stanley Lemons's argument that they "were primarily responsible for whatever Progressive impulse still existed in an essentially conservative decade."[60] Kristi Andersen concurs by observing that "women extended the life of Progressivism."[61]

Such positive assessments of social feminists' efforts, especially when combined with the legislation that followed them, would seem to bode well for American women's eventual political equality and integration. Yet there seems to be general agreement among scholars that American feminism actually declined in the 1920s. While many observers explain this decline by pointing to the diffusion of American women's efforts into multiple causes, an additional explanation might be found in the sentiment expressed by the same president, Calvin Coolidge, who seemed so willing to help in his first message to Congress. Indeed, as Coolidge's sixth annual message reveals, this president may have in fact been *too* willing to help women.

In a section of his December 4, 1928, message to Congress entitled, "Women and Children," Coolidge offered the following single sentence. "The Federal Government should continue its solicitous care for the 8,500,000 women wage earners and its efforts in behalf of the public health, which is reducing infant mortality and improving the bodily and mental conditions of our citizens."[62] On its face, this request probably does not sound offensive to modern-day readers, and it almost certainly would not have surprised Congress. Coolidge had previously argued for a minimum wage law to protect women workers and had spoken about "Mothers' Aid" in similar addresses. And, to be clear, it is not my intention to suggest that Coolidge was in any way insincere or otherwise suspect in these appeals. Instead, I mean to call attention to the logic behind them and the subtle ways that Coolidge's request might possibly have reinforced some perceptions about U.S. women's capabilities and, more specifically, their assumed economic and political agency.

American women, Coolidge's 1928 request suggests, needed nothing less than "solicitous care" from the federal government—not "assistance," not "help," not "education," not "money," nor even, as in the example mentioned previously, "Mothers' Aid." A presidential request for "solicitous care" signals something different than these other terms might have: a type of concern that is self-consciously patriarchal and even slightly officious. In this discourse assistance is offered purposefully, to be sure, but also somewhat patronizingly.

Such an interpretation of Coolidge's phrasing is supported by the close reading of some of his other discourse, in which a gendered hierarchy implicit in his logic becomes even clearer. In his third annual message to Congress, for example, President Coolidge discussed immigration restrictions by observing that "the standard which we apply to our inhabitants is that of manhood, not place of birth." This standard, he continued, is "applied in order that we may not have a larger annual increment of good people within our borders than we can weave into our economic fabric."[63] In light of this standard, what does it mean when women and children are assumed to need "solicitous care"? Are women somehow suddenly inferior citizens, in marked contrast to the days before suffrage when they were framed as models of civic virtue? And what does women's weaker economic status, both presumed and real, signify within such a logic? Does their presumed inability to "weave into the economic fabric" also somehow reinforce the perception of some kind of essentialized inferiority?

Whatever its implications, Coolidge's call for solicitous care for women and children was repeated by his successor, Herbert Hoover. President Hoover used his first annual message to Congress to call for "an extensive and valuable program of constructive social service, in education, home building, protection to women and children, employment, public health, recreation, and many other directions." Here the protection of women and children is placed within a broader laundry list of policy goals, all with the stated purpose of supporting "one of the most precious possessions of the American people: that is, local and individual responsibility."[64] Yet it is not clear, within this rhetoric at least, how women themselves could exercise individual responsibility.

However beneficent and even responsive the notion of "solicitous care" might have been for American women's material needs at the time, discourse like Coolidge's and Hoover's seems to rhetorically divorce women from the possibility of individual agency and economic self-sufficiency. While there is no denying the tremendous economic challenges that women of this era did in fact face, my point here is that this rhetoric seemed to suggest that American women's fate should be viewed more as the responsibility of the federal government rather than of American women themselves. If so, such discourse may have contributed to the idea that women were necessarily weaker and less industrious than men, a curious shift away from the productive, hard-working women featured in Wilson's rhetoric just a few years before. Likewise, if the civil religious rhetoric of American national identity so frequently used by presidents can also be associated with themes related to the Protestant work ethic, then the suggestion that women needed extra "solicitous care" for their economic well-being may also have distanced them somehow from the ideal of a U.S. citizen.

Theme Four: Women as Equal Citizens

In 1937, when Franklin Roosevelt delivered his second inaugural address, he seemed to avoid the mistake that Woodrow Wilson had made in 1913. Whereas Wilson had incurred the early feminists' wrath by omitting any discussion of women's political agency, Roosevelt spoke of women as full-fledged U.S. citizens three times in the same sentence. "Overwhelmingly, we of the Republic are men and women of good will; men and women who have more than warm hearts of dedication; men and women who have cool heads and willing hands of practical purpose as well. They will insist that every agency of popular government use effective instruments to carry out their will," the president assured a presumably anxious audience.[65] In addition to featuring egalitarian language that would make Warren Harding proud, President Roosevelt's words are also conspicuous because of what they did *not* feature.

Simply put, at first glance this instance of Roosevelt's rhetoric seemed to attribute no special characteristics or distinctions to American women. Missing here, for instance, were the ghosts of true womanhood and Republican motherhood that had so obviously haunted the rhetoric of the pre-suffrage era. Absent as well were the rhetorical tokens of gender-specific gratitude for feminized industry that Wilson had used to publicly explain his eventual advocacy of women's suffrage. And gone, too, was the blatant solicitousness that had peppered the messages of Coolidge and Hoover. In his second inaugural address President Roosevelt had portrayed American men and women as equal political agents, with "warm hearts, cool heads, and willing hands" equally eager to work within a governmental system to overcome the economic crisis.

In some senses, FDR's relative inclusiveness in his inaugural address may not be all that remarkable. After all, his was the first mass-mediated presidency, during which his words were broadcast to a radio audience comprising both men and women. His presidency was also during a time in which women's needs may have been presumed to be more important to the executive branch, if only because of the first lady's assumed influence. Whatever its root causes, the unequivocal egalitarianism heard in Roosevelt's second inaugural address was not necessarily repeated in his state of the union messages. There we can hear thematic traces of some of his predecessor's portrayals of American women. In 1935, for example, he used his second annual message to promise "definite recommendations" to address the "broad problem of livelihood" facing the nation, which included "unemployment insurance and old-age insurance, of benefits for children, for mothers, for the handicapped, for maternity care, and for other aspects of dependency and illness where a beginning can now be made."[66] Here one might hear faint echoes of Coolidge's women in need of solicitous care.

Likewise, in his ninth annual message, delivered in 1942, Roosevelt sounded slightly more Wilsonian: "Production for war is based on men and women— the human hands and brains which collectively we call Labor. Our workers are ready to stand long hours; to turn out more in a day's work; to keep the wheels turning and the fires burning 24 hours a day, and 7 days a week."[67] He repeated this characterization of women as men's industrious equals when he gave his 1943 state of the union message: "As spokesmen for the United States Government," he said, "you and I take off our hats to those responsible for American production—to the owners, managers, and supervisors, to the draftsmen and engineers, to the workers—men and women—in factories and arsenals and shipyards and mines and mills and forests—and railroads and on highways."[68] And again the following year: "National service . . . will be a means by which every man and woman can find that inner satisfaction which comes from making the fullest possible contribution to victory."[69]

The next year, 1945, Roosevelt also spoke explicitly of women's role in the war effort, yet here his tone took a slight turn back into Coolidge's rhetoric of special care, as he expresses his concern for women in one occupation in particular: "The present shortage of Army nurses is reflected in undue strain on the existing force. . . . It is tragic that the gallant women who have volunteered for service as nurses should be so overworked." Additionally, in the next sentence Roosevelt came close to invoking the discourse of separate spheres that would have suggested that there was something unique and even patriotic about American women's capacity for care-giving. "It is tragic," the president continued, "that our wounded men should ever want for the best possible nursing care."[70]

In these examples of Franklin Roosevelt's references to American women, one can perhaps get a better sense of how more than one of the four themes (discussed here as being more or less discrete) can be incorporated into one chief executive's discourse. Taking Roosevelt's state of the union messages as a whole, women are portrayed as capable citizens who nevertheless need help in facing "broad problem[s] of livelihood" and as "workers" in "national service" who are "gallant" but "overworked" in caring for the male citizen soldiers of the day. Such polysemy in formal presidential references to American women would also be featured in some of Roosevelt's successors' executive discourse, as I will discuss shortly. Yet in Roosevelt's case, these blended themes suggest that, even as U.S. women were beginning to make economic and legislative gains, the president still had difficulty talking about them without incorporating some of the rhetoric of the past.

To be sure, there were moments when certain presidents seemed to break free from previous stereotypes. One of these moments was during the Truman administration. In Truman's 1946 state of the union message, in which he referred to the "year of decision" when the world moved "from war to peace," the president made it clear that American women were part of this movement. Yet instead of thanking women alone for their wartime industry at home, à la Wilson perhaps, Truman noted that American soldiers were "supported by the millions of Americans in private life—men and women in industry, in commerce, on the farms, and in all manner of activity on the home front—who contributed their brains and their brawn in arming, equipping, and feeding them." In this statement, the president portrayed U.S. women and men as equally representative of American national character, an observation that Truman underscored in the subsequent sentence: "The country was brought through four years of peril by an effort that was truly national in character."[71]

Because Truman made this speech at the beginning of the Cold War years, some might assume that the president's progressive rhetoric signaled a particular strategy. Mary L. Dudziak's book *Cold War Civil Rights* suggested that presidents and their administrations tried to sound progressive on civil rights during the Cold War years as part of a propaganda battle against the Soviets, and in this speech Truman might have been especially careful to portray the United States as unified and egalitarian. No matter what his motives were, it may be instructive to contrast Truman's message about U.S. women with some of the others that were being offered during the 1940s and 1950s. In 1942, for example, in the best-selling book *Generation of Vipers,* author Philip Wylie accused U.S. housewives of psychologically ruining their sons and mercilessly controlling their husbands. Women who worked outside of the home were also subject to intense criticism during this period, most notably through the book *Modern Woman: The Lost Sex,* in which social scientists Marynia Farnham and Ferdinand Lundberg connected a whole host of social problems to women's absence from the home. In light of these sorts of messages, Truman's unambiguous rhetoric on U.S. women in this 1946 speech may have been preferable to what much of the rest of the culture had to offer.

BYGONE THEMES AND MULTIPLE MEANINGS:
MORE RECENT PORTRAYALS OF AMERICAN WOMEN

If, as Lois Banner has argued, American feminism came "of age" during the period from 1945 to 1984, then certainly its adolescence was a difficult one.[72] As noted, from the 1940s forward, women's changing roles in the United States were loudly contested. Perhaps no book captured what it was like to be a middle-class woman in the United States in the 1950s better than Betty Friedan's celebrated *The Feminine Mystique,* first published in 1963. Today, of course, many observers associate Friedan's work with the beginnings of the twentieth-century feminist movement in the United States, in which leaders strove to gain government attention to their cause, most notably through the fight for an equal rights amendment to the Constitution. By the late 1970s, as feminists and antifeminists alike galvanized their efforts around the campaign for passage or defeat of the Equal Rights Amendment (ERA), public debate and mixed messages about the appropriate roles for American women became even more pronounced. Jane Mansbridge has argued that both sides' arguments were filled with much exaggeration and ideological purity.[73] Yet what was new about these arguments was perhaps not as significant as what was not. By some accounts, these debates recalled lines of argumentation plucked directly from a previous era. For instance, some legislators voiced concerns that the ERA would "destroy the family," thus echoing those who had forecast a similar outcome as the result of women's suffrage.[74]

Even before all of this debate had reached its peak, President Dwight Eisenhower was avoiding the topic of women's rights per se in his inaugural and state of the union addresses. Sounding faintly like Calvin Coolidge, Ike preferred to advocate for better maternal and child health in several of his state of the union addresses.[75] By comparison, John F. Kennedy may have sounded remarkably progressive, especially in his third annual message when he referred to "more men and women in the work force."[76] By the time Richard Nixon gave his 1971 state of the union address, the president used images of regular male and female citizens alike to point to not hope but despair: "As everything seems to have grown bigger and more complex in America, as forces that shape our lives seem to have grown more distant and impersonal, a great feeling of frustration has swept across the land. Whether it is the workingman who feels neglected, the black man who feels oppressed, or the mother concerned about her children, there has been a growing feeling that 'things are in the saddle, and ride mankind.'"[77] One positive way to read these remarks is to note that this president was at least an equal opportunity pessimist. His typical citizens include a "mother" alongside a "workingman" and a "black man," all proto-types offered as token identities for individual citizens. Yet one wonders, per-haps, if Nixon's categories are mutually exclusive and thus somewhat essen-tialist: if working men cannot somehow also be black, if black men cannot also worry about their children, and if women's feelings of neglect and frustration are not as politically significant as men's. To be fair, one could read these words as suggesting that Nixon was at least portraying women as equal citizens. Yet Nixon's references to these three groups in particular might also be read as corresponding with the more stratified categories of citizens maintained else-where within presidents' rhetoric of shared beliefs. As I have suggested in two previous chapters, some types of citizens have been subtly yet consistently represented as being less capable of participating in the ideological world of U.S. nationalism than white males are. In the case of U.S. women, rhetoric such as Nixon's can promote something of a mixed message. Women are si-multaneously part of this world, sharing in national identity in general and the national mood in particular in this example, but also somehow removed from it, still locked into a separate sphere where their worries are reserved for their children.

Nixon's successor Gerald Ford may have sensed this ambivalence, not just among women but among other groups of increasingly vocal citizens during the 1960s and 1970s. In the conclusion of his 1974 address to a joint session of Congress, Ford said,

> The truth is I am the people's man, for you acted in their name, and I accepted and began my new and solemn trust with a promise to serve all the people and do the best I can for America. When I say all the people, I mean exactly that. To the limits of my strength and ability, I will be the President of black, brown, red, and white Americans, of young and old, of women's liberationists and male chauvinists—and all the rest of us in-between, of the poor and the rich, of native sons and new refugees, of those who work in lathes or at desks or in mines or in the fields, of Christians, Jews, Muslims, Buddhists, and atheists, if there really are any atheists after what we have all been through.[78]

It is hard to imagine a more sociologically accurate yet rhetorically inept de-scription of "the American people" in the 1970s. Ford's rhetoric definitely shows the signs of its era, for no president before the 1960s would have felt compelled to offer such specificity. On one hand, then, Ford had little choice but to mention all of the groups that he did, and he had to reference the nation's internal tensions of race and religion, generation and gender. On the other hand, however, consider how deftly President Ford disassociated "all the people" from these sources of discontent. "All the rest of us," he offered, are "in-between."

In some respects, "in-between" may be a fitting way to characterize more recent chief executives' depictions of American women. Women still took care of the nation's children and homes, still worked industriously, still needed special care and governmental assistance at times, and yet still represented egalitarian values and thus reflected the nation's charter. Like Ford's America, perhaps, women are portrayed in his speech as being torn between their multiple roles and thus suffering some internal conflict. As such, they do not seem at all like the Puritan faithful, who not only believed wholeheartedly in their mission but also believed that Providence would ensure its success. Instead, modern American women are portrayed as believing in and preserving high morals but also as still somehow beyond the pale since they do not yet know exactly their place in society or political life. Thus, American women may have been able to embody and understand these Puritan principles in ways that immigrant newcomers could not, but they also needed assistance in their practical pursuits in the same ways that Native and African Americans were assumed to. In this sense, American women have been portrayed as being particularly "in-between." They may not be feared as foreigners, but they are often represented in presidential inaugural addresses and state of the union messages as "foreign" to the political efficacy commonly ascribed to American men.

Several of Ronald Reagan's state of the union addresses can be read as making this last suggestion quite clearly, particularly when we consider the blended themes often found in his descriptions of U.S. women in these texts. In his 1983 address to Congress, for example, he promised to bring "working mothers' . . . ordeal to an end" so that the nation could "build a better future for ourselves and our children."[79] Here, perhaps, one can hear a type of solicitous care from a previous era, but also the faint echoes of an even older notion of true womanhood that would make the idea of a mother working outside of the home anathema to the American people. A year later, in his 1984 state of the union message, Reagan offered one of his characteristic anecdotes about American citizens to evoke a more Wilsonian image of American womanhood. He singled out Barbara Proctor, "who rose from the ghetto to build a multi-million dollar advertising agency in Chicago," and praised her for her industriousness. "People like these are the heroes for the eighties," the president proclaimed, without discussing whether or not Proctor was married or a parent and, if so, certainly without discussing what she might have done with her children during her celebrated rise.[80]

Reagan did speak about children a few lines later, and when he did so he invoked Coolidge's notions of solicitous care. "Opportunities for all Americans will increase if we move forward in fair housing and work to ensure women's rights, provide for equitable treatment in pension benefits and individual retirement accounts, facilitate child care, and enforce delinquent parent support payments," he explained.[81] While these goals are admirable, and would presumably benefit all Americans indeed, this discourse may portray women as being especially needy. Who, after all, needs "rights," "child care," and "parent support payments" more—men or women? Similarly, in a section of his 1985 state of the union message devoted to the nation's crime rate, Reagan's prototypical victims are women in two of the three cases, and a woman and a man together in the third, as he lists "the woman who must run to her car after shopping at night" as a victim, just like the "couple" who "drap[e] their door with locks and chains" and the "decent cleaning woman who can't ride a subway home without being afraid."[82]

Yet all of these images of women came from a man who, in his 1986 state of the union message, used the story of a young girl's heroism to illustrate the true nature of the American people. Recognizing "Shelby Butler, honor student and member of her school's safety patrol," the president recounted her tale: "Seeing another girl freeze in terror before an out-of-control school bus, she risked her life and pulled her to safety. With bravery like yours, Shelby, America need never fear for her future."[83] Here President Reagan did something that Grover Cleveland, Woodrow Wilson, Calvin Coolidge, and most of their executive brethren would never have done: He offered a young girl as an idealized exemplar of American national identity—indeed, as the hope of an entire nation.

In his 1989 inaugural address, George H. W. Bush also spoke of American men's and women's hopes, and more specifically, of "what matters" in their hearts. "We cannot hope to leave our children a bigger car, a bigger bank account," the president proclaimed. Instead, "We must hope to give them a sense of what it means to be a loyal friend, a loving parent, a citizen who leaves his home, his neighborhood, and his town better than he found it. What do we want the men and women who work with us to say when we are no longer there? That we were more driven to succeed than anyone around us? Or that we stopped to ask if a sick child had gotten better, and stayed a moment there to trade a word of friendship?" In this passage the president sounds egalitarian enough ("the men and women who work with us"), especially if one overlooks the universal "he" in his discussion of the average citizen. Seconds later, however, Bush's pronoun changed as he linked these individual questions to the nation's mission:

America is never wholly herself unless she is engaged in high moral principle. We as a people have such a purpose today. It is to make kinder the face of the Nation and gentler the face of the world. My friends, we have work to do. There are the homeless, lost and roaming. There are the children who have nothing, no love, no normalcy. There are those who cannot free themselves of enslavement to whatever addiction—drugs, welfare, the demoralization that rules the slums. There is crime to be conquered, the rough crime of the streets. There are young women to be helped who are about to become mothers of children they can't care for and might not love. They need our care, our guidance, and our education, though we bless them for choosing life.[84]

Here women are on the list of those who need solicitous care indeed. Grouped with the homeless, the "children who have nothing," the addicted, and those victimized by "the rough crime of the streets," the young women the presidents seeks to help are portrayed as decidedly passive. Although teenage pregnancy is certainly a serious social problem, Bush's articulation of these women's needs—"they need our care, our guidance, and our education"—is remarkably similar to the types of things that presidents said about new immigrants and former slaves almost one hundred years before. Indeed, this was not the only time a century-old sensibility appeared in the president's discourse. Later in this same speech, when the president recalled "the woman who will tell her sons the words of the battle hymns" during patriotic celebrations, he also invoked the Revolutionary War–era notion of Republican motherhood.[85]

By the time Bush's successor William J. Clinton took office in 1993, political commentators had made much of the "soccer moms" and "angry white men" who were predicted to swing national and state elections. Nevertheless, in his first inaugural address, Clinton made no such distinctions about male and female political agency. Referring to the need for "each generation of Americans" to "define what it means to be an American," the president thanked previous generations of Americans, the "millions of men and women whose steadfastness and sacrifice triumphed over Depression, fascism, and Communism."[86] Implicit in his gratitude, and explicit in later passages of this same speech, was his pledge to promote the "dramatic change" that Thomas Jefferson had written was so vital to democracy. Although Clinton would prove to have a different kind of "woman problem" during his executive tenure, in his state of the union messages there was indeed a hint of discursive change as he talked about children's welfare as a concern for both mothers and fathers, of teen pregnancy as a concern for "all Americans."[87] Only time will tell if his successors can similarly manage to avoid the themes of the past as they discuss gender roles in some of their most formal and public presidential rhetoric.

CHAPTER 6

Implications of Presidents' Rhetoric of Shared Beliefs

In this book I have asked how U.S. presidents have constructed American national identity from 1885 to 2000. In doing so, I have considered the following questions: How have chief executives defined American identity in such a highly heterogeneous, pluralistic culture? How have they explained the more symbolic aspects of U.S. citizenship to a rapidly diversifying public? And why have they operated as they have in all of these matters?

To situate insights into such matters within a general historical context, I examined a collection of presidential rhetoric issued over a 115-year period of rapid and substantial demographic change within the United States. When Grover Cleveland took office in 1885, for example, the nation was only beginning to absorb a dramatic influx of newcomers, with the first federal immigration restrictions still fresh on the books. By 1992 the U.S. population had more than quadrupled, and even though immigration laws had similarly multiplied, U.S. citizens still demanded even tighter prohibitions against newcomers at the twentieth century's end.[1] During this same period of time, chief executives went from having to craft solutions to the "Indian problem" to formulating ways of protecting African Americans' and other minorities' civil rights. Likewise, they also had to preside over significant changes in U.S. women's roles in society before and long after women's suffrage. How did chief executives cope with such profound American differences, and, perhaps more importantly, how did they explain these changes to their constituents?

To see how U.S. presidents have discussed such matters before national audiences, I have analyzed two of their most formal and ritualistic sets of discourse, inaugural addresses and state of the union messages, both of which provide a recurring forum in which presidents may address questions of national identity and discuss current affairs. Although some observers might argue that there is a bias in analyzing just these two genres, I would respond that this bias is itself meaningful. If we can find such an obvious mixture of inclusive and exclusive themes in these two largely epideictic and/or ritualistic types of addresses—the delivery of which becomes a historic moment when one would think that presidents would be putting on their very best faces, at least discursively—then what does that tell us? My answer is that the contradictions of Myrdal's "American Dilemma" are written clearly on the face of some of the nation's most ideal-driven texts and that they have been there throughout the twentieth century.

More specifically, my conclusion that presidents have used a civil religious rhetoric of American nationalism to promote national unity might also mean that chief executives have dealt with topics of diversity largely through rhetorical indirection. That is, they have not addressed difference outright but instead treated it in highly symbolic yet strategic ways:

- Presidents have defined American identity ideationally, explaining that the civil religion requires citizens to transcend their differences and that they can do so only by adopting a set of proper attitudes.
- Presidents have argued that newcomers must ultimately be restricted because they cannot truly understand American beliefs, thereby making America a haven for the enlightened (that is, those who are already here).
- Presidents have recommended that Native and African Americans need re-education and governmental assistance to learn American ways, thereby making citizenship achievable primarily via institutional remedies.
- Presidents have used a complex and often polysemic discourse to discuss American women's political roles, thereby situating women simultaneously within and outside of the world of American shared beliefs.

Through these modes of indirection, redirection, and hybridization, presidents have encouraged citizens to pay less attention to their diversity by using stratagems that recur with astonishing regularity from 1885 to 2000 regardless of individual leaders' party affiliations or legislative agendas. Even if the American people have expressed anxiety about diversity at various points during their history, then, their presidents have been considerably more stoic about such matters. Carefully and consistently, they have called up images of a peaceful, attitudinally homogeneous citizenry. Before speculating about whether this rhetoric can or should continue into the twenty-first century, let us briefly consider some of the possible implications of these findings for three distinct but related areas: the study of U.S. democracy, the U.S. presidency, and the critical-historical analysis of presidential rhetoric.

MAKING DIVERSITY SAFE FOR DEMOCRACY (AND VICE VERSA)

Although democracy and diversity have long been thought of as fundamentally incompatible, my reading attempted to provide insights into how and why the concept and the condition have been able to coexist within the United States. Robert Dahl has noted that classical democratic principles were originally formulated within homogeneous city-states, places where the very idea of difference was "anathema."[2] Indeed, in the centuries since democracy first spread to nation-states, the notion that ethnically, religiously, and otherwise diverse people could share political beliefs has been sorely tested. Even in the United States, as Roderick Hart has noted, pluralism has been proven to be "genuinely untidy."[3]

If, as Dahl has suggested, such messiness is merely an inevitable consequence of large-scale democratic politics, my analysis has revealed how U.S. presidents have deployed rhetoric to contain it.[4] Instead of attempting to vitiate diversity altogether, presidents have accommodated it in part by advancing a definition of national identity that demands new ways of thinking and minimizes ancient allegiances. Such rhetoric has problems, as we have seen, yet it may also have benefits. Because I have considered its weaknesses in greater detail in previous chapters, it might be fruitful to compare this overall strategy to some real-world alternatives.

U.S. presidents could have, for example, promoted a more unabashedly ethnic criterion for national identity. After all, most of the nation's founders were of northern European descent, and ethnic homogeneity was the standard for citizenship in pre-modern democracies, just as it is in some modern nation-states today. Recently, as the citizens of the former Yugoslavia struggled to establish a democratic government, they (and their leaders) chose to fight a bloody civil war rather than to acknowledge, and accept, ethnically diverse people as equal citizens. Balkan democracies, it would seem, can serve one particular lineage of people if they live in clearly demarcated, separated regions.[5] Similarly, as the people of the former Soviet Union struggle with the changes wrought by communism's fall, some politicians in Russia have argued that only those with authentic Russian roots can claim citizenship.[6] (One need not look too far back into world history to understand the danger of this type of nationalism, nor does one need to look abroad to realize that nationalist chauvinisms now thrive in parts of the United States as well.) In contrast to these examples, American presidents have emphasized a more ideational model, thereby inhibiting some of the dangerous and regressive aspects of the ethnic paradigm.

Alternatively, U.S. chief executives could have tried to deal with the citizenry's diversity by creating even more divisions. We have seen here how some presidents have, indeed, occasionally taken such a tack, implying that some citizens are superior to others, with new immigrants being perceived as "less American" than their predecessors, for example. By way of contrast, however, it may be important to recall that other democracies have embraced far more explicit distinctions. During the days of apartheid in South Africa, for example, the white upper class established a system of differentiation so strict that the majority of the population had no voice at all. Similarly, in India, where a caste system still exists, citizens cannot use their political voice to escape its rigid, historic confinements. Even in Great Britain, whose parliamentary democracy is often considered most similar to the U.S. government, social and class-based differences are so ingrained that democratically elected leaders are sometimes considered traitors for merely appearing to agree with their ideological opponents.[7] In comparison, although U.S. presidents have sometimes reinforced divisions among their constituents, they have simultaneously offered the promise that differences *can* be overcome in the United States.

Given this range of global options, then, perhaps Americans ought to be thankful for the presidential platitudes of American national identity. Insipid as such messages may seem at times, it is also the case that they reify the conception of the American people as "one public" in which participatory democracy is at least possible.[8] To be sure, over time, this one public has not really been one public at all but instead has evoked the model of the public sphere that Geoff Eley has characterized as "the structured setting where cultural and ideological contest or negotiation among a variety of publics takes place."[9]

Perhaps, then, what we have seen in this analysis is an institutionalized version of one side of this type of ongoing dialectic. Even when members of what Nancy Fraser has called "subaltern counterpublics" have challenged the prevailing idioms of national identity in the United States, chief executives have resisted this protest by clinging to their civil religious models of identity. Subaltern groups and social theorists alike may express outrage at this resistance, and it may even strike some observers as being antidemocratic. But there is no denying that democracy and diversity do seem to have coexisted less tumultuously in the United States than in other parts of the world. Perhaps this relative success can be attributed in part to the rhetorical ambivalence presidents have shown toward multiculturalism's threat to the symbolic unity of the United States.

THEORIZING THE PRESIDENCY: DIVERSITY AS AN INSTITUTIONAL CONSTRAINT

For most students of American democracy, the presidency is hard to ignore as a central mechanism of its governance. Indeed, within both political science and political communication, like-minded scholars have created a field of literature known as presidency studies. My analysis contributes directly to that literature by specifically addressing one of the ways in which we might better theorize the constraints of executive office.

Summarizing past presidential scholarship, George Edwards, John Kessel, and Bert Rockman have chronicled its development in three basic stages. First was a "wave . . . largely focused on the legal structures and the roles of the presidency," they report. In this wave scholars "saw presidential roles as responding to external conditions and thus expanding beyond strictly legal definitions."[10] Next came widespread interest in the "political psychoanalysis" of individual presidents, exemplified in James David Barber's well-known comparative study, *The Presidential Character: Predicting Performance in the White House.* A third body of work incorporated elements of the first two by focusing on the "exercise of presidential power and the operation of the White House," especially via the analysis of particular administrations.[11]

Despite these different approaches, Edwards, Kessel, and Rockman claim that presidential scholarship has yielded few theoretical contributions thus far. Most scholars, they suggest, have been so preoccupied with either purely institutional or merely individual constraints that they have not focused on larger questions. Presidential scholarship has thus been "tied either to an unchanging subject, that is, formal powers, or to an idiosyncratic one, that is, presidents."[12] To escape these tendencies, Edwards, Kessel, and Rockman recommend that future thinkers be "guided by some larger theoretical concerns and include systematically gathered data."[13]

But perhaps presidential scholarship seems atheoretical not because it overestimates the constraints facing a president but because previous thinkers have *underestimated* the constraints, thereby obscuring the larger universe of forces bearing down on the office and its individual officeholders. Specifically, most observers have failed to notice that presidents are constrained not only by material and political factors but also by cultural, symbolic, and rhetorical ones.

Presidents inherit both problems and policies from their predecessors, and these inheritances establish parameters that, along with constitutional provisions and congressional assistance, dictate much of what a chief executive can or cannot do. Yet presidents' actions are also constrained by what they can and cannot *say*. As we have seen here, these options can be greatly compromised by cultural logics, by the facts of history, and, of course, by public opinion. This reading of the presidency has suggested that, due to such forces, chief executives often do not have power over their own words. We have seen how this situation has developed vis-à-vis diversity, but the same could be said for other topics as well. Perhaps presidents are similarly trapped into deploying logics of indirection when discussing the national economy, for example, or foreign affairs.[14] To formulate more comprehensive theories of presidential agency, we might seek to learn more about the ineffable but no less ideological conditions that influence presidents' decisions and, over time, affect the institution itself.

To be clear, I am not advocating here a return to psychobiographical studies. I agree with Edwards et al. that the focus on individual character does not necessarily advance an understanding of the presidency's more enduring dilemmas. Indeed, to understand chief executives' rhetorical choices in this study, I have viewed specific presidents less as individuals than as vessels for the cultural logics of their day as well as the institutional constraints placed on their public discourse. Although presidential speech is clearly more than simply a barometer of public opinion, it provides a unique opportunity to learn about the ongoing negotiation between leaders and those they lead.[15]

This book has shown, for example, how the public can "write" the presidency, not merely by voting for one candidate rather than another, but also by predetermining its leaders' rhetorical choices. During the late 1800s and the early 1900s, for instance, widespread public outrage forced presidents to talk about immigration restrictions, a topic they had consistently avoided at other times even though immigration has been a constant force in U.S. history. *How* they could speak about it, however, was constrained by the fact that many of their constituents came from foreign soil themselves. Not surprisingly, then, chief executives routinely chose to talk about the dangers of new immigrants with their "suspicious" mindsets, rooted merely in "foreignness" rather than any specific ethnic culture.

We have also seen how presidents have tried to "write" or construct the citizenry in specific ways. While they have usually promoted inclusion by explaining American identity as ideational, at times they have implied that even ideational identities are not equally available to all, thereby contributing to the perception that the "real" American people are somehow nonethnic and/or nonracial. This latter assumption still thrives in several arenas: among racist groups, most obviously, but also in contemporary political discourse (as in would-be presidential candidate Patrick Buchanan's 1992 call to "take back our cities, take back our culture, take back our country" from, presumably, minorities) and even in academic fields, where "ethnic studies" typically cover only non-Caucasian groups, which suggests that northern European ancestry precludes ethnicity.

While it is important to recognize the consequences of these cultural negotiations, we must also realize that the symbolic transaction between leader and led is extremely complex. It has no clear beginning or end, meaning that analyses like this one must always have somewhat arbitrary parameters. As complicated as this interplay is in American politics, a rhetorical perspective offers one of the best vantage points for viewing it since a modern democracy functions with the support of powerful symbols.

Likewise, presidential rhetoric is situated discourse. In addition to responding directly to immediate exigencies, it occurs within an established institutional tradition, meaning that observers can "map" both changes and continuities in presidential arguments across time. Scholars seeking more complete theories of the presidency's enduring features may want to pay closer attention to these long-term patterns. They show how presidents have used the rhetorical resources available to them, as we have seen, but they also show how these same rhetorics have "used" presidents, a possibility with implications for the study of political communication.

PRESIDENTIAL RHETORIC AND QUESTIONS
OF INDIVIDUAL AGENCY

One of the goals of this analysis has been to suggest that, in some senses at least, presidential rhetoric may vary little from president to president. Although I have largely relied on modernist assumptions and methodologies in undertaking this reading, the conclusion that presidential rhetoric may not be all that individualized evokes some postmodern notions, especially those associated with the work of Jacques Derrida and Michel Foucault. These thinkers have suggested, among other things, that human symbol-use is never a purely expressive act. All symbols are loaded symbols, they have said, imprinted both by their past usage, with Derridean "traces" revealing the "logic of repeated inscription without simple origin," according to Peggy Kamuf, and by their past users, with Foucault's genealogical methods inviting us to uncover their ideological histories.[16]

These insights would seem especially suited to the study of presidential rhetoric, but so far most scholars interested in traditional studies of elite discourse have been reluctant to embrace them. While some scholars may reject such insights on philosophical or political grounds (for being overly relativistic or nihilistic, for example), there may be additional reasons for such inattention. Rhetorical critics, for example, may have avoided this model because it undermines their historical focus on a speaker's agency. Most such scholars continue to mount investigations based on either implicitly Aristotelian or literary models of discourse in order to privilege a speaker's (authorial) intent, motive, or historical consequence. They may study rhetoric in order to understand its effects (e.g., Did Robert Kennedy's speech keep mourners from rioting after Martin Luther King, Jr.'s death?) or its organic composition (e.g., What devices did King use in his "I Have a Dream" speech?). Even the sparsely attended Coatesville Address should be studied, Edwin Black argued long ago, so that readers might understand the speaker's inventional choices.[17] In any of these cases, rhetoric is perceived as the means through which a speaker creates something or purposefully contributes to an ongoing cultural dialectic. So popular is this paradigm that even the often incompatible public address scholars and ideological critics continue to follow its assumptions today.

This study also began with such beliefs. My initial question ("How have presidents constructed American national identity?") supposed that presidents must respond to their constituency's diversity as they would to any other rhetorical situation: by choosing to say certain things to certain audiences faced with certain exigencies.[18] Like all speakers in a democracy, chief executives are assumed to have a seemingly unending array of responses available to them, with presidents' additional powers and resources making their final decisions especially noteworthy. Given this model of invention, we would have expected to find wildly divergent approaches to diversity. "Silent Cal" Coolidge might have responded with few words, for example, while Franklin Roosevelt might have been expected to detail specific programs to combat prejudice.

Repeatedly throughout this analysis, however, I found evidence that presidents do *not* have unlimited rhetorical options. Despite their individual skills, constraints, and preferences—the same variables studied ad infinitum by most students of public address—presidential responses to diversity have been surprisingly uniform. This repetition may itself be strategic, as I have already discussed, but it may also be that presidents' rhetorical strategies do not reflect purely idiosyncratic choices.

Why might this be the case? Ideological critics may suggest structural answers. Discourse is heavily influenced by economics, gender, or other transcendent conditions of the context in which it is produced, they might argue.[19] While these explanations certainly account for many discursive tendencies, the insights offered by poststructural theorists such as Derrida and Foucault also provide additional clues. The production of meaning is so complex, they suggest, that it cannot be adequately understood as the result of structural forces or the choices of an individual speaker. For them, the creation of meaning is more likely to occur in the more ambiguous middle spaces between structures and agents, where other, less obvious forces may intervene as well. Rather than being viewed as an unlimited, renewable resource speakers can use to get things done, rhetoric is, from this perspective, an ancient map, somehow always and already present, revealing the paths of past users, paths that are dug deep enough to limit future travelers' options.

To gain a fuller understanding of why and how presidential rhetoric works, then, we may need more complete views of this map. Because speech is a human and ephemeral activity, its avenues often seem arbitrary, making it important to know about an individual speaker's actions. But we also need longitudinal and comparative studies to see why alternative routes are so rarely taken. The need for comparative studies of elite discourses is especially acute because they are presumed to serve the interests of the state over time. In addition to facilitating our understanding of the presidency, such long-term views provide insights into the slow mutations or maintenance of official logics as well as the cultural, ideological, and other factors forging their expression.

This investigation has provided one model for how this work might be done. Throughout this analysis I have not ignored the historical circumstances of past speeches altogether, nor have I completely overlooked the interests of specific speakers. Yet I have tried to limit such discussions in order to emphasize an alternative, "aerial" view of this discursive landscape. More specifically, I have tried to show how a longitudinal view might be used to examine how cultural meanings are reproduced over time. In this case, we have seen how the American people's diversity has affected the individual styles of white male orators by, ironically, limiting the ways in which they can speak of American national identity.

To study the impact of diversity on political communication in the United States, we need not confine ourselves to speeches given by members of historically neglected groups. We can also listen to the words of "dead white males," but we must do so in new and different ways, including some that incorporate postmodern impulses into otherwise traditional analyses. While postmodernism may not easily translate into a politics, it can help us understand how discursive strategies from the past can affect rhetorical choices and, ultimately, political realities.

To promote such an enterprise, there must be a great deal of additional work. Future studies, for example, might look for other situations or topics on which presidential responses have been curiously limited. One could also investigate other institutional commentaries on American diversity. How, for example, have the mass media influenced or responded to presidential messages on difference? Have television shows or other forms of popular culture supported the ideational definition of American citizenship? If not, what models of identity and/or diversity have they implicitly embraced? Similarly, one could extend the time line used here to examine more closely how these cultural definitions developed earlier in American history. Are they related to British conceptions of citizenship popular in colonial times?[20] How did the first U.S. presidents explain American citizenship and/or promote tolerance in a nation still being conceived?

While this last type of study might help us better understand the symbolic parameters that seem to have guided presidential talk for the past one hundred or so years, there is also a bit of evidence that one recent president may have tried to strike out in a slightly new direction. To conclude this chapter, I discuss Bill Clinton's first inaugural address, which may have contained some challenges to the status quo in presidential discourse and offered a vision of how national community might be both imagined and achieved in the future.

THE FUTURE OF THE RHETORIC OF SHARED BELIEFS

Given my charge that past scholars have overemphasized rhetorical agency, the suggestion that Bill Clinton somehow single-handedly broke with rhetorical tradition might seem odd. If Clinton's first inaugural speech does represent a significant change from its forebears, such a shift would presumably not be the result of the president's choices alone but would reflect a shift in the national zeitgeist. Before looking more closely at what Clinton said in January,

1993, let us consider why he might have been inclined to reject past arguments about American identity.

Karlyn Kohrs Campbell and Kathleen Jamieson have noted that, in addition to an inaugural address's obviously epideictic functions, the speech also gives presidents a forum to "set forth the political principles that will govern the new administration."[21] While presidents typically do not detail specific policies in these speeches, they may use the occasion to review the broad issues they hope to address while in office. Individual presidents may consider several different factors when deciding how to do so, including how urgent a particular item may seem or how much of a mandate a president has when addressing these issues.[22] At some level, though, presidents *must* discuss the nation's problems and their solutions in these speeches.[23]

By the time Bill Clinton assumed the presidency, however, he could not discuss the same problems his predecessors had confronted. Chief executives from Cleveland to Bush had repeatedly implied that the nation's most pressing threats came from *outside* the citizenry, including both foreign nations and foreign ideologies (e.g., communism). During his inaugural address, for example, Woodrow Wilson asked the American people for "tolerance . . . and your united aid" as the nation entered World War I, just as Richard Nixon later asked Americans to unite to "[help] make the world safe for mankind" in an age of nuclear rivalry. Even George H. W. Bush, celebrating the democratic "new breezes" blowing throughout the world, warned that the United States must still "stay strong and protect the peace" against those who would stifle it.[24]

Even when these presidents spoke of domestic problems, their expressed adversaries were frequently impersonal, structural forces (including economics) that could still be portrayed as external agencies. In his 1889 inaugural address, for example, instead of discussing the lingering, divisive problems of the Civil War, Benjamin Harrison spoke of them as financial dilemmas that could be solved through protective tariffs.[25] Almost one hundred years later, Ronald Reagan also made a financial argument when he vowed to lead the fight against an "economic affliction of great proportions." Reagan asked the citizenry to participate in this crusade in much the same way young Martin Treptow had helped his country during World War I. The president explained:

> [Treptow] was killed trying to carry a message between battalions under heavy
> artillery fire. We're told that on his body was found a diary. On the flyleaf under
> the heading, "My Pledge," he had written these words: "America must win this

war. Therefore I will work, I will save, I will sacrifice, I will endure, I will fight cheerfully and do my utmost, as if the issue of the whole struggle depended on me alone." The crisis we are facing today does not require of us the kind of sacrifice that Martin Treptow and so many thousands of others were called upon to make. It does require, however, our best effort and our willingness to believe in ourselves and to believe in our capacity to perform great deeds, to believe that together with God's help we can and will resolve the problems which now confront us.[26]

Although he was not asking for the same kinds of sacrifices made by Treptow and his generation, Reagan urged his constituents to become warriors none-theless, directing their collective attention toward a common cause. (Although the enemy's exact nature is unclear in this passage, elsewhere in the speech Reagan names "government [as] the problem.")[27] Like previous presidents, Reagan gave the American people an external "Other" against which to unite, a dangerous enemy whose threats made their internal differences comparatively insignificant.

If this "Other" was the problem, belief in American ideals was Reagan's solution. This solution was the same one, of course, offered most commonly by presidents from 1885 to 1992, as we have seen. If all citizens would simply unite in shared beliefs, by "[believing] in ourselves" and "[believing] in our capacity to perform great deeds," then all other problems would be inconse-quential, Reagan suggested. Indeed, even though the problems Reagan spoke of here "[threatened] to shatter the lives of millions of our people," the presi-dent pledged that such problems "could be solved through faith and a can-do attitude." "And after all, why shouldn't we believe that?" Reagan concluded. "We are Americans."[28]

When Bill Clinton took the presidential oath, however, the American people did not appear to agree on what being an American meant. They had no real or imagined foreign foes against which to rally. The Cold War was over, the Berlin Wall had been torn down, and all other vital signs of communism seemed dead as well. Even the economy seemed better—far better, in fact, than it had been the last time a Democrat had been elected president. Simi-larly, the more recent problems cited by Ronald Reagan appeared to be on their way to resolution. With little certainty about who or what their mutual enemies might be, the American people appeared less confidant about what they had in common. Indeed, many seemed convinced that their main adver-saries were their fellow citizens.

Despite signs of a general economic upturn in 1993, there was widespread dissatisfaction and fear among the "middle class" and the "working poor," terms characterizing only some of the distinct "types" of Americans eager to voice their mounting frustrations. Likewise, many citizens were deeply worried about civil rights. The previous year's trial of Los Angeles police officers accused of beating Rodney King and the riots that ensued renewed widespread doubts about the possibility of racial harmony in the United States.

In addition to Americans being separated along economic and racial lines, new divisions were coming to the fore in the early 1990s. In Colorado, for example, after state courts barred homosexuals from suing for discrimination in 1992, gay rights groups and supporters intensified their national political initiatives. A year earlier, Senate hearings on charges of sexual harassment against a Supreme Court nominee had brought issues of race, gender, *and* class to the front pages of national newspapers and into daily conversations. Even as these specific events and their divisive effects were unfolding, antipathies toward immigration were increasing, as were worries about the North American Free Trade Agreement (NAFTA) and other foreign trade policies. During the two years leading up to Clinton's bid for the presidency, then, very practical problems of diversity figured prominently on the national scene.

One person who seemed particularly unnerved by such matters was the incumbent president, George H. W. Bush. Despite his considerable political experience and foreign policy successes, Bush often had trouble portraying himself as sensitive to the American people's diverse needs. Even his own campaign's efforts to present him as a "regular guy" could not overcome his background of blue-blooded, old-monied privilege. Bush had played baseball in his youth but had done so at Yale University, a bastion of all-white secret societies and Puritan sobriety. Bush listened to country music and ate pork rinds, true, but he allegedly had never seen a grocery store scanner. The president even had a "mixed marriage" in his immediate family, but he spoke of its results, his own grandchildren, as "the little brown ones."

As one might expect, Bush's less patrician Democratic challenger in the 1992 race directed much of his rhetorical energy toward matters of diversity. Candidate Clinton repeatedly promised to make "government look more like America," presumably by filling the cabinet and other advisory positions with people from diverse backgrounds. Policy-wise, he pledged support for homosexuals in the military and seemed genuinely supportive of women (although his later impeachment revealed a darker side to his relationships with women). Clinton also suggested that his administration would protect affirmative action programs. When campaigning, Clinton eagerly embraced matters of diversity, radiating as much empathy as he could to as many different types of citizens as he could find. No matter what one's past background or current problems, this candidate wanted voters to know that he could "feel their pain."

Given this historical and cultural context, it makes considerable sense that the new president's inaugural address might differ from previous ones. If Clinton were going to fulfill even some of the campaign promises he had made, he would have to both acknowledge and affirm the American people's differences rather than avoid such matters, as his predecessors had. Such prior avoidance made a certain amount of sense, of course, when a new chief executive was expected to denounce civic disharmonies and "reconstitute the people" as a single entity. So how could Clinton make his address sound appropriately presidential, resonating with "epideictic timelessness," while also showing he was a leader suited for a time-of-difference?[29]

Clinton met such challenges by arguing that the American people needed a new way of thinking to guide them into the next century. They were gathered, after all, "at the edge of the twenty-first century," as he noted early in these remarks. It is not uncommon, of course, for new presidents to note the uniquely historic circumstances of their inaugurations, nor is it unusual for them to talk about the challenges of the day. But rather than just outlining his guiding principles or general goals, Clinton argued that the American people themselves needed to face this new day's demands. "Powerful and profound forces are shaking and remaking our world," he explained, "and the urgent question of our time is whether we can make change our friend and not our enemy."[30]

What needed changing, Clinton suggested, was not national policy nor the American people's attitude, which he praised as being ever "restless, questing, [and] hopeful."[31] Instead, there needed to be a change in the things that the American people felt "restless, questing, [and] hopeful" about. That is, while his predecessors had routinely asked their audiences to renew their commitment to traditional American values, Mr. Clinton asked his audience to reconsider the ways in which they put these values into practice.

To be clear, the new president took no radical position his first day in office. He did not ask his audience to burn flags, repudiate capitalism, or renounce their religious beliefs. He did, however, subtly suggest that it was time for the American people to reconsider their civil religious faith and its implications for mass citizenship.

Presidents have incorporated the civil religion into their discussions of citizenship for centuries, as we have already seen. American citizens have believed that they are "God's chosen people," blessed with unique gifts and burdened with moral and global responsibilities. This definition has encouraged the American people to overlook their more earthy differences, as I have also argued, and to see American identity as both ideational and enduring. To speak differently about difference, then, Bill Clinton would have to somehow challenge this rhetorical behemoth.

Before he could guide the American people through such a major shift, however, Clinton needed motivating material. He supplied this motivation by subtly questioning the civil religion's basic premise—that the United States necessarily holds a special place in the world. Instead of assuring the American people that they were uniquely blessed by the Creator, Clinton admitted that the United States was just as vulnerable as other countries to the "ancient hatreds and new plagues" spreading rapidly over the earth. Indeed, according to the president, the nation might be even *more* susceptible to such ills after the Cold War.[32]

Previous presidents, the reader will recall, had told the American people that they were immune to such atavistic impulses. They argued that God, who had "at all times been revealed in our country's history," had protected his chosen people by imbuing them with a special disposition of rational detachment from the rest of the world's tribalisms.[33] Likewise, many chief executives had said that God had charged the American people with advancing this principled restraint around the world, thereby, in George H. W. Bush's words, "mak[ing] kinder the face of the Nation and gentler the face of the World." "America is never wholly herself," Bush explained, "unless she is engaged in high moral principle."[34]

In Clinton's first inaugural, however, such shared beliefs were portrayed as luxuries rather than national priorities. To be clear, I am not claiming that he abandoned the civil religion altogether; he began his speech by retelling the founders' declaration of "our purposes to the Almighty" and ended it, as most presidents do, by asking for God's help. But when he spoke of the values that the American people were assumed to share, President Clinton also implied that such supernatural favor alone was insufficient insurance in the new world. Things had changed greatly since the founders' days, he implied, and his constituents were far less concerned about global missions than "an economy that is still the world's strongest but is weakened by business failures, stagnant wages, increasing inequality, and deep divisions among our own people." These fears, combined with new technologies, had perhaps diminished the American people's capacity for principled restraint, Clinton suggested: "When George Washington first took the oath I have just sworn to uphold, news traveled slowly across the land by horseback and across the ocean by boat. Now, the sights and sounds of this ceremony are broadcast instantaneously to billions around the world. Communications and commerce are global. Investment is mobile. Technology is almost magical. And ambition for a better life is now universal."[35] Although the American people's "ambition for a better life" might seem to be evidence of national successes, Clinton went on to treat this yearning as something of a threat to the American people. Such striving was no longer the spiritual hallmark of the American people alone, he seemed to warn, but a driving force behind international economic competition as well. U.S. citizens would now have to compete for their rewards, not merely receive them as a God-given birthright.

According to Clinton, then, the current intensity of global competition was forcing Americans to reconsider their beliefs, some of which had become obsolete. "There is no longer a clear division between what is foreign and what is domestic," the president explained: "The world economy, the world environment, the world AIDS crisis, the world arms race: they affect us all. Today, as an older order passes, the new world is more free but less stable. Communism's collapse has called forth old animosities and new dangers. Clearly, America must continue to lead the world we did so much to make."[36] Even in calling for America to lead the world, a prototypical civil religious plea, Clinton warned his listeners against overconfidence. The days when the United States "[made] the world" are over, he argued.

In addition to urging the American people to reconsider their country's global positioning, the president asked them to view themselves anew. As I argued in chapter 2, one of the most significant benefits of civil religious rhetoric has been its usefulness for promoting zealous yet ideational definitions of national identity in the United States. Citizenship has allegedly been available to anyone willing to accept these ideals. Once accepted into the community of believers, this logic continues, a citizen's main obligations can become highly individualistic. Citizens should support American ideals, for example, but keep to themselves while other, newer citizens struggle to learn American ways, a message we saw repeatedly in presidential rhetoric on the inclusion of Native and African Americans. In urging citizens to overlook difference, then, civil religious models of citizenship also prompt the American people to see diversity as either someone else's problem or as an affliction that must be purged.

Clinton criticized this model of disengagement. In a clearly interventionist mode, the president detailed the negative consequences of avoiding issues of diversity:

This new world has already enriched the lives of millions of Americans who are able to compete and win in it. But when most people are working harder for less, when others cannot work at all, when the cost of health care devastates families and threatens to bankrupt our enterprises, great and small, when the fear of crime robs law-abiding citizens of their freedom, and when millions of poor children cannot even imagine the lives we are calling them to lead, we have not made change our friend. We know we have to face hard truths and take strong steps, but we have not done so; instead we have drifted.[37]

After years of being ignored, Clinton implied, the facts of the United States' demographic diversity had grown into debilitating American anxieties. Fears about international trade competition, economic stratification, insufficient health care, and skyrocketing crime and poverty rates had conspired to produce problems. All of these vicissitudes were associated with the increasing socioeconomic diversification of the American people, Clinton implies, the same "hard truths" the American people had been loath to face. As these problems grew, the nation's inattention to them had "eroded our resources, fractured our economy and [has] shaken our confidence," the new president observed.[38] Without yet mentioning the word "diversity," Clinton suggested that the citizenry's past blindness to its own differences had seriously crippled the nation's strength.

To "renew America," Clinton continued, the citizenry must reject these old ideas and adopt new ones. Specifically, they must become more self-reliant, acknowledging their differences as well as their mutual responsibilities. "We must be bold," Clinton warned, "[and] it will not be easy," but the American people have no choice if their nation is to succeed in the next century: "It will require sacrifice, but it can be done fairly, not choosing sacrifice for its own sake, but for our own sake. We must provide for our Nation the way a family provides for its children. . . . We must do what America does best: offer more opportunity to all and demand more responsibility from all. It is time to break the bad habit of expecting something for nothing from our Government or from each other. Let us all take more responsibility not only for ourselves and our families but for our communities and our country."[39]

The idea of citizen responsibility is hardly new, of course, but by associating it with the conscious rejection of previous models of national identity, Clinton infused his talk with a new urgency. Lyndon Johnson, for example, had also called for the American people to "[work] shoulder to shoulder" to cure their own ills, but he had also said that "our destiny in the midst of change will rest on the *unchanged character of our people and their faith"* (emphasis added).[40] Bill Clinton, in contrast, called for the American people to change both their character and their faith by addressing long-ignored "truths" about themselves. Their collective character *had* changed, Clinton argued, and it was time to acknowledge it. No longer, for example, could the nation's citizens expect the government to manage its "minority problems." The rest of the nation would have to attend to such matters as well, Clinton implied.

Clinton also rejected an alternative, more conservative model of shared citizen responsibilities. As I have previously discussed, Ronald Reagan had argued in his first inaugural address, for example, that the American people must all "bear the burden" of their troubles, but he also argued that such sharing was evidence that all Americans were essentially the same:

> The solutions we seek must be equitable, with no one group singled out to pay a higher price. We hear much of special interest groups. Well, our concern must be for a special interest group that has been too long neglected. It knows no sectional boundaries or ethnic and racial lines. It is made up of men and women who raise our food, patrol our streets, man our mines and factories, teach our children, and heal us when we're sick—professionals, industrialists, shopkeepers, clerks, cabbies, and truck-drivers. They are, in short, "We the people," this breed called Americans.[41]

Like Reagan's speech, Clinton's implied that constituents were all quite "American," but that did not mean they had the same needs or resources. Indeed, when Clinton invoked the magnanimous "idea of America" in his first inaugural address, he did so to make the point that it must be "tempered by the knowledge that, but for fate, we, the fortunate, and the unfortunate might have been each other."[42] Clinton did not reduce all Americans to a single class, to be sure, but he did make the rather paradoxical argument that the people's differences would not make them less united. Indeed, they would make themselves even stronger if they acknowledged their own diversity.

Under his watch, the new president implied, the long-ignored facts of American difference would be addressed outright. Individuals would be responsible not only for themselves but also for each other. Americans need not abandon their shared beliefs altogether to accept this new logic, for all their actions should be guided by an overarching belief that "our Nation can summon from its myriad diversity the deepest measures of unity."[43] This faith was, in fact, the foundation of the American people's "new covenant," Clinton's label for his different but no less spiritual way of thinking about American national identity. Using this interactive metaphor, Clinton challenged the old ideational model of citizenship in which patriotism is expressed by shared beliefs, and thus decidedly intellectual criteria, with one that championed commitment, candor, responsibility, and, most importantly, *behavioral* action. "My fellow Americans, you, too, must play your part in our renewal. . . . In serving we recognize a simple but powerful truth: We need each other, and we must care for one another," the president implored. Through their works as well as their faith, then, American citizens would ensure that the nation could continue its "long, heroic journey" to "go forever upward."[44]

As heard on that January morning in 1993, Clinton's first inaugural address may not have sounded like a major departure from those of his predecessors. He did, in fact, meet all of the generic requirements of this occasion, making his speech sound conventional enough even to well-informed listeners. Indeed, some commentators have suggested that Clinton's words were too traditional, while others have labeled the speech "contemplative" and even "flat." "One combs the address in vain," Halford Ryan laments, "for hints of political principles or for ways to right the wrongs that Clinton had excoriated in the 1992 campaign."[45]

I disagree. There is evidence here that Clinton offered hints of both new political principles and solutions in this speech. The new president may not have provided a detailed list of policy innovations, but he did something subtle and significant nonetheless. He rejected the old model of a national union based solely on shared beliefs because it was inattentive to difference, and he introduced a new, more ecumenical model that defined American national identity in terms of relational, not solely ideational, criteria. This latter shift enabled him to end the long-standing presidential silence on the merits of American diversity and argue that facing its "truths" was a necessary step in strengthening the nation.

Even after Clinton's presidency, it is still hard to tell how successful he was at promoting a new "idea of America" that could better accommodate diversity. Speaking candidly about difference is not inherently good; the Ku Klux Klan, for example, has been nothing if not forthcoming about its views. Nevertheless, Clinton continued to recommend such frankness throughout his presidency. Speaking in Austin, Texas, on October 16, 1995, the same day that Louis Farrakhan held the Million Man March in Washington, D.C., the president acknowledged the country's deep racial divisions, warning that "the rift we see before us is tearing at the heart of America." There were many reasons for this split, he argued: "Some are rooted in the awful history and stubborn persistence of racism. Some are rooted in the different ways we experience the threats of modern life to personal security, family values, and strong communities. Some are rooted in the fact that we still haven't learned to talk frankly, to listen carefully, and to work together across racial lines."[46] To change this last condition, which is the only condition individual citizens could in fact change, the American people would have to make a decision:

> Today we face a choice—one way leads to further separation and bitterness and more lost futures. The other way, the path of courage and wisdom, leads to unity, to reconciliation, and a rich opportunity for all Americans to make the most out of the lives God gave them. This moment in which the racial divide is so clearly out in the open need not be a setback for us. It presents us with a great opportunity, and we dare not let it pass us by. . . . Abraham Lincoln reminded us that a house divided against itself cannot stand. When divisions have threatened to bring our house down, somehow we have always moved together to shore it up. My fellow Americans, our house is the greatest democracy in human history. And with its racial and ethnic diversity, it has beaten the odds of human history. But we know that divisions remain, and we still have work to do. The two worlds we now see each contain both truths and distortions. Both black and white Americans must face this, for honesty is the only gateway to the many acts of reconciliation that will unite our worlds at last into one America.[47]

The "path of courage and wisdom" that this president advocated, the one that would lead to a united and reconciled America, was paved with talk, with honest, direct conversation about the American people's differences:

> Today I ask every governor, every mayor, every business leader, every church leader, every civic leader, every union steward, every student leader—most importantly, every citizen—in every workplace and learning place and meeting place all across America to take personal responsibility for reaching out to people of different races; for taking time to sit down and talk through this issue; to have the courage to speak honestly and frankly; and then to have the discipline to listen quietly with an open mind and an open heart, as others do the same.[48]

For the American people to "clean our house of racism," Clinton reiterated in his closing remarks, he would "do [his] part, but you, my fellow citizens, must do yours."[49]

No matter how impassioned or overdue this presidential charge may have been, Clinton was correct when suggesting that presidents alone could not eliminate the discontents of diversity and craft a more inclusive rhetoric of American nationalism than the one we have seen here. Indeed, events in both the 1996 and the 2000 presidential campaigns suggested that voters are increasingly demanding such forthrightness, meaning that future presidents would have little choice but to confront such matters directly. In 1996, for example, Republican nominee Bob Dole was harshly criticized for refusing to speak to NAACP members in July. He later told convention-goers at the National Association of Black Journalists' annual meeting in August that he was "sorry about that" and that he was now going to try harder than ever to "earn" the black vote. "I deeply believe that the Republican Party will never be whole until it earns the broad support of African Americans and others by speaking to their hopes," Dole announced. And while he "wouldn't profess to know" African Americans' problems, the candidate explained that because he himself was "a member of a minority group called the disabled," he would fight for a "simple vision for America" in which "equality of opportunity" was guaranteed for all.[50] Four years later at the Republican National Convention in 2000, featured speaker Colin Powell would recite almost exactly these words in an effort to convince the nation that his party's candidate, George W. Bush, cared about diversity too.

In 1996 or 2000, few observers were presumably surprised to hear presidents, and especially presidential candidates, make such pledges. After all, the cynic would argue, political figures will always tell voters what they want to hear. For better or worse, then, the people that Ronald Reagan invoked as "this breed called Americans" will ultimately have to decide which vision of democratic political community will prevail from one century into the next. The American people can choose to seek new types of talk—and the future leaders to speak it—that help them imagine themselves as being both diverse and united. Or they can reaffirm their support of tradition by electing leaders who espouse the shared beliefs hypothesis that has historically promoted national unity even as it has excluded certain types of people.

This latter option is certainly consistent with the contradiction between "American Creed" and "American Deeds" that so perplexed Gunnar Myrdal and countless other observers. My analysis suggests that presidential rhetoric is uniquely equipped to facilitate and even promote this contradiction. Yet presidential rhetoric is also ultimately democratic rhetoric. When the American people start trying to work out this contradiction, perhaps their chief executives will have little choice but to follow.

Notes

INTRODUCTION: PRESIDENTIAL RHETORIC AND THE CHALLENGE OF A DIVERSE DEMOCRACY

1. See McGee, "In Search of 'The People.'"
2. Anderson, *Imagined Communities*, 6.
3. Walzer, *What It Means to Be an American*, 6–7.
4. Ibid.
5. George W. Bush, "Special Address to a Joint Session of Congress and the American People," Sept. 20, 2001, available online at www.whitehouse.gov/news/releases/2001/09/20010920-8.html.
6. See Hargrove, *The President as Leader*.
7. See Wills, *Lincoln at Gettysburg*.
8. Lerner, *America as a Civilization*, 77–79.
9. Smith, *Civic Ideals*, 6.
10. Gellner, *Culture, Identity, and Politics*, 9.
11. Charland, "Constitutive Rhetoric," 134.
12. See McGee, "In Search of 'The People.'"
13. Charland, "Constitutive Rhetoric," 134.
14. Ibid., 147.
15. Bakhtin, *Speech Genres and Other Late Essays*, 65.
16. Geertz, *The Interpretation of Cultures*, 11.
17. Williams, *The Sociology of Culture*, 12.
18. Campbell and Jamieson, *Deeds Done in Words*, 6–7.
19. See Hart, "The Functions of Human Communication in the Maintenance of Human Values."
20. Sorensen, *Kennedy*, 245.
21. Campbell and Jamieson, *Deeds Done in Words*, 14.
22. Campbell and Jamieson, "Inaugurating the Presidency," 203.
23. Campbell and Jamieson, *Deeds Done in Words*, 54.
24. Ibid., 53.
25. Ibid., 52–53.
26. Ibid., 52.
27. See Anderson, *Imagined Communities*, 37–46.
28. See Black, "The Second Persona," and Wander, "The Ideological Turn in Rhetorical Theory."

29. In Garth Pauley's *The Modern Presidency and Civil Rights,* for example, the author traces the development and aftermath of four such occasions: Harry Truman's address to the NAACP on June 29, 1947; Dwight Eisenhower's national address on Sept. 24, 1957; John F. Kennedy's speech of June 11, 1963; and Lyndon Johnson's voting rights message of March 15, 1965. Similar scholarship includes Mary L. Dudziak's *Cold War Civil Rights,* Russell L. Riley's *The Presidency and the Politics of Racial Inequality,* and Kenneth O'Reilly's *Nixon's Piano.*

30. In this statement I am obviously omitting longitudinal accounts from other fields, including Riley's *The Presidency and the Politics of Racial Inequality* and O'Reilly's *Nixon's Piano,* as mentioned in note 29.

31. See, for example, James A. Morone's "The Struggle for American Culture."

32. Anderson, *Imagined Communities,* 9–36.

33. Ibid., 30. Anderson illustrates this state-fostered national imagination with a provocative analysis of both European and Indonesian texts of this period.

34. Anderson, *Imagined Communities,* 36.

35. Ibid., 43.

36. Ibid., 47.

37. Ibid., 63.

38. Ibid., 59.

39. Kraut, *The Huddled Masses,* 20–21.

40. Tulis, *The Rhetorical Presidency,* 18.

41. Kraut, *The Huddled Masses,* 20–21.

42. Tulis, *The Rhetorical Presidency,* 110–11, 117–24.

43. Ibid., 112–14, 128.

44. Ibid., 125.

45. Woodrow Wilson, "Leaderless Government," address before the Virginia Bar Association, Aug. 4, 1897, in Ray Stannard Baker and William E. Dodd, eds., *The Public Papers of Woodrow Wilson,* vol. 1, *College and State* (New York: Harper and Brothers, 1925), 339, cited in Tulis, *The Rhetorical Presidency,* 117.

46. Kernell, *Going Public,* viii.

47. Fisher, "Rhetorical Fiction and the Presidency," 120.

48. Elshtain, "Democracy and the Politics of Difference," 9.

49. Dahl, *Democracy and Its Critics,* 1.

50. Ibid., 235.

CHAPTER 1. THE RIDDLE OF THE "AMERICAN PEOPLE"

1. Myrdal, *An American Dilemma,* 3.

2. Myrdal quoted in Southern, *Gunnar Myrdal and Black-White Relations,* 8.

3. Fuchs, *The American Kaleidoscope,* 154.

4. Perlmutter, *Divided We Fall,* 36.

5. Ibid., 238.

6. Myrdal, *An American Dilemma,* 3.

7. See, for example, Henry Steele Commager's *The Search for a Usable Past* and Luther S. Luedtke's introduction to *Making America.*

8. See, for example, Arthur M. Schlesinger, Jr.'s *The Disuniting of America* and Michael Novak's *Unmeltable Ethnics.*

9. See Southern, *Gunnar Myrdal and Black-White Relations.*

10. See Smith, *Civic Ideals;* Foner, ed., *The New American History;* and Thelen and Hoxie, eds., *Discovering America.*

11. See Morone, "The Struggle for American Culture."

12. David Southern notes that many of Myrdal's colleagues tried to discourage him from such an "optimistic perception of social reform" necessitated by the American creed. Sociologist Donald Young "argued constantly with him," Southern writes, "about the efficacy of the Creed. Myrdal asserted that if the discrepancy between the creed and the deed were exposed, it would die like a germ in powerful sunlight. Young parried with the idea that a strong creed on sexual behavior existed, and yet it failed to stop thousands from going out on the town on Saturday night" (Southern, *Gunnar Myrdal and Black-White Relations,* 33–34).

13. Myrdal quoted in Hargrove, *The President as Leader,* 22.

14. Bercovitch, "The Rites of Assent," 6.

15. Tracing the recurrence of this presumption within scholarly literature reveals how central some level of ideological, attitudinal, or even psychological agreement within the citizenry has been to most accounts of American nationalism. For an excellent and more complete intellectual history of this literature, see Luedtke, *Making America.*

16. St. John de Crevecouer, "Letter III: What Is an American?," 44.

17. Tocqueville, *Democracy in America,* 509; Morone, "The Struggle for American Culture," 425.

18. Gleason, "American Identity and Americanization," 62–63.

19. See, for example, Bernard Bailyn's *The Ideological Origins of the American Revolution.*

20. Lipset, *American Exceptionalism,* 18.

21. Bryce quoted in Mann, *The One and the Many,* 46.

22. Mann, *The One and the Many,* 47.

23. Welter, "On Studying the National Mind," 66.

24. Commager, *The Search for a Usable Past,* 183.

25. Lind, *The Next American Nation,* 364.

26. See, for example, Perry Miller's *Nature's Nation.*

27. Bellah, *The Broken Covenant,* 6.

28. Ibid., 12.

29. Winthrop quoted in Bellah, *The Broken Covenant,* 12.

30. Bercovitch, "The Rites of Assent," 8.

31. See, for example, Roderick P. Hart's *The Political Pulpit* and Robert Jewett's *The Captain America Complex.*

32. Bercovitch, "The Rites of Assent," 10–11.

33. For the original use of the term "civil religion," see Robert N. Bellah's article "Civil Religion in America." In *Paddy and the Republic,* Dale T. Knobel quotes nineteenth-century orator Charles B. Boynton as proclaiming that "Puritanism, Protestantism, and True Americanism are only different terms to designate the same set of principles" (5). See also Lind, *The Next American Nation,* 17–54.

34. Lerner, *America as a Civilization,* 103.

35. Ibid., 104.

36. Slotkin, *The Fatal Environment,* 16.

37. Turner quoted in Mattson and Marion, *Frederick Jackson Turner*, xix.

38. Turner's work initiated, according to Luther Luedtke, the "professional study of American character," defined broadly as the search for "reasonable and valid generalizations" about "who we are." See Luedtke, *Making America*, 8.

39. Santayana, *Character and Opinion in the United States*, viii.

40. See Frederick Merk's *Manifest Destiny and Mission in American History*, Ray Allen Billington's *Westward Expansion*, and John Brinckerhoff Jackson's *American Space*.

41. See, for example, Wilbur Jacobs's argument that Turner's work promoted a version of U.S. history that treated Native Americans unfairly (Jacobs, "The Fatal Confrontation," 283–309).

42. Steinbeck, *America and the Americans*, 29. See also Lerner, *America as a Civilization*, 98–99.

43. See, for example, Shelley et al., *Political Geography of the United States*.

44. Luedtke probably understates the case when he notes that "the social and psychological milieu in the United States between the First and Second World Wars did not lend itself to an impartial study of the American character" (Luedtke, *Making America*, 8).

45. For a discussion of immigration policy and nativist scholarship during this period, see Luedtke, *Making America*, 9–10.

46. Luedtke, *Making America*, 10.

47. Higham quoted in Luedtke, *Making America*, 11. See also, for example, Richard Hofstadter's 1948 work, *The American Political Tradition and the Men Who Made It*.

48. Notable examples include Henry Steele Commager's *The American Mind*, Geoffrey Gorer's *The American People*, Harold Laski's *The American Democracy*, Merle Curti's *American Paradox*, Hans Kohn's *American Nationalism*, and Louis Hartz's *The Liberal Tradition in America*.

49. See Smith, *Civic Ideals*, 17.

50. Hochschild, *Facing Up to the American Dream*, xix.

51. Hartz, *The Liberal Tradition in America*, 9.

52. Lipset, *American Exceptionalism*, 19.

53. Morone, "The Struggle for American Culture," 426.

54. Smith, *Civic Ideals*, 1.

55. See Wood, *The Creation of the American Republic, 1776–1787*.

56. Quoted in Smith, *Civic Ideals*, 84.

57. Smith, *Civic Ideals*, 83–84. Also, see Drukman, *Community and Purpose in America*.

58. Smith, *Civic Ideals*, 8–9.

59. Santayana, *Character and Opinion in the United States*, 175.

60. Albert and Williams quoted in Luedtke, *Making America*, 20.

61. For a description of his research subjects, see Wolfe, *One Nation, After All*, 33.

62. Wolfe, *One Nation, After All*, 38.

63. See, for example, Glazer, "Individualism and Equality in the United States," 292–307. See also Kammen, ed., *The Contrapuntal Civilization*, and Bellah et al., *Habits of the Heart*.

64. Erikson, *Childhood and Society*, 265.

65. For a concise version of the critique regarding a lack of rigorous methodology, see Jones, "American Studies: The Myth of Methodology."

66. See Mead, *Mind, Self & Society from the Standpoint of a Social Behaviorist*.

67. Lerner, *America as a Civilization*, 11.

68. Elston, "The Great Migration," 28.

69. See Daniels, *Coming to America*.

70. Zinn, *A People's History of the United States*, 24.

71. See Morone, "The Struggle for American Culture," 25. See also Salvatore, *We All Got History*.

72. See, for example, Arthur M. Schlesinger, Jr.'s *The Disuniting of America*.

73. John Higham, "Beyond Pluralism: The Historian as American Prophet," paper delivered at Organization of American Historians meeting, April, 1983, quoted in Levine, *The Unpredictable Past*, 5–6.

74. See, for example, Charles Taylor's "The Politics of Recognition."

75. Young, *Justice and the Politics of Difference*, 172.

76. Young writes that "my 'affinity group' in a given social situation comprises those people with whom I feel the most comfortable, who are more familiar. Affinity names that manner of sharing assumptions, affective bonding, and networking that recognizably differentiates groups from one another, but not according to some common nature. The salience of a particular person's group affinities may shift according to the social situation or changes in her or his life" (Young, *Justice and the Politics of Difference*, 182).

77. See Jennifer Hochschild's *Facing Up to the American Dream*.

78. Bellah et al., *Habits of the Heart*, 143.

79. Tocqueville, *Democracy in America*, 508.

80. According to James Bronowski and Bruce Mazlish, "[In] *Wealth of Nations*, Smith stated that the wealth of a community increases with the amount of work which it puts out. But . . . he traced everything back to original labor. He did not say merely that wealth was added to a bale of wool when you made it into a cloth; he traced the labor back to the shepherd, and then to the man who sowed the grass on which the sheep fed, and so on in an exhaustive and complete fashion" (Bronowski and Mazlish, *The Western Intellectual Tradition*, 348).

81. Bronowski and Mazlish, *The Western Intellectual Tradition*, 352.

82. For a detailed account of the ways in which the automotive industry symbolized the strength of the United States in the 1950s, see Halberstam, *The Fifties*, 116–30.

83. For an interesting historical account arguing that the "end of morality" resulted in an increase in self-interest in America during the twentieth century, see James Lincoln Collier's *The Rise of Selfishness in America*.

84. Lasch, *The Culture of Narcissism*, xvi.

85. The term "techno-economic" was coined by Daniel Bell to stress the marriage of technology and economics in the modern state (Bell, *The Cultural Contradictions of Capitalism*, 165).

86. Berger, Berger, and Kellner, *The Homeless Mind*, 37–38.

87. Slater, *The Pursuit of Loneliness*, 9–10.

88. Nisbet, *The Making of Modern Society*, 82.

89. Baltzell, ed., *The Search for Community in Modern America*, 3. Classic examples of sociological studies based on this assumption include Robert Lynd and Helen Lynd's 1929 *Middletown: A Study in American Culture*, as well as many of the studies that emerged from Robert Park's students at the University of Chicago in the 1920s and 1930s.

90. See Putnam, "Tuning In, Tuning Out."

91. Kanter, *Commitment and Community*, 172–73.

92. Buchanan's statement quoted in Morone, "The Struggle for American Culture," 425.

93. See, for example, Wolfe, *One Nation, After All*.

94. See Morone, "The Struggle for American Culture," 430, and the introductory chapter to Smith, *Civic Ideals.*

95. Lipset writes, "The emphasis in the American value system, in the American creed, has been on the individual. Citizens have been expected to demand and protect their rights on a personal basis. The exceptional focus on law here as compared to Europe, derived from the Constitution and the Bill of Rights, has stressed rights against the state and other powers. America began and *continues as* the most anti-statist, legalistic, and rights-oriented nation" (emphasis added) (Lipset, *American Exceptionalism,* 21).

96. Lipset, *American Exceptionalism,* 31.

97. Condit and Lucaites, *Crafting Equality,* xii–xiii.

98. Ibid., 217.

99. Geertz, *The Interpretation of Cultures,* 29.

100. Hart, "The Functions of Human Communication in the Maintenance of Human Values," 756, 757.

101. See Somers, "The Privatization of Citizenship: How to Unthink a Knowledge Culture," 124–25.

CHAPTER 2. A PRESIDENTIAL RHETORIC
OF SHARED BELIEFS

1. See, for example, Rogers Smith's *Civic Ideals* and Rosina Lippi-Green's *English with an Accent.*

2. For a more detailed account of the uses and implications of the notion of Americans as "God's chosen people," see the classic work by Conrad E. Cherry, *God's New Israel: Religious Interpretations of American Destiny.*

3. Washington's first inaugural address quoted Lott, ed., *The Presidents Speak,* 5.

4. See Bellah, "Civil Religion in America."

5. Cleveland quoted in Lott, *The Presidents Speak,* 153.

6. Harrison quoted in Lott, *The Presidents Speak,* 162.

7. Woodrow Wilson, "Eighth Annual Message," in Israel, ed., *The State of the Union Messages of the Presidents,* 3:2609.

8. Franklin Roosevelt quoted in Lott, *The Presidents Speak,* 237.

9. Reagan, "Inaugural Address," Jan. 21, 1985, 5.

10. Perhaps the best known works in this vein are Sacvan Bercovitch's analyses of the rhetorical and symbolic uses of the Puritan errand into the wilderness. See, for example, his articles "The Typology of America's Mission," and "The Rites of Assent." See also Hart, *The Political Pulpit.*

11. Bellah, "Civil Religion in America," 7, 8.

12. Ibid.

13. Ibid., 8.

14. See Jewett, *The Captain America Complex.*

15. Theodore Roosevelt quoted in Lott, *The Presidents Speak,* 185.

16. Bercovitch, "The Rites of Assent," 7–13.

17. Clinton, "Address before a Joint Session of Congress on the State of the Union," Jan. 27, 2000, 140.

18. Lawrence Fuchs is one of the few observers to write about this potential function when he argues that the civil religion sanctifies the civic culture. See Fuchs, *The American Kaleidoscope*.

19. Gal 3:23–29.

20. Ford, "Address before a Joint Session of the Congress Reporting on the State of the Union," Jan. 19, 1976, 31.

21. Wilson quoted in Lott, *The Presidents Speak*, 203–204.

22. Ibid., 204.

23. Ibid., 205.

24. See Jewett, *The Captain America Complex*.

25. Johnson, "Inaugural Address," Jan. 20, 1965, 72.

26. Ibid., 73.

27. Ibid., 71, 73.

28. Harding quoted in Lott, *The Presidents Speak*, 209.

29. Ibid., 207.

30. Ibid., 209.

31. Daniels, *Coming to America*, 281.

32. Coolidge quoted in Lott, *The Presidents Speak*, 216.

33. Ibid., 218.

34. See, for example, Eugene Genovese's ground-breaking work *Roll, Jordan, Roll: The World the Slaves Made*, which is about slaves' use of spirituals and Christian logic.

35. Hart, *The Political Pulpit*, 96.

36. Reagan, "Inaugural Address," Jan. 21, 1985, 57.

37. Hoover quoted in Lott, *The Presidents Speak*, 223.

38. Kennedy quoted in Lott, *The Presidents Speak*, 269.

39. Carter, "Address to a Joint Session of Congress on the State of the Union," Jan. 23, 1980, 194.

40. Fairbanks, "The Priestly Functions of the Presidency," 214.

41. Miller, *The Unmaking of Americans*, 23–24.

42. Black, *Rhetorical Questions*, 18.

43. Wald, *Religion and Politics in the United States*, 51.

44. Clinton, "Address to a Joint Session of Congress on the State of the Union," Jan. 23, 1996, 86.

45. For a similar argument by Kenneth Wald about the ways in which "certain types of faith actually depress political involvement" in the United States, see Wald, *Religion and Politics in the United States*, 31–32.

CHAPTER 3. IMMIGRATION AND PRESIDENTS' RHETORIC OF SHARED BELIEFS

1. Kraut, *The Huddled Masses*, 2. According to Kraut, Lazarus wrote the poem to help raise money for the statue's pedestal. "Only years later," he notes, "would the public come to share her understanding of the statue's symbolic importance" (2).

2. Johnson, "Inaugural Address," Jan. 20, 1965, 72.

3. Daniels, *Coming to America,* 265.

4. Ibid.

5. Kraut, *The Huddled Masses,* 149.

6. See, for example, Marouf A. Hasian, Jr.'s *the Rhetoric of Eugenics in Anglo-American Thought.*

7. Walker quoted in Kraut, *The Huddled Masses,* 151.

8. Nativist slogans and phrased mentioned in Kraut, *The Huddled Masses,* 153.

9. Despite its considerable political power, the IRL would ultimately be unsuccessful in many of its attempts, including a major initiative to create a literacy test as the primary criterion for citizenship. Nevertheless, the group campaigned for such reforms for twenty-two years. See Daniels, *Coming to America,* 276.

10. Kraut, *The Huddled Masses,* 52.

11. Ibid., 176–77.

12. Albert Johnson quoted in Daniels, "Two Cheers for Immigration," 23.

13. Daniels, "Two Cheers for Immigration," 25.

14. Ibid., 26–28.

15. Roosevelt quotation cited in Daniels, "Two Cheers for Immigration," 28.

16. Daniels, "Two Cheers for Immigration," 36.

17. Ibid., 42.

18. For an in-depth view, see David Reimers's book, *Unwelcome Strangers.*

19. Daniels, "Two Cheers for Immigration," 49.

20. Morganthau, "America: Still a Melting Pot?" 19.

21. Graham, "The Unfinished Reform," 179.

22. Lee et al., "Proposition 187 in Its Historical and Economic Contexts."

23. From 1871 to 1880, more than 2.5 million people immigrated to the United States. During the next decade (from 1881 to 1890), more than 5 million newcomers arrived. See Daniels, *Coming to America,* 124.

24. Benjamin Harrison quoted in Lott, *The Presidents Speak,* 155.

25. "Mill fires were lighted at the funeral pile [*sic*] of slavery. The emancipation proclamation was heard in the depths of the earth as well as in the sky; men were made free, and material things became our better servants" (Harrison quoted in Lott, *The Presidents Speak,* 157).

26. Harrison quoted Lott, *The Presidents Speak,* 159.

27. Ibid.

28. In some of the literature produced by the Immigration Restriction League, for example, the following rhetorical question provides a clear example of commonly perceived hierarchies of value among races: "Do Americans want their country . . . to be peopled by British, German and Scandinavian stock, historically free, energetic and progressive, or by Slav, Latin and Asiatic races, historically down-trodden, atavistic, and stagnant?" (quoted in Daniels, *Coming to America,* 276).

29. This popular observation was reinforced by new legislation, such as the Chinese Exclusion Act, passed by an overwhelming majority in Congress in 1882. Originally meant to appease organized labor's complaints about unfair competition, the act has been regarded by several historians as the "hinge on which American immigration policy turned." By 1892, the Supreme Court had ruled that the "exclusion of a particular class of immigrants was constitutional," setting the precedent for more than forty years of strict restrictions and quotas based on nationality (Daniels, *Coming to America,* 265–77).

30. Cleveland quoted in Lott, *The Presidents Speak,* 154.

31. McKinley spoke specifically about the need for "international bimetallism" to protect the "integrity of the currency," and he advocated a tariff act for foreign trade (McKinley quoted in Lott, *The Presidents Speak,* 171).

32. McKinley quoted in Lott, *The Presidents Speak,* 174.

33. Ibid., 175.

34. To be sure, immigration was perceived as worrisome to some citizens because of a perceived increase in "anarchists" within the immigrant population. For more information, see Daniels, *Coming to America,* 200–201.

35. McKinley quoted in Lott, *The Presidents Speak,* 175.

36. Kraut, *The Huddled Masses,* 148.

37. For the idea of the uniquely "American God," see Merelman, *Making Something of Ourselves,* 4.

38. Richard Merelman writes, "So firm was the Puritan vision that it actually required the practice of intolerance. The many Puritan acts of religious persecution, most notably the Salem witch-hunts, may offend the modern mind, but as [Arthur] Miller observed, 'To allow no dissent from the truth was exactly the reason they had come to America'" (Merelman, *Making Something of Ourselves,* 5).

39. Grover Cleveland came closest to making this suggestion, perhaps, in his second annual message, when he advocated stricter immigration restrictions by suggesting that they would in fact protect the Chinese.

40. Calvin Coolidge, "First Annual Message," Dec. 6, 1923, in Israel, ed., *The State of the Union Messages of the Presidents,* 3:2651.

41. Ibid.

42. I will address only two of these reasons here. First, "native-born" Americans do not necessarily have any greater understanding or appreciation for democracy than immigrants might. Indeed, the introduction of democratic practices in places like Haiti and the former Soviet Union have suggested that non-Americans participate in democratic government even more than the American people, if their dismal voting records are any indication. Second, even if immigrants were confused by a new political philosophy when they arrived, they soon learned that the everyday machinations of politics in a democracy were largely the same as those in the societies they had left. Regardless of the many counterarguments against this notion, the fact remains that Coolidge's statements reflected contemporary (and continuing) nativist prejudice that marked all foreigners as suspect.

43. Benjamin Harrison quoted in Lott, *The Presidents Speak,* 159.

44. Kraut, *The Huddled Masses,* 176.

45. See Daniels, "Two Cheers for Immigration," 24.

46. Hoover, "Address to a Joint Session of Congress on the State of the Union," Dec. 2, 1930, 520.

47. Daniels, "Two Cheers for Immigration," 25.

48. Ibid.

49. In 1940, however, Roosevelt signed the Alien Registration Act, which "required all aliens to register, be fingerprinted, and keep the government informed of their address" (quoted in Daniels, "Two Cheers for Immigration," 30).

50. Daniels, "Two Cheers for Immigration," 29.

51. Harry S. Truman, "Message to the Congress on the State of the Union and on the Budget for 1947," Jan. 6, 1947, 10.

52. Graham, "The Unfinished Reform," 140–41.

53. Ibid., 142.

54. Eisenhower, "Annual Message to the Congress on the State of the Union," Jan. 12, 1961, 929.

55. Daniels, *Coming to America*, 338–39.

56. Johnson's 1964 state of the union message, quoted in Israel, ed., *The State of the Union Messages of the Presidents*, 3:3160.

57. Graham, "The Unfinished Reform," 152.

58. Daniels, *Coming to America*, 388.

59. Reagan, "Address before a Joint Session of the Congress on the State of the Union," Feb. 6, 1985, 130.

60. Ibid.

61. George H. W. Bush, "Address before a Joint Session of the Congress on the State of the Union," Jan. 31, 1990, 135.

62. Clinton, "Address before a Joint Session of the Congress on the State of the Union," Jan. 24, 1995, 80–81.

63. Harrison quoted in Lott, *The Presidents Speak*, 159.

CHAPTER 4. RACE AND PRESIDENTS' RHETORIC OF SHARED BELIEFS

1. Gottlieb, "Racial Split at the End, as at the Start," A-1.

2. Ibid.

3. Clinton, "Remarks at the University of Texas at Austin," Oct. 16, 1995, 1600–1606.

4. Faulkner, *American Political and Social History,* 46.

5. See Shklar, *American Citizenship.*

6. Ellison quoted in West, *Race Matters,* 1.

7. See West, *Race Matters,* for example, or Bell, *The Cultural Contradictions of Capitalism.*

8. West, *Race Matters,* 3.

9. Schlesinger, ed., *The Almanac of American History,* 219–23.

10. Cleveland quoted in Israel, ed., *The State of the Union Messages of the Presidents,* 2:1545.

11. Ibid.

12. Ibid.

13. Ibid.

14. Harrison quoted in Israel, ed., *The State of the Union Messages of the Presidents,* 2:1692.

15. Cleveland quoted in Lott, *The Presidents Speak,* 167.

16. Ibid.

17. McKinley quoted in Israel, ed., *The State of the Union Messages of the Presidents,* 2:1876–77.

18. Ibid., 2:1877.

19. Israel, ed., *The State of the Union Messages of the Presidents,* 2:1877–78.

20. Theodore Roosevelt quoted in Israel, ed., *The State of the Union Messages of the Presidents,* 2:2047.

21. Ibid.

22. Ibid., 2:2071.

23. Cleveland quoted in Israel, ed., *The State of the Union Messages of the Presidents*, 2:1802.

24. McKinley quoted in Israel, ed., *The State of the Union Messages of the Presidents*, 2:1969.

25. Ibid.

26. See Lott, *The Presidents Speak*, 174.

27. As I discussed in the previous chapter, presidents frequently asserted that immigrants were inherently "lawless" and thus a threat to the citizenry.

28. Theodore Roosevelt quoted in Israel, ed., *The State of the Union Messages of the Presidents*, 3:2200, 2201.

29. Ibid., 3:2201.

30. Ibid. In *Crafting Equality: America's Anglo-African Word*, Celeste Condit and John Lucaites argue that this particular passage of Roosevelt's is significant because it demonstrates the president's "adoption of the African-American's conception of Equality as a relationship of humans founded on 'no distinction on the basis of color.'" While this may be true, Roosevelt's rhetoric quickly undid itself, I argue here, by subtly reinforcing these very distinctions. See Condit and Lucaites, *Crafting Equality*, 164.

31. Taft quoted in Lott, *The Presidents Speak*, 195.

32. Ibid.

33. Indeed, some scholars have interpreted Taft's "both negroes and whites" statement as a reference to the Ku Klux Klan, whose ranks were growing rapidly and whose members frequently intimidated blacks to keep them from voting.

34. Taft quoted in Lott, *The Presidents Speak*, 195–96.

35. Condit and Lucaites have noted that presidents in office after the 1896 *Plessy v. Ferguson* decision responded to its "separate but equal" compromise in "distinctly different ways." I am arguing here, however, that whether presidential responses were "egalitarian" or not, to use their parlance, they still spoke exemptively on the subject of inclusion. Indeed, this tendency may be even more remarkable in presidents remembered as progressive on racial issues. As Condit and Lucaites point out, "the deep chasm in the American public vocabulary" on race "undermin[ed] the best intentions of the best of leaders" (Condit and Lucaites, *Crafting Equality*, 167).

36. Woodrow Wilson devoted most of his two inaugural addresses as well as his eight state of the union messages to foreign policy and, later, the war itself. (Warren Harding, in office for only two years before his death, referred to slavery as an "ambiguity" within the nation's otherwise clear "organic law," thus bespeaking his sympathy for the southern states.)

37. From 1910 to 1920, Chicago's black population grew by more than 150 percent, Cleveland's by more than 300 percent, and Detroit's by 600 percent (Norton et. al., *A People and a Nation*, 664).

38. Norton et al., *A People and a Nation*, 664.

39. Ibid., 665.

40. Coolidge's inaugural address, Mar. 4, 1925, quoted in Lott, *The Presidents Speak*, 221.

41. In every one of his state of the union messages, Coolidge elaborately praised African Americans' "progress" and "advancement." In fact, he frequently spoke of the historical significance of African Americans' advancements, noting once that "history does not anywhere record so much progress made in the same length of time as that which has been accomplished by the Negro race in the United States since the Emancipation Proclamation" (Coolidge quoted in Israel, ed., *The State of the Union Messages of the Presidents*, 3:2722).

42. Coolidge quoted in Israel, ed., *The State of the Union Messages of the Presidents,* 3:2689.

43. Ibid.

44. Ibid., 3:2688-89.

45. Pauley, *The Modern Presidency and Civil Rights,* 24. For Roosevelt's references, see Israel, ed., *The State of the Union Messages of the Presidents,* 3:2809, 2851, and 2865, although the context for this last reference suggests that the president's remarks were directed more at "racial discrimination" that targeted Jewish people.

46. Eisenhower quoted in Israel, ed., *The State of the Union Messages of the Presidents,* 3:3066.

47. Kennedy quoted in Israel, ed., *The State of the Union Messages of the Presidents,* 3:3135.

48. Johnson quoted in Israel, ed., *The State of the Union Messages of the Presidents,* 3:3159.

49. Nixon, "Address on the State of the Union Delivered before a Joint Session of Congress," Jan. 20, 1972, 38.

50. Reagan, "Inaugural Address," Jan. 20, 1981, 1.

51. Ibid., 1-2.

52. While Reagan's statement appears to employ the same argument that was behind the abstract ideational rhetoric of earlier presidents, it is actually quite different. Because his predecessors had already introduced particularity into national addresses, Reagan could not avoid it altogether, meaning that he could not use a purely ideational discourse. In this passage, for example, the president did not claim that Americans were Americans because of their shared beliefs or blessings, as most chief executives had. Instead, he offered a shared identity of particular action, naming Americans by what they *did* (raising food, patrolling shores, mining, etc.). He thus spoke specifically of difference without falling into essentialist logics, a phenomenon I explore in greater detail in chapter 5.

53. This void in Reagan's language might also be symptomatic of other aspects of his legacy, according to John Brenkman. In trying to account for why "American political opinion has shifted dramatically to the right since the Reagan-Bush era," Brenkman has argued that "Reaganism succeeded in dislocating a value painstakingly established in the years following the Second World War. Reaganism excised racial justice from public discourse, transforming this powerful, tenuously shared expression of a common good into a tabooed slogan" (Brenkman, "Race Publics," 4).

54. Reagan, "Inaugural Address," Jan. 20, 1981, 2.

55. Carcasson and Rice, "The Promise and Failure of President Clinton's Race Initiative of 1997-1998," 244.

56. Clinton, "Inaugural Address," Jan. 20, 1997, 33.

57. Clinton, "Address before a Joint Session of Congress on the State of the Union," Feb. 4, 1997, 116.

58. Ibid.

59. Ibid., 117.

CHAPTER 5. GENDER AND PRESIDENTS' RHETORIC OF SHARED BELIEFS

1. Campbell, *Man Cannot Speak for Her,* 1:173.

2. Ibid., 173-74.

3. This language comes directly from Shaw and her contemporaries. On June 22, 1917, according to Campbell, feminist protestors marched at the White House carrying a banner that read, "WE SHALL FIGHT FOR THE THINGS WHICH WE HAVE ALWAYS HELD NEAREST OUR HEARTS—FOR DEMOCRACY, FOR THE RIGHT OF THOSE WHO SUBMIT TO AUTHORITY TO HAVE A VOICE IN THEIR OWN GOVERNMENT—President Wilson's War Message, April 2, 1917." The protestors were intent on showing the hypocrisy of Wilson's approach to women's suffrage (Campbell, *Man Cannot Speak for Her,* 1:175).

4. Within communication studies, for instance, many researchers have analyzed the early U.S. feminists as leaders of a social movement whose strategies and persuasive discourse merit further study. Campbell's *Man Cannot Speak for Her* is perhaps the best-known example of this type of scholarship, and there are numerous historical and biographical studies written by scholars from multiple disciplines who also share a movement-oriented focus. Authors of such works often emphasize the "great women" of the past in order to explore what they did, or did not do, or said, or did not say, that might help explain their movement's successes, failures, and subsequent influence on American society.

   Another group of influential studies has focused on the public policy results of women's integration into U.S. politics. More specifically, these scholars have studied the institutional and legislative processes through which women's rights have been interpreted throughout American history. Notable examples of this work include Noralee Frankel and Nancy Dye's volume *Gender, Class, Race, and Reform in the Progressive Era* as well as the more broadly and contemporarily focused *Women in American Law* by Judith A. Baer. Works like these attempt to document the influences and processes through which the United States has moved, if dubiously at times, from "patriarchy toward equality" in the decades after women's suffrage became a reality. Even though, as Baer is quick to point out, the "law cannot do everything," researchers who share her focus write about what institutions (including courts and legislatures) have done, and have not done, to maintain and/or change women's historically disadvantaged position within American society.

5. For a more detailed theoretical defense of my vantage point, see Beasley, "Engendering Democratic Change."

6. See Kerber, *Women of the Republic.*

7. Ryan, *Womanhood in America,* 1.

8. Skocpol, *Protecting Soldiers and Mothers,* 321.

9. In volume 2 of *Democracy in America* Tocqueville writes, "In America, more than anywhere else in the world, care has been taken constantly to trace clearly distinct spheres of action for the two sexes, and both are required to keep in step, but along paths that are never the same. You will never find American women in charge of the external relations of the family, managing a business, or interfering with politics; but they are also never obliged to undertake rough laborers' work or any task requiring hard physical exertion. No family is so poor that it makes an exception to this rule. If the American woman is never allowed to leave the quiet sphere of domestic duties, she is also never forced to do so" (Tocqueville, *Democracy in America,* 601).

10. Ryan, *Womanhood in America,* 4. By 1890, historian Lois Banner writes, "Many states had modified the common law doctrine . . . under which wives had been chattels of their husbands" to give "wives control over their inherited property and their earnings" (Banner, *Women in Modern America,* 1).

11. Ryan, *Womanhood in America*, 5. In *Gender and Higher Education in the Progressive Era*, Lynn D. Gordon argues that women's increasing attendance at American universities between 1880 and 1920 forced significant and lasting changes within higher education in the United States.

12. See, for example, Hewitt, "Feminist Friends."

13. See, for example, Bordin, *Woman and Temperance*.

14. For more information regarding the farm and labor organizations, see Ryan, *Womanhood in America*, 16. On community-building work, see Lerner's introduction to her edited volume *The Female Experience*, xxxiii. See also Tilly and Gurin, eds., *Women, Politics, and Change*, 9.

15. Ryan, *Womanhood in America*, 16

16. Banner, *Women in Modern America*, 6; Shannon, *Between the Wars*, 113.

17. Braxton, *Women, Sex, and Race*, 79–81.

18. To be clear, some American women could and did vote before 1920. As historian David A. Shannon explains, "States had always had the power to grant the franchise to women. . . . By 1900 women voted in Wyoming, Utah, Idaho, and Colorado. In the next fifteen years seven other states, all of them in the West, extended the vote to women" (Shannon, *Between the Wars*, 111).

19. Campbell, introduction to *Man Cannot Speak for Her*, 2:xx.

20. Skocpol, *Protecting Soldiers and Mothers*, 322–23.

21. Ibid., 322.

22. Sapiro, *The Political Integration of Women*, 18.

23. Cleveland quoted in Israel, ed., *The State of the Union Messages of the Presidents*, 2:1594.

24. Theodore Roosevelt quoted in Israel, ed., *The State of the Union Messages of the Presidents*, 2:2007.

25. Cleveland quoted in Israel, ed., *The State of the Union Messages of the Presidents*, 2:1550.

26. Ibid., 2:1551.

27. Ibid.

28. McKinley quoted in Israel, ed., *The State of the Union Messages of the Presidents*, 3:1894.

29. Ibid., 2:1858, 1882.

30. For a more thorough discussion of the gendered nature of cultural discourses of American citizenship, see Dana D. Nelson's *National Manhood*.

31. Theodore Roosevelt quoted in Israel, ed., *The State of the Union Messages of the Presidents*, 2:2016, 2023.

32. Ibid., 2:2053.

33. Ibid., 3:2144.

34. Nelson, *National Manhood*, 1–28.

35. Bolt, *The Women's Movements in the United States and Britain*, 244–45.

36. Flexner, *Century of Struggle*, 269.

37. Ibid., 271.

38. Wilson quoted in Flexner, *Century of Struggle*, 272.

39. In fact, it was probably politically expedient for Wilson and others to do so. "Between 1890 and the First World War," Banner explains, the "majority of organized women probably did not support" suffrage. The movement was effectively dead by 1912, she writes, citing journalist Rheta Childe Dorr's observation that around this time, "no newspaper or magazine editor would have printed an article on the subject. No politician gave it a thought" (Banner,

Women in Modern America, 99). It seems unlikely, then, that national suffrage by itself could have changed the way presidents talked about America in their most public addresses.

40. Wilson quoted in Israel, ed., *The State of the Union Messages of the Presidents,* 3:2589, 2590.

41. For a description of the effigy incident, see Bolt, *The Women's Movements in the United States and Britain,* 244.

42. Wilson quoted in Israel, ed., *The State of the Union Messages of the Presidents,* 3:2590.

43. Harding quoted in Israel, ed., *The State of the Union Messages of the Presidents,* 3:2623.

44. Banner, *Women in Modern America,* 131.

45. Brown, *Setting a Course,* 51.

46. Murray, *The Harding Era,* 66.

47. Harding quoted in Lott, *The Presidents Speak,* 211.

48. Kerber, "The Republican Mother," 188.

49. Andersen, *After Suffrage,* 23.

50. Ibid., 27.

51. Kerber, *Women of the Republic,* 229–30.

52. Andersen, *After Suffrage,* 27.

53. Mrs. Frank O. Immler, "Women's Natural Disbarments from Political Science: A Reply," *American Magazine of Civics* (March, 1896): 277, cited in R. Edwards, *Angels in the Machinery,* 162.

54. Harding quoted in Lott, *The Presidents Speak,* 209.

55. Ibid., 212.

56. For Coolidge's endorsement of suffrage while serving in the U.S. Senate, see McCoy, *Calvin Coolidge,* 49. For her view of Coolidge's domestic agenda, see Deutsch, "From Ballots to Breadlines, 1920–1940," 421.

57. Brown, *Setting a Course,* 6.

58. Coolidge quoted in Israel, ed., *The State of the Union Messages of the Presidents,* 3:2650.

59. Banner, *Women in Modern America,* 139.

60. Ibid., 140.

61. Andersen, *After Suffrage,* 153.

62. Coolidge quoted in Israel, ed., *The State of the Union Messages of the Presidents,* 3:2740.

63. Ibid., 3:2679.

64. Hoover quoted in Israel, ed., *The State of the Union Messages of the Presidents,* 3:2765.

65. Franklin D. Roosevelt, "Second Inaugural Address," Jan. 20, 1937, quoted in Lott, *The Presidents Speak,* 240.

66. Franklin D. Roosevelt quoted in Israel, ed., *The State of the Union Messages of the Presidents,* 3:2813–14.

67. Ibid., 3:2864.

68. Ibid., 3:2872.

69. Ibid., 3:2879.

70. Ibid., 3:2888.

71. Truman, "Annual Message to the Congress on the State of the Union," 38.

72. Banner, *Women in Modern America,* ix.

73. See Mansbridge, *Why We Lost the ERA.*

74. Mathews and De Hart, *Sex, Gender, and the Politics of ERA,* vii–xv.

75. See Eisenhower's second, third, and fourth annual messages in Israel, ed., *The State of the Union Messages of the Presidents,* 3:3032, 3048, and 3064, respectively.

76. Kennedy quoted in Israel, ed., *The State of the Union Messages of the Presidents,* 3:3159.

77. Nixon, "State of the Union Address," Jan. 22, 1971, 51.

78. Ford, "Address to a Joint Session of the Congress," Aug. 12, 1974, 13. Ford gave this address shortly after assuming the presidency, and I used it as a supplement to his inaugural address.

79. Reagan, "Address before a Joint Session of the Congress on the State of the Union," Jan. 25, 1983, 109–10.

80. Ibid., Jan. 25, 1984, 87.

81. Ibid., 92.

82. Ibid., Feb. 6, 1985, 103.

83. Ibid., Feb. 4, 1986, 130.

84. George H. W. Bush, "Inaugural Address," Jan. 20, 1989, 2.

85. Ibid., 3.

86. Clinton, "Inaugural Address," Jan. 20, 1993, 1.

87. See Clinton, "Address to a Joint Session of Congress on the State of the Union," Jan. 23, 1996, 81.

CHAPTER 6. IMPLICATIONS OF PRESIDENTS' RHETORIC OF SHARED BELIEFS

1. On the quadrupling of the U.S. population see Norton et al., *A People and a Nation,* A-16.

2. Dahl, *Democracy, Liberty, and Equality,* 235.

3. Hart, *Seducing America,* 143.

4. See Dahl, *Democracy and Its Critics,* 213–310.

5. For a more elaborate analysis of the roots and early stages of this conflict, see Misha Glenny's *The Fall of Yugoslavia.*

6. See, for example, White, Pravda, and Gitelman, eds., *Developments in Russian and Post-Soviet Politics.*

7. Recently, for example, Labour Party leader and, subsequently, prime minister Tony Blair has received widespread criticism for agreeing with (and even advancing) some of former Conservative prime minister Margaret Thatcher's arguments about the merits of a free market. See, for example, "Spot the Europhile," 54.

8. See Fraser, "Rethinking the Public Sphere," 70.

9. Eley, "Nations, Publics, and Political Cultures," 302.

10. Edwards, Kessel, and Rockman, eds., *Researching the Presidency,* 3–4.

11. Ibid.

12. Ibid.

13. Ibid., 5. To "catalyze" this effort, Edwards, Kessel, and Rockman edited *Researching the Presidency* as a collection of various perspectives and guidelines for future scholarship, which, they and their contributing authors suggest, might be guided by theories of leadership, cognition, organizations, or institutions, for example.

14. Both presidential and rhetorical scholars have analyzed case studies of how presidents have handled these topics at specific times. Doris Graber's 1968 work, *Public Opinion, the President, and Foreign Policy,* for example, documented the impact of public opinion on four

different chief executives' decision-making. I am encouraging more comparative and qualitative approaches to these topics to see if and/or how rhetorical patterns constrain presidential actions.

15. Even if presidential speech were merely a barometer of public opinion, scholars already have less complicated sources of public opinion data, from polls and marketing information, for example.

16. Kamuf, ed., introduction to "Speech and Phenomenon," *The Derrida Reader,* 7.

17. See Black, *Rhetorical Criticism.*

18. See Bitzer, "The Rhetorical Situation."

19. See, for example, Wander, "The Ideological Turn in Rhetorical Theory," *16.*

20. *Andrew W. Robertson took up this question in his 1995 study, The Language of Democracy: Political Rhetoric in the United States and Britain, 1790–1900.* This work focuses on election coverage in British and U.S. colonial newspapers.

21. Campbell and Jamieson, *Deeds Done in Words,* 15.

22. Second-term presidents, for instance, are presumably less likely to talk about specific national difficulties than are leaders beginning a first term, as incumbents are more likely to refer to their own previous successes and progress.

23. See Bitzer, "The Rhetorical Situation," 6.

24. Wilson, "Inaugural Address," Mar. 5, 1917, quoted in Lott, *The Inaugural Addresses of the American Presidents,* 205; Nixon, "Inaugural Address," Jan. 29, 1969, 1; George H. W. Bush, "Inaugural Address," Jan. 20, 1989, 1.

25. Benjamin Harrison, quoted in Lott, ed., *The Presidents Speak,* 156–57.

26. Reagan, "Inaugural Address," Jan. 20, 1981, 4.

27. Ibid., 1.

28. Ibid., 4.

29. The quoted phrases are from Campbell and Jamieson, "Inaugurating the Presidency," 206.

30. Clinton, "Inaugural Address," Jan. 20, 1993, 1.

31. Ibid.

32. President Clinton stated, "Today, a generation raised in the shadows of the cold war assumes new responsibilities in a world warmed by the sunshine of freedom but threatened still by ancient hatreds and new plagues" (Clinton, "Inaugural Address," Jan. 20, 1993, 1).

33. The quotation is from Grover Cleveland's first inaugural address, Mar. 4, 1885, in Lott, *The Presidents Speak,* 153. On "rational detachment" from tribalisms, see, for example, Theodore Roosevelt's inaugural address, Mar. 4, 1905, in Lott, *The Presidents Speak,* 185.

34. George H. W. Bush, "Inaugural Address," Jan. 20, 1989, 2.

35. Clinton, "Inaugural Address," Jan. 20, 1993, 1.

36. Ibid.

37. Ibid.

38. Ibid.

39. Ibid.

40. Johnson, "Inaugural Address," Jan. 20, 1965, 72–73.

41. Reagan, "Inaugural Address," Jan. 20, 1981, 1.

42. Clinton, "Inaugural Address," Jan. 20, 1993, 2.

43. Ibid., 1.

44. Ibid.

45. Ryan, "President Bill Clinton's Inaugural Address, 1993," 300.

46. Clinton, "Remarks at the University of Texas at Austin," Oct. 16, 1995, 1601.

47. Ibid.

48. Ibid., 1603.

49. Ibid., 1605.

50. Dole, "Excerpts from Dole and Kemp's Remarks to Convention of Black Journalists," A-8.

Bibliography

Andersen, Kristi. *After Suffrage: Women in Partisan and Electoral Politics before the New Deal.* Chicago: University of Chicago Press, 1996.

Anderson, Benedict R. O. *Imagined Communities: Reflections on the Origin and Spread of Nationalism.* 2nd ed., revised and expanded. London: Verso, 1991.

Baer, Judith A. *Women in American Law: The Struggle toward Equality from the New Deal to the Present.* 2nd ed. New York: Holmes and Meier, 1996.

Bailyn, Bernard. *The Ideological Origins of the American Revolution.* Cambridge, Mass.: Belknap Press of Harvard University Press, 1967.

Bakhtin, Mikhail. *Speech Genres and Other Late Essays.* Translated by Vern W. McGee. Austin: University of Texas Press, 1986.

Baltzell, E. Digby, ed. *The Search for Community in Modern America.* New York: Harper and Row, 1968.

Banner, Lois W. *Women in Modern America: A Brief History.* 2nd ed. San Diego: Harcourt Brace Jovanovich, 1984.

Barber, James David. *The Presidential Character: Predicting Performance in the White House.* Englewood Cliffs, N.J.: Prentice-Hall, 1972, 1977.

Beasley, Vanessa B. "Engendering Democratic Change: How Three U.S. Presidents Discussed Female Suffrage." *Rhetoric & Public Affairs* 5, no. 1 (2002): 79–86.

Bell, Daniel. *The Cultural Contradictions of Capitalism.* New York: Basic Books, 1978.

Bellah, Robert N. *The Broken Covenant: American Civil Religion in a Time of Trial.* New York: Seabury Press, 1975.

———. "Civil Religion in America." *Daedalus* 96 (Winter, 1967): 1–21.

Bellah, Robert N., Richard Madsen, William M. Sullivan, Ann Swidler, and Steven M. Tipton. *Habits of the Heart: Individualism and Commitment in American Life.* Berkeley: University of California Press, 1985.

Bercovitch, Sacvan. "The Rites of Assent." In *The American Self: Myth, Ideology, and Popular Culture,* edited by Sam B. Girgus, 5–42. Albuquerque: University of New Mexico Press, 1981.

———. "The Typology of America's Mission." *American Quarterly* 30 (1978): 135–55.

Berger, Peter L., Brigitte Berger, and Hansfried Kellner. *The Homeless Mind: Modernization and Consciousness.* New York: Vintage Books, 1974.

Billington, Ray Allen, with James Blaine Hedges. *Westward Expansion: A History of the American Frontier.* 2nd ed. New York: Macmillan, 1960.

Bitzer, Lloyd. "The Rhetorical Situation." *Philosophy and Rhetoric* 1, no. 1 (Winter, 1968): 1–14.

Black, Edwin. *Rhetorical Criticism: A Study in Method.* New York: Macmillan, 1965.

——. *Rhetorical Questions: Studies in Public Discourse.* Chicago: University of Chicago Press, 1992.

——. "The Second Persona." *Quarterly Journal of Speech* 56 (1970): 109–19.

Bolt, Christine. *The Women's Movements in the United States and Britain from the 1790s to the 1920s.* Amherst: University of Massachusetts Press, 1993.

Bordin, Ruth. *Woman and Temperance: The Quest for Power and Liberty, 1873–1900.* Philadelphia: Temple University Press, 1981.

Braxton, Bernard. *Women, Sex, and Race: A Realistic View of Sexism and Racism.* Washington, D.C.: Verta Press, 1973.

Brenkman, John. "Race Publics: Civic illiberalism, or Race after Reagan." *Transition* 66 (1995): 4–36.

Bronowski, James, and Bruce Mazlish. *The Western Intellectual Tradition, from Leonardo to Hegel.* New York: Harper Press, 1960.

Brown, Dorothy M. *Setting a Course: American Women in the 1920s.* Boston: Twayne Publishers, G. K. Hall and Company, 1987.

Bush, George H. W. "Address before a Joint Session of the Congress on the State of the Union." January 31, 1990. In *Public Papers of the Presidents of the United States.* Washington, D.C.: U.S. Government Printing Office, 1991.

——. "Inaugural Address." January 20, 1989. In *Public Papers of the Presidents of the United States.* Washington, D.C.: U.S. Government Printing Office, 1990.

Campbell, Karlyn Kohrs. *Man Cannot Speak for Her.* 2 vols. Westport, Conn.: Greenwood Press, 1989.

Campbell, Karlyn Kohrs, and Kathleen Hall Jamieson. *Deeds Done in Words: Presidential Rhetoric and the Genres of Governance.* Chicago: University of Chicago Press, 1990.

——. "Inaugurating the Presidency." In *Form, Genre, and the Study of Political Discourse,* edited by Herbert W. Simons and Aram A. Aghazarian, 394–411. Columbia: University of South Carolina Press, 1986.

Carcasson, Martin, and Mitchell F. Rice. "The Promise and Failure of President Clinton's Race Initiative of 1997–1998: A Rhetorical Perspective." *Rhetoric & Public Affairs* 2, no. 2 (1999): 243–74.

Carter, Jimmy. "Address to a Joint Session of Congress on the State of the Union." January 23, 1980. In *Public Papers of the Presidents of the United States.* Washington, D.C.: U.S. Government Printing Office, 1981.

Charland, Maurice. "Constitutive Rhetoric: The Case of the *Peuple Quebeçois.*" *Quarterly Journal of Speech* 73 (1987): 134–47.

Cherry, Conrad E. *God's New Israel: Religious Interpretations of American Destiny.* Englewood Cliffs, N.J.: Prentice-Hall, 1971.

Clinton, William J. "Address before a Joint Session of the Congress on the State of the Union." January 24, 1995. In *Public Papers of the Presidents of the United States.* Washington, D.C.: U.S. Government Printing Office, 1996.

——. "Address to a Joint Session of Congress on the State of the Union." January 23, 1996. In *Public Papers of the Presidents of the United States.* Washington, D.C.: U.S. Government Printing Office, 1997.

————. "Address before a Joint Session of Congress on the State of the Union." February 4, 1997. In *Public Papers of the Presidents of the United States.* Washington, D.C.: U.S. Government Printing Office, 1998.

————. "Address before a Joint Session of Congress on the State of the Union." January 27, 2000. In *Public Papers of the Presidents of the United States.* Washington, D.C.: U.S. Government Printing Office, 2001.

————. "Inaugural Address." January 20, 1993. In *Public Papers of the Presidents of the United States.* Washington, D.C.: U.S. Government Printing Office, 1994.

————. "Inaugural Address." January 20, 1997. *Public Papers of the Presidents of the United States.* Washington, D.C.: U.S. Government Printing Office, 1998.

————. "Remarks at the University of Texas at Austin." White House Press Release, October 16, 1995. In *Public Papers of the Presidents of the United States.* Washington, D.C.: U.S. Government Printing Office, 1996.

Collier, James Lincoln. *The Rise of Selfishness in America.* New York: Oxford University Press, 1991.

Commager, Henry Steele. *The American Mind: An Interpretation of American Thought and Character since the 1880s.* New Haven, Conn.: Yale University Press, 1950.

————. *The Search for a Usable Past and Other Essays in Historiography.* New York: Knopf, 1967.

Condit, Celeste M., and John L. Lucaites. *Crafting Equality: America's Anglo-African Word.* Chicago: University of Chicago Press, 1993.

Curti, Merle Eugene. *American Paradox: The Conflict of Thought and Action.* New Brunswick, N.J.: Rutgers University Press, 1956.

Dahl, Robert. *Democracy and Its Critics.* New Haven, Conn.: Yale University Press, 1989.

————. *Democracy, Liberty, and Equality.* Oslo: Norwegian University Press, 1986.

Daniels, Roger. *Coming to America: A History of Immigration and Ethnicity in American Life.* New York: Harper Perennial, 1991.

————. "Two Cheers for Immigration." In *Debating American Immigration, 1882–Present,* edited by Roger Daniels and Otis L. Graham, 5–88. Lanham, Md.: Rowman and Littlefield, 2001.

Deutsch, Sarah Jane. "From Ballots to Breadlines, 1920–1940." In *No Small Courage: A History of Women in the United States,* edited by Nancy F. Cott, 413–72. Oxford: Oxford University Press, 2000.

Dole, Bob. "Excerpts from Dole and Kemp's Remarks to Convention of Black Journalists." *New York Times,* August 24, 1996, A-8.

Drukman, Mason. *Community and Purpose in America: An Analysis of American Political Theory.* New York: McGraw-Hill, 1971.

Dudziak, Mary L. *Cold War Civil Rights: Race and the Image of American Democracy.* Princeton, N.J.: Princeton University Press, 2000.

Edwards, George C., III, John H. Kessel, and Bert A. Rockman, eds. *Researching the Presidency: Vital Questions, New Approaches.* Pittsburgh: University of Pittsburgh Press, 1993.

Edwards, Rebecca. *Angels in the Machinery: Gender in American Party Politics from the Civil War to the Progressive Era.* New York: Oxford University Press, 1997.

Eisenhower, Dwight D. "Annual Message to the Congress on the State of the Union." January 12, 1961. In *Public Papers of the Presidents of the United States.* Washington D.C.: U.S. Government Printing Office, 1961.

Eley, Geoff. "Nations, Publics, and Political Cultures." In *Habermas and the Public Sphere,* edited by Craig Calhoun, 289–339. Cambridge, Mass.: MIT Press, 1992.

Elshtain, Jean Bethke. "Democracy and the Politics of Difference." *The Responsive Community* 4, no. 2 (Spring, 1994): 9.

Elston, John. "The Great Migration." *Time,* special issue, Fall, 1993, 28.

Erikson, Erik. *Childhood and Society.* 2nd ed., revised and enlarged. New York: Norton, 1963.

Fairbanks, James David. "The Priestly Functions of the Presidency: A Discussion of the Literature on Civil Religion and Its Implications for the Study of Presidential Leadership." *Presidential Studies Quarterly* 11, no. 2 (Spring, 1981): 214–32.

Faulkner, Harold Underwood. *American Political and Social History.* New York: Appleton-Century-Crofts, 1952.

Fisher, Walter. "Rhetorical Fiction and the Presidency." *Quarterly Journal of Speech* 66 (April, 1980): 120.

Flexner, Eleanor. *Century of Struggle: The Woman's Rights Movement in the United States.* Rev. ed. Cambridge, Mass.: Belknap Press of Harvard University Press, 1975.

Foner, Eric, ed. *The New American History.* Philadelphia: Temple University Press, 1990.

Ford, Gerald R. "Address before a Joint Session of the Congress." August 12, 1974. In *Public Papers of the Presidents of the United States.* Washington, D.C.: U.S. Government Printing Office, 1975.

———. "Address before a Joint Session of the Congress, Reporting on the State of the Union." January 19, 1976. In *Public Papers of the Presidents of the United States.* Washington, D.C.: U.S. Government Printing Office, 1977.

Frankel, Noralee, and Nancy Dye, eds. *Gender, Class, Race, and Reform in the Progressive Era.* Lexington: University Press of Kentucky, 1991.

Fraser, Nancy. "Rethinking the Public Sphere: A Contribution to the Critique of Actually Existing Democracy." *Social Text* 25/26 (1991): 56–70.

Friedan, Betty. *The Feminine Mystique.* 1963. Reprint, New York: Dell, 1970.

Fuchs, Lawrence H. *The American Kaleidoscope: Race, Ethnicity, and the Civic Culture.* Hanover, N.H.: Wesleyan University Press, 1990.

Geertz, Clifford. *The Interpretation of Cultures: Selected Essays.* New York: Basic Books, 1973.

Gellner, Ernest. *Culture, Identity, and Politics.* Cambridge: Cambridge University Press, 1987.

Genovese, Eugene. *Roll, Jordan, Roll: The World the Slaves Made.* New York: Pantheon Books, 1974.

Germino, Dante. *The Inaugural Addresses of American Presidents: The Public Philosophy and Rhetoric.* Lanham, Md.: University Press of America, 1984.

Glazer, Nathan. "Individualism and Equality in the United States." In *Making America: The Society and Culture of the United States,* edited by Luther S. Luedtke, 292–307. Chapel Hill: University of North Carolina Press, 1992.

Gleason, Philip. "American Identity and Americanization." In *Concepts of Ethnicity,* edited by William Peterson, Michael Novak, and Philip Gleason, 57–143. Cambridge, Mass.: Belknap Press of Harvard University Press, 1982.

Glenny, Misha. *The Fall of Yugoslavia: The Third Balkan War.* New ed. New York: Penguin Books, 1993.

Gordon, Lynn D. *Gender and Higher Education in the Progressive Era.* New Haven, Conn.: Yale University Press, 1990.

Gorer, Geoffrey. *The American People: A Study in National Character.* New York: Norton, 1948.

Gottlieb, Martin. "Racial Split at the End, as at the Start." *New York Times,* October 4, 1995, A-1.

Graber, Doris. *Public Opinion, the President, and Foreign Policy: Four Case Studies from the Formative Years.* New York: Holt, Rinehart, and Winston, 1968.

Graham, Otis L. "The Unfinished Reform: Regulating Immigration in the National Interest." In *Debating American Immigration, 1882–Present,* edited by Roger Daniels and Otis L. Graham, 89–185. Lanham, Md.: Rowman and Littlefield, 2001.

Gurko, Miriam. *The Ladies of Seneca Falls: The Birth of the Woman's Rights Movement.* New York: Macmillan, 1974.

Halberstam, David. *The Fifties.* New York: Villard Books, 1993.

Hargrove, Erwin C. *The President as Leader: Appealing to the Better Angels of Our Nature.* Lawrence: University Press of Kansas, 1998.

Hart, Roderick P. "The Functions of Human Communication in the Maintenance of Human Values." In *The Handbook of Rhetorical and Communication Theory,* edited by Carroll C. Arnold and John Waite Bowers, 749–91. *Boston: Allyn and Bacon, 1984.*

———. *The Political Pulpit.* West Lafayette, Ind.: Purdue University Press, 1977.

———. *Seducing America: How Television Charms the Modern Voter.* New York: Oxford University Press, 1994.

Hartz, Louis. *The Liberal Tradition in America: An Interpretation of American Political Thought since the Revolution.* New York: Harcourt, Brace, 1955.

Hasian, Marouf A., Jr. *The Rhetoric of Eugenics in Anglo-American Thought.* Athens: University of Georgia Press, 1996.

Hewitt, Nancy A. "Feminist Friends: Agrarian Quakers and the Emergence of Women's Rights in America." *Feminist Studies* 12, no. 1 (Spring, 1986): 27–49.

Hochschild, Jennifer. *Facing Up to the American Dream: Race, Class, and the Soul of the Nation.* Princeton, N.J.: Princeton University Press, 1995.

Hofstadter, Richard. *The American Political Tradition and the Men Who Made It.* New York: Knopf, 1948.

Hoover, Herbert. "Address to a Joint Session of Congress on the State of the Union." December 2, 1930. In *Public Papers of the Presidents of the United States.* Washington, D.C.: U.S. Government Printing Office, 1976.

Israel, Fred L., ed. *The State of the Union Messages of the Presidents, 1790–1966.* 3 vols. New York: Chelsea House, 1966.

Jackson, John Brinckerhoff. *American Space: The Centennial Years, 1865–1876.* New York: Norton, 1972.

Jacobs, Wilbur. "The Fatal Confrontation." *Pacific Historical Review* 40 (1971): 283–309.

Jewett, Robert. *The Captain America Complex: The Dilemma of Zealous Nationalism.* Philadelphia: Westminster Press, 1973. Reprint, Santa Fe, N.Mex.: Bear & Company, 1984.

Johnson, Lyndon Baines. "Inaugural Address." January 20, 1965. *Public Papers of the Presidents of the United States.* Washington, D.C.: U.S. Government Printing Office, 1966.

Jones, Joel. "American Studies: The Myth of Methodology." *American Quarterly* 31 (1979): 382–87.

Kammen, Michael, ed. *The Contrapuntal Civilization: Essays toward a New Understanding of the American Experience.* New York: Crowell, 1971.

Kamuf, Peggy, ed. *The Derrida Reader: Between the Blinds,* by Jacques Derrida. New York: Columbia University Press, 1991.

Kanter, Rosabeth Moss. *Commitment and Community: Communes and Utopias in Sociological Perspective.* Cambridge, Mass.: Harvard University Press, 1972.

Kerber, Linda K. "The Republican Mother: Women and the Enlightenment—An American Perspective." *American Quarterly* 281 (1976): 187–205.

———. *Women of the Republic: Intellect and Ideology in Revolutionary America.* Chapel Hill: University of North Carolina Press, 1980.

Kernell, Samuel. *Going Public: New Strategies of Presidential Leadership.* Washington, D.C.: Congressional Quarterly Press, 1986.

Knobel, Dale T. *Paddy and the Republic: Ethnicity and Nationality in Antebellum America.* Middletown, Conn.: Wesleyan University Press, 1986.

Kohn, Hans. *American Nationalism: An Interpretative Essay.* New York: Macmillan, 1957.

Kraut, Alan M. *The Huddled Masses: The Immigrant in American Society, 1880–1921.* Arlington Heights, Ill.: Harlan Davidson, 1982.

Lasch, Christopher. *The Culture of Narcissism: American Life in an Age of Diminishing Expectations.* New York: Norton, 1978.

Laski, Harold. *The American Democracy: A Commentary and an Interpretation.* New York: Viking Press, 1948.

Lee, Wen Shu, Philip Wander, Sandra Torres, and Mary Jo Gonzales. "Proposition 187 in Its Historical and Economic Contexts." Paper presented at the annual meeting of the Speech Communication Association, San Antonio, Tex., November, 1995.

Lerner, Gerda, ed. *The Female Experience: An American Documentary.* Indianapolis: Bobbs-Merrill Educational Publishing, 1977.

Lerner, Max. *America as a Civilization: Life and Thought in the United States Today.* 3rd ed. New York: Henry Holt, 1987.

Levine, Lawrence W. *The Unpredictable Past: Explorations in American Cultural History.* New York: Oxford University Press, 1993.

Lind, Michael. *The Next American Nation: The New Nationalism and the Fourth American Revolution.* New York: Free Press, 1995.

Lippi-Green, Rosina. *English with an Accent: Language, Ideology, and Discrimination in the United States.* London: Routledge, 1997.

Lipset, Seymour Martin. *American Exceptionalism: A Double-Edged Sword.* New York: Norton, 1996.

Lott, Davis Newton, ed. *The Inaugural Addresses of the American Presidents, from Washington to Kennedy.* New York: Holt, Rinehart, and Winston, 1961.

———. *The Presidents Speak: The Inaugural Addresses of the American Presidents, from Washington to Nixon.* 3rd ed. New York: Holt, Rhinehart, and Winston, 1969.

Luedtke, Luther S., ed. *Making America: The Society and Culture of the United States.* Chapel Hill: University of North Carolina Press, 1992.

Lundberg, Ferdinand, and Marynia Farnham. *Modern Woman: The Lost Sex.* New York: Grosset and Dunlap, 1947.

Mann, Arthur. *The One and the Many: Reflections on the American Identity.* Chicago: University of Chicago Press, 1979.

Mansbridge, Jane J. *Why We Lost the ERA.* Chicago: University of Chicago Press, 1986.

Martin, Theodora Penny. *The Sound of Our Own Voices: Women's Study Clubs, 1869–1910.* Boston: Beacon Press, 1987.

Mathews, Donald G., and Jane Sherron De Hart. *Sex, Gender, and the Politics of ERA: A State and the Nation.* New York: Oxford University Press, 1990.

Mattson, Vernon E., and William E. Marion. *Frederick Jackson Turner: A Reference Guide.* Boston: G. K. Hall, 1985.

McCoy, Donald R. *Calvin Coolidge: The Quiet President.* New York: Macmillan, 1967.

McGee, Michael. "In Search of 'The People': A Rhetorical Alternative." *Quarterly Journal of Speech* 61 (1975): 235–49.

Mead, George Herbert. *Mind, Self & Society from the Standpoint of a Social Behaviorist.* Chicago: University of Chicago Press, 1934.

Medhurst, Martin J. *Dwight D. Eisenhower: Strategic Communicator.* Westport, Conn.: Greenwood Press, 1993.

Merelman, Richard. *Making Something of Ourselves: On Culture and Politics in the United States.* Berkeley: University of California Press, 1984.

Merk, Frederick, with Lois Bannister Merk. *Manifest Destiny and Mission in American History: A Reinterpretation.* New York: Knopf, 1963.

Miller, John J. *The Unmaking of Americans: How Multiculturalism Has Undermined the Assimilation Ethic.* New York: Free Press, 1998.

Miller, Perry. *Nature's Nation.* Cambridge, Mass.: Belknap Press of Harvard University Press, 1967.

Morganthau, Tom. "America: Still a Melting Pot?" *Newsweek,* August 9, 1993.

Morone, James A. "The Struggle for American Culture." *PS: Political Science and Politics* 29 (September, 1996): 425–30.

Murray, Robert K. *The Harding Era: Warren G. Harding and His Administration.* Minneapolis: University of Minnesota Press, 1969.

Myrdal, Gunnar. *An American Dilemma: The Negro Problem and American Democracy.* Vol. 1. New York: Harper and Brothers, 1944.

Nelson, Dana D. *National Manhood: Capitalist Citizenship and the Imagined Fraternity of White Men.* Durham, N.C.: Duke University Press, 1998.

New Standard Revised Bible. Nashville: National Council of Churches, 1989.

Nisbet, Robert. *The Making of Modern Society.* Brighton, England: Wheatsheaf Books, 1986.

Nixon, Richard M. "Address on the State of the Union Delivered before a Joint Session of Congress." January 20, 1972. In *Public Papers of the Presidents of the United States.* Washington, D.C.: U.S. Government Printing Office, 1973.

———. "Inaugural Address." January 20, 1969. In *Public Papers of the Presidents of the United States.* Washington, D.C.: U.S. Government Printing Office, 1970.

————. "State of the Union Address." January 22, 1971. In *Public Papers of the Presidents of the United States*. Washington, D.C.: U.S. Government Printing Office, 1972.

Norton, Mary Beth, et al. *A People and a Nation: A History of the United States.* 2nd ed. Boston: Houghton Mifflin, 1986.

Novak, Michael. *Unmeltable Ethnics: Politics and Culture in American Life.* 2nd ed. New Brunswick, N.J.: Transaction Publishers, 1996.

O'Neill, William L. *Everyone Was Brave: The Rise and Fall of Feminism in America.* Chicago: Quadrangle Books, 1969.

O'Reilly, Kenneth. *Nixon's Piano: Presidents and Racial Politics from Washington to Clinton.* New York: Free Press, 1995.

Pauley, Garth E. *The Modern Presidency and Civil Rights: Rhetoric on Race from Roosevelt to Nixon.* College Station: Texas A&M University Press, 2001.

Perlmutter, Philip. *Divided We Fall: A History of Ethnic, Religious, and Racial Prejudice in America.* Ames: Iowa State University Press, 1992.

"Public Papers and Messages of the Presidents." American Reference Library CD-ROM. Orem, Utah: Western Standard Publishing, 1998.

Putnam, Robert D. "Tuning in, Tuning Out: The Strange Disappearance of Social Capital in America." *PS: Political Science and Politics* 28 (December, 1995): 664–83.

Rascoe, Peggy. *Relations of Rescue: The Search for Female Moral Authority in the American West, 1874–1939.* New York: Oxford University Press, 1990.

Reagan, Ronald. "Address before a Joint Session of the Congress on the State of the Union." February 6, 1985. In *Public Papers of the Presidents of the United States.* Washington: U.S. Government Printing Office, 1986.

————. "Address to a Joint Session of Congress on the State of the Union." January 25, 1983. In *Public Papers of the Presidents of the United States.* Washington, D.C.: U.S. Government Printing Office, 1984.

————. "Inaugural Address." January 20, 1981. In *Public Papers of the Presidents of the United States.* Washington, D.C.: U.S. Government Printing Office, 1982.

————. "Inaugural Address." January 21, 1985. In *Public Papers of the Presidents of the United States.* Washington D.C.: U.S. Government Printing Office, 1986.

————. "State of the Union Address." January 25, 1984. In *Public Papers of the Presidents of the United States.* Washington, D.C.: U.S. Government Printing Office, 1984.

————. "State of the Union Address." February 6, 1985. In *Public Papers of the Presidents of the United States.* Washington, D.C.: U.S. Government Printing Office, 1985.

————. "State of the Union Address." February 4, 1986. In *Public Papers of the Presidents of the United States.* Washington, D.C.: U.S. Government Printing Office, 1987.

Reimers, David. *Unwelcome Strangers: American Identity and the Turn against Immigration.* New York: Columbia University Press, 1998.

Riley, Russell L. *The Presidency and the Politics of Racial Inequality: Nation-keeping from 1831 to 1965.* New York: Columbia University Press, 1999.

Robertson, Andrew W. *The Language of Democracy: Political Rhetoric in the United States and Britain, 1790–1900.* Ithaca, N.Y.: Cornell University Press, 1995.

Rosenberg, Rosalind. *Beyond Separate Spheres: Intellectual Roots of Modern Feminism.* New Haven, Conn.: Yale University Press, 1982.

Ryan, Halford. "President Bill Clinton's Inaugural Address, 1993." In *The Inaugural Addresses of Twentieth-Century American Presidents,* edited by Halford Ryan. Westport, Conn.: Praeger, 1993.

Ryan, Mary P. *Womanhood in America: From Colonial Times to the Present.* New York: New Viewpoints, 1975.

Salvatore, Nick. *We All Got History: The Memory Books of Amos Webber.* New York: Times Books, 1996.

Santayana, George. *Character and Opinion in the United States.* New York: Scribner's Sons, 1920.

Sapiro, Virginia. *The Political Integration of Women: Roles, Socialization, and Politics.* Urbana: University of Illinois Press, 1983.

Schlesinger, Arthur M., Jr., ed. *The Almanac of American History.* New York: Putnam, 1983.

———. *The Disuniting of America: Reflections on a Multicultural Society.* Rev. and enlarged ed. New York: Norton, 1998.

Scott, Anne Firor. *Natural Allies: Women's Associations in American History.* Urbana: University of Illinois Press, 1991.

Shannon, David. *Between the Wars: America, 1919–1941.* 2nd ed. Boston: Houghton Mifflin, 1979.

Shelley, Fred M., et al. *Political Geography of the United States.* New York: Guilford Press, 1996.

Shklar, Judith. *American Citizenship: The Quest for Inclusion.* Cambridge, Mass.: Harvard University Press, 1991.

Skocpol, Theda. *Protecting Soldiers and Mothers: The Political Origins of Social Policy in the United States.* Cambridge, Mass.: Belknap Press of Harvard University Press, 1992.

Slater, Philip. *The Pursuit of Loneliness: American Culture at the Breaking Point.* Rev. ed. Boston: Beacon Press, 1976.

Slotkin, Richard. *The Fatal Environment: The Myth of the Frontier in the Age of Industrialization, 1800–1890.* New York: Atheneum, 1985.

Smith, Rogers. *Civic Ideals: Conflicting Visions of Citizenship in U.S. History.* New Haven, Conn.: Yale University Press, 1997.

Somers, Margaret R. "The Privatization of Citizenship: How to Unthink a Knowledge Culture." In *Beyond the Cultural Turn: New Directions in the Study of Society and Culture,* edited by Victoria E. Bonnell and Lynn Hunt, 121–61. Berkeley: University of California Press, 1999.

Sorensen, Theodore C. *Kennedy.* New York: Harper and Row, 1965.

Southern, David W. *Gunnar Myrdal and Black-White Relations: The Use and Abuse of an American Dilemma, 1944–1969.* Baton Rouge: Louisiana State Press, 1987.

"Spot the Europhile." *The Economist,* June 22, 1996.

Steinbeck, John. *America and the Americans.* New York: Viking Press, 1966.

St. John de Crevecoeur, J. Hector. "Letter III: What Is an American?" In *Letters from an American Farmer,* edited with an introduction and notes by Susan Manning, 40–82. New York: Oxford University Press, 1997.

Taylor, Charles. "The Politics of Recognition." In *Multiculturalism: Examining the Politics of Recognition,* edited by Amy Gutmann, 3–73. Princeton, N.J.: Princeton University Press, 1994.

Thelen, David, and Frederick E. Hoxie, eds. *Discovering America: Essays on the Search for an Identity.* Urbana: University of Illinois Press, 1994.

Tilly, Louise, and Patricia Gurin, eds. Introduction to *Women, Politics, and Change.* New York: Russell Sage Foundation, 1990.

Tocqueville, Alexis de. *Democracy in America.* Edited by J. P. Mayer and M. Lerner. Translated by G. Lawrence. 2 vols. New York: Harper and Row, 1966.

Truman, Harry S. "Message to the Congress on the State of the Union and on the Budget for 1947." January 6, 1947. In *Public Papers of the Presidents of the United States.* Washington, D.C.: U.S. Government Printing Office, 1948.

Tulis, Jeffrey K. *The Rhetorical Presidency.* Princeton, N.J.: Princeton University Press, 1987.

Wald, Kenneth D. *Religion and Politics in the United States.* New York: St. Martin's Press, 1987.

Wald, Priscilla. *Constituting Americans: Cultural Anxiety and Narrative Form.* Durham, N.C.: Duke University Press, 1995.

Walzer, Michael. *What It Means to Be an American.* New York: Marsilio, 1992.

Wander, Philip. "The Ideological Turn in Rhetorical Theory." *Central States Speech Journal* 35 (1984): 1–18.

Welter, Rush. "On Studying the National Mind." In *New Directions in American Intellectual History,* edited by John Higham and Paul K. Conkin, 64–82. Baltimore: Johns Hopkins University Press, 1979.

West, Cornel. *Race Matters.* Boston: Beacon Press, 1993.

White, Stephen, Alex Pravda, and Zvi Gitelman, eds. *Developments in Russian and Post-Soviet Politics.* 3rd ed. Durham, N.C.: Duke University Press, 1994.

Williams, Raymond. *The Sociology of Culture.* New York: Schocken Books, 1982; Chicago: University of Chicago Press, 1995.

Wills, Garry. *Inventing America: Jefferson's Declaration of Independence.* Garden City, N.Y.: Doubleday, 1978.

———. *Lincoln at Gettysburg: The Words That Remade America.* New York: Simon and Schuster, 1992.

Wolfe, Alan. *One Nation, After All: What Middle-Class Americans Really Think about God, Country, Family, Racism, Welfare, Immigration, Homosexuality, Work, the Right, the Left and Each Other.* New York: Viking, 1998.

Wood, Gordon S. *The Creation of the American Republic, 1776–1787.* New York: Norton, 1969.

Wylie, Philip. *Generation of Vipers.* New York: Farrar and Rinehart, 1942.

Young, Iris Marion. *Justice and the Politics of Difference.* Princeton, N.J.: Princeton University Press, 1990.

Zarefsky, David. *President Johnson's War on Poverty: Rhetoric and History.* University: University of Alabama Press, 1986.

Zinn, Howard. *A People's History of the United States.* New York: Harper and Row, 1980.

Index

ISBN 1-58544-277-1

90000